The Nature of Choice

AMS Studies in Modern Society:
Political and Social Issues: No. 18

Other Titles in This Series:

ISSN 0275-8407

The Nature of Choice

AND OTHER SELECTED WRITINGS

Anita J. Faatz

AMS PRESS, INC.
New York

Library of Congress Cataloging in Publication Data

Faatz, Anita J. (Anita Josephine)
  The Nature of Choice, and Other Selected Writings.

  (AMS Studies in Modern Society: Political and Social
Issues, ISSN 0275-8407; No. 18)
  Includes index.
  1. Social case work—Addresses, essays, lectures.
2. Choice (Psychology)—Addresses, essays, lectures.
I. Title. II. Series: AMS studies in modern society;
no. 18.
HV43.F23   1985   361.3′2   83-72424
ISBN 0-404-16043-3

MANUFACTURED IN THE UNITED STATES OF AMERICA

TO

VIRGINIA P. ROBINSON

WITH GRATITUDE

CONTENTS

FOREWORD

The publication of the work of Dr. Anita Faatz marks the final project of the Otto Rank Association of which she was a founder and the executive director during the entire period of its existence. The decision by the Board of Directors to publish this book affirms its recognition of her enormous contribution and of her selfless devotion. She has carried the Association over the years, dealt with the complex administrative details, planned its annual conferences, edited its *Journal,* and sustained by newsletters and personal correspondence a relationship to all of its members as well as with others interested in Otto Rank and functional casework. One is awed at the incredible productivity and the unceasing creativity manifested in these achievements.

We can take pride in the fact that these efforts have indeed kept alive and in the forefront the incisive and revolutionary ideas of Otto Rank, ideas which provide a basis for understanding and conducting the complex processes of therapy, helping in general, teaching, and creativity in the arts. More than that, Otto Rank provided a firm basis for self-understanding and the development of a personal philosophy.

The decision by the entire membership to discontinue the Association was not one easily made. Declining membership and income in the face of escalating costs, the imminent retirement of Anita Faatz and the emergence of strong local groups interested in sustaining, applying, and developing Otto Rank's thinking, brought the Board and membership to the conclusion that the purpose of the founders of the Association had been realized. We concluded that the continuing work could be best achieved through the local groups without the growing cost of a national organization.

Through a generous and unexpected legacy from Miss Abigail Brownell, a former member, the Association was able to plan its ending to include a final conference, produce a final volume of its *Journal,* and carry through the publication of this book. The balance of assets have been contributed to the Rare Book and Manuscript Library at Columbia University to strengthen, expand, and make more widely useful its collection of the writings of Otto Rank and related contributors. The papers, correspondence, and publications of the Otto Rank Association have been added to that collection.

One may validly question the justification of the publication of a book of writings originally published many years ago, given the present surfeit of publications in psychology and the helping fields. Dr. Faatz's underlying theme of the ultimate responsibility of the individual for making the choices necessary for his own as well as communal survival is as timely today as it has ever been. The confrontation between social limitation and the individual freedom to choose is at the forefront of human concerns today, as is the potential for such choice despite social, psychological, and physical limitations. Dr. Faatz has made a rare contribution to understanding that polarity and to finding the means of facilitating the individual's capacity to make such choices. The profound insights she offers are as timely as they have ever been. One may paraphrase Otto Rank and say of Dr. Faatz's work that it deals not just with knowledge but with life. Never has it been more important to affirm the freedom of the individual to make choices and to will creatively.

I wish to use this occasion to express my own gratitude for the long and close association with Dr. Faatz afforded by my role as president these past eight years. I have been enriched by this experience and have seen in her life an ideal for making one's mature years creative and productive. She is, indeed, a rare and unusual person with whom every connection becomes enriching. It is that quality which perfuses and unifies her life and work.

SAUL HOFSTEIN, D.S.W.

PREFACE
Forty Years, 1943 to 1983

Collected in this volume are subjects so diverse that one may well wonder what unity brings them together. Surely the likeness is not to be found in the subject matter—ranging from policy in public welfare to *The Secret Sharer* as Conrad gives it to us. Neither is the unity only in the factor that one author has written them all.

I pose this question to myself because I feel an underlying idea that gripped my attention in the early 1940s and continues even today. "Choice" is the magnet, the central entity that creates the idea that runs through all of this writing. Even though many years have passed, I feel now in memory those fragments of reality that awakened my interest in choice in those early days. And it seems as if I have been following the finest of threads through obstacles of all description, until the conclusion emerges that learning and growing come only through the process I have attempted to describe.

If I were to write at length about "choice" today, there are many words that I would reexamine and perhaps even restate. I am not as sure as I was then that no matter what the circumstances may be, one can create a life-fulfilling attitude toward them. In the original Preface to *The Nature of Choice* I wrote, "I have had to give up the assumption that the capacity to choose is innate and natural to the self, on behalf of the acknowledgment that the mature capacity to choose is earned through growth," And I added, "the quality of inner freedom is rare." I am still challenged by these thoughts.

*   *   *

In the closing years of one's life, there could be no richer gift than that which now comes to me from The Otto Rank Association. I owe to it and its devoted membership my thanks for twenty years of unmatched pleasure in relationships and memorable occasions. To have that experience brought to a conclusion, first by a celebration at the last annual meeting, by a final issue of the *Journal,* and now in a book that contains all of my writings, is a source of deep satisfaction

My thanks go to its Board of Directors, which shaped and made real this publication; to its able president, Dr. Saul Hofstein, who took over the difficult presidency at the time of Miss Robinson's death; to Dr. Ruth Wells who designed and saw through to conclusion the imaginative plan for the Rank Fund now housed at Columbia University, Rare Book and Manuscript Library.

To Jacob Hechler we owe a very special kind of thanks: He took on the arduous task of seeking out the publisher, providing the printed work to be included, conveying his own belief in, and enthusiasm for, the work he was presenting. Step by step he piloted this publication through to conclusion, including even the preparation of the Index. Only the fact that he has a depth of thought, sensitive and true, and is himself an accomplished author, could have made this possible.

Lastly, I am grateful for my life experiences, for the learning experience which brought me to the Pennsylvania School of Social Work, for the teaching experience throughout which I had the remarkable opportunity to be helped in process by Virginia P. Robinson and Jessie Taft, when "experience and psychological understanding were simultaneous."

*   *   *

In ending I cannot resist the temptation to say a word about "choice" in the process of aging—for indeed aging is a process as truly as any other phase of life. One must surely come to realize, as one moves into age 80 and beyond, that reality choices become more and more limited; that inner and outer resources of the self diminish. And that the ultimate recognition of "yielding" comes in the form of acceptance: acceptance of changes that come unwanted and unasked for. Still the truth remains that one finds one's own relation to what must be; that inner change is possible no matter what the age. I have always believed in living as a process; I do so now more than ever.

ANITA J. FAATZ

Doylestown, February 1984

[4]

THE NATURE OF CHOICE IN

CASEWORK PROCESS

The Nature of Choice
in
Casework Process

by

Anita J. Faatz

Introduction by VIRGINIA P. ROBINSON

THE UNIVERSITY OF NORTH CAROLINA PRESS
Chapel Hill

[1953]

CONTENTS

INTRODUCTION

THE PUBLICATION of a new book in the field of social casework, whose literature is limited for the most part to
the conference paper, the short article, or brief pamphlet, is
an event of significance for this professional field. I am honored by the invitation of the University of North Carolina
Press, its publisher, to introduce this book. For myself, in my
position of professor emeritus on the faculty of the University of Pennsylvania School of Social Work where I have been
in active teaching and administrative positions for many
years, I welcome this opportunity to express to social workers
and to the North Carolina Press my appreciation of the continuity which this volume establishes for the theory and
practice of the functional point of view in social casework.

The title which Miss Faatz has chosen for this book is
immediately challenging and suggestive, not only to the professional caseworker but to every human being who approaches the problem of living and choosing in the world
today with curiosity as to the nature of his own choices and
concern for the continuity and integrity of the self that makes
those choices. The title of Part I, "Continuity and Change,"
and the chapters which develop it, express a sense of continuity underlying change and development that is rare in
this young professional field whose definition is still in the
making. The "search for the therapeutic factor" in casework
process, the beginnings of which were heralded in the publication by the North Carolina Press in 1930 of my book,
A Changing Psychology in Social Casework, has been carried by Miss Faatz through two decades of development
with a clear and undeviating sense of direction. That this
historical evaluation can be affirmed by the two people
whose names are most closely associated with this search and
with the discovery of function is evidence of the accuracy

with which Miss Faatz has absorbed and appraised the past as she carries it into the present.

But the more important contribution of this book lies not in the historical background of Part I but in the dynamic and original description of process in Part II. The debt to Rank's contribution to psychological understanding of inner experience and relationship process is acknowledged fully and precisely by Miss Faatz in her Preface, but the process she describes grows immediately and authentically out of her own experience in the helping processes of casework, of supervision, of teaching, and administration. Her point of view has true individuality at the same time that it comprehends and expresses universal meaning.

Miss Faatz has limited her discussion to the helping processes of social casework not only because it is in this practice that her experience and her competence lie but even more because of the singular importance which the problem of choice has assumed in this field. As she sees it, the conflict between freedom of choice and external compulsion constitutes the basic dilemma in which this helping profession is entangled, determining differences and conflicts in practice as well as in theoretical opinions. To my knowledge this problem has never been grappled with so fundamentally as in this volume. The psychological solution to which this analysis points, "the ultimate single nature of choice," must be read in full and cannot be summarized. Only those individuals who are willing to go beneath the surface of conventional attitudes and externally determined choices to examine the long slow process of internal choosing will read this book to the end. Those who lend themselves to reading in this way will find this book deeply rewarding not only for an understanding of social casework practice but for finer understanding of helping processes in any profession or of any life experience in which the problem of the relationship between self and other has become conscious.

VIRGINIA P. ROBINSON

P A R T   I

CONTINUITY AND CHANGE: A DEVELOPMENTAL VIEW OF EMERGING CASEWORK PROCESS

> . . . The organism which lives is a thing that endures. Its past, in its entirety, is prolonged into its present, and abides there, actual and acting.
>
> HENRI BERGSON

CHAPTER I

ASPECTS OF PROCESS IN THE DEVELOPMENT OF A PROFESSION

IN UNDERTAKING to present a comprehensive view of case-work process at this time, a special problem arises, and a very interesting one, out of a consideration of past, present, and future, so far as casework practice is concerned. The problem is one of assessing accurately where we now stand, for a purpose related wholly to the on-going movement. Social phenomena in their growth processes, like the growth process of the individual, reflect developmental phases, now highly accelerated, now slowing to a halt; now gathering substance upon a plateau; now backward, now caught in immobility; and now again suddenly illuminated by the swift shock of momentary understanding. To articulate the known is to possess it more fully. To possess it more fully is to gather in and consolidate the substance and strength of what is, in order that it can be given more generously to the evolution of what can be.

Whereas the title of this book suggests a partial consideration of casework process—that part which I have called the nature of choice in this process—it is in fact a consideration of the whole in a very particular sense. The nature of choice constitutes a central focus at the core of the subject which operates to hold the detail in constant relation to a central idea, so that no outer boundary or limitation is necessary. No case material has been utilized, and in consequence the reader must supply his own illustration. No particular field of casework practice has been held in mind. This discussion is in every sense of the word an exploration of the common base which underlies all casework helping; it does not develop in any detail the specific differences in particular casework services, important as these differences are. Simultaneously there is a common and universal base in which all helping process rests and there is a distinguishable and fine and precise difference in each function which operates with crucial importance in the helping process.

One aspect of this problem of assessing where we are today arises on account of the clear indication that the field of casework practice is comprised of two distinct and opposite points of view,[1] and when this is acknowledged, it becomes equally clear that few if any generalizations will apply to the whole of casework. What is described here is the professional practice now solidly established with distinction and precision as the functional method of helping. The differences existing in point of view in the casework field today are dealt with only on occasion as illuminating contrast, especially in Part I dealing with the development of functional practice, where it is just this divergence which clarifies the two opposite directions in which casework thought and practice have moved.

Another aspect of this problem of assessing the situation today originates from the discouragement which caseworkers often feel on account of the attitude of the public in relation to casework practice, an attitude which at times seems hardly to know that such a thing as casework exists; or, when it does become aware of this fact, is often impelled to attack because of the change and difference which social work represents. It is natural enough that the caseworker's whole relation to the field should be colored by the fact that casework is seldom if ever wholeheartedly wanted by other professions, and that the effort to establish itself as a profession has been an uphill climb. But caseworkers are coming to realize more and more that this is but an inevitable phase of reaction to difference, to change, to fear of what the psychological represents. This is nothing to despair of, so long as the prominence of the problem does not obscure the reality of the remarkable, phenomenal growth in casework practice which has in fact taken place. For the first thing which might be said about casework at the present time is that the development, especially during the past twenty years, has been swift and substantial both in extension of casework method to new services, and particularly in breadth and depth of psychological concept and understanding of a skill which can be taught and learned in responsible process.

Roughly speaking, the term casework has been in use for some fifty years as a means of designating a method of helping which takes place between individual helper and one seeking help. Immediately, when one uses the words individual helper, the necessity arises to add the further observation that this helping takes place always in a social agency setting, as representative of an agency. But at this point this added fact obscures the meaning, in that here we are considering only the one single isolated fact that casework is a process between two individuals, in contrast to other social work processes which concern themselves with numbers of people and with economic and social programs of various sorts. In this respect, namely, that casework is devoted to the one, to the importance of the single, separate life expression, there can be no difference of opinion.

At times, however, there has been a great dissatisfaction with the lack of precise definition for the term casework, and efforts continue in many quarters to force into the mold of logical and watertight definition that which defies every attempt to define. This pressure toward definition has at times been a very compelling one. Its origin is both inner and outer: inner in the sense that it reflects the conflict of the individual caseworker who, trying to help but baffled and unsuccessful in his efforts, projects this discomfort upon the profession in terms of a conceptual drive to define and to prove in absolutes. In turn, this projected pressure becomes a group phenomenon, so that the profession as a whole has at times turned against itself this fierce attack to force a kind of definition and a kind of proof which its longing for sureness seeks in the external world.

It marks a singular advance both in the profession and in the individual helper, that this compelling pressure to define has at last given way to the greater strength of a wholly different kind of precision. There is a kind of definition which is organic, which holds its unity and identity through a central core of concept and reality, which admits its complexity and its life movement, and does violence to neither by force of the human intellect. To some who are oriented within the older natural science philosophy, with its reliance upon precise definition and proof, and its veneration of reason and logic to the exclusion of emotion, the inability on the part of casework to lend itself to precise definition is viewed as evidence of flaw and failure, requiring some day to be corrected if casework is to reach its scientific stature. But to others this capitulation to the intrinsic nature of casework reflects an acknowledgment that casework belongs with that philosophical movement in human experience which seeks new ways to comprehend the dynamics of living, and at last acknowledges the inescapable fact that life will not yield its meaning to him who would attempt to force it into the rigid mold of causal determinism. Wherever the life process has been genuinely understood, this result has come about through a deep devotion to the effort to understand the way it is: imbued with change as well as permanence, tinged by the irrational as powerfully as by the rational, given meaning by emotion, heightened by fear and guilt and evil as truly as by its opposites, and always, in its swift flight in time, defying the effort to arrest its movement or hold it in the hand. Within the helping person who is genuinely related to this process there lies at bottom this deep capitulation to, and admission of, the limitation to understanding; but precisely on this account, paradoxically, new understanding is the reward.

The Development of a Profession

That casework can be described in terms of what it does, the kinds of problems with which it deals, the setting of the social agency in which it is located, the characteristics of the clients who come, goes without saying. It can also be communicated in psychological principle and concept, and its process can be known in ways far more reliable than words alone afford. The nature of growth within the helping person which the casework skill demands can be known and communicated provided always that the reader brings to this task a willingness to seek within his own experience for the understanding which the written word can only suggest; and provided too there is readiness to yield some measure of the tight organization of the self in order to welcome and entertain the impact of the new and unfamiliar idea. Casework does express itself in a new and different language and this too is a sign of its developing maturity.

Casework is a method, a way of helping, not a result or a quality. In its intent and purpose and practical result it is frankly therapeutic. This statement can always be counted upon to arouse doubt and sometimes shock and fear, often projected outward in the question, "But what, then, differentiates casework from psychotherapy?" Actually, the fear is an unavoidable reaction to the character of the responsibility and the nature of the psychological task which the caseworker undertakes. Wherever the difference between casework and therapy may lie, it is not on the score of the value of the therapeutic results. Throughout this discussion from first word to last we speak of a process which aims to help the individual free the temporarily restricted life impulse in order that it can seek out its own natural growth potential, and thus discover the new expressions of self capable of coping with the life reality. The word therapeutic is a life-giving, growth-producing word. It belongs to real life experience, as well as to the special aspect of life created especially for therapeutic purposes. The sense of healing, of unity in contrast to division, of well-being; of the "I," the self whole and unified, is as possible in the common course of a life experience as it is in a process consciously created for this purpose.

But those who come to social agencies are locked in this very inability to discover and affirm the capacity equated with the life element in the self. When we undertake to help, we undertake to create a situation precisely and responsibly established for this purpose. Being an unreal situation, it must be time limited, and because of its very limitation in time, it affords the possibility for the therapeutic results. What this process can be, how it comes about that one human being can use another for the purpose of releasing the source of new life within the self, is the subject matter with which this book deals. Surely it must be said, how serious a purpose this is, what deep responsibility it asks of the one who undertakes it; for as helping persons we do indeed effect change in the one who seeks help, and the only thing which makes it possible at all is that it comes about through his own will and choice.

In the discussion of historical development which follows, it has not been my intention to attempt anything like a complete examination of the history of social work, nor even of the more limited area of casework, during the years under consideration. Instead my purpose is to identify the origin of those concepts which appear and are explored in Part II of this book. By this means, ideas assume the fullness and depth which evolution in thought and practice affords. What is written in these pages attempts to take possession of that which is already known and understood, and, by tracing the development of a concept, to gain the illumination which only the comparison of past and present can afford.

CHAPTER II

THE SPECIAL QUALITIES OF
THE INDIVIDUAL UNIT

T HE TITLE of this chapter is a quotation which has singular significance as a focus for this swift view of the developmental phases in social casework across the span of some seventy years, from 1880 to 1950.[1] The words were originally used by a person who had no connection with social work, Secretary of the Interior Franklin K. Lane,[2] who, at the time of his retirement, in looking back at and evaluating the period in which he had served as a government official, characterized the times as distinguished by "the search for the special qualities of the individual unit."[3]

This comment would have gone unnoticed and unmarked in social work history had it not been that Miss Mary E. Richmond, at the peak of her career in 1920, in a paper read at the National Conference of Social Work entitled "Some Next Steps in Social Treatment," selected these words of Secretary Lane to express her own conviction that indeed the progress of social work in the twenty years of her greatest activity had been marked by exactly this search for the "special qualities of the individual unit."[4]

It may seem precipitate to plunge thus into the middle of a seventy-year span of development without proceeding in the usual chronological sequence; yet the reason for so doing is that from this earliest forty-year period, from 1880 to 1920, scarcely anything remains of importance for today's casework practice except this one trend of opposing forces, one side of which is represented by Miss Richmond's 1920 paper. All other facts and details are of historical interest only, interesting for what they were at the time and for the devoted service of many vigorous and creative personalities. But today there survives in social work a similar conflict of opposing tendencies and a vital issue which is the same as that of which Miss Richmond spoke, and the same as that which can be found in National Conference deliberations in every year from 1880 on.

This struggle of opposing tendencies, together constituting an unbroken trend in time, is the struggle between the individual and the social, the one and the many, the psychological and the economic, the inner experience and the external event. The developmental view of social work shows what we have seldom been willing to admit, that no great personality in social work has been able to carry both these opposing tendencies in equal development within the self, but that leadership in social work has flourished through individuals who have carried with passionate devotion either one side or the other of this conflict. One can select from the contemporary scene almost any content in world affairs to examine this same fundamental point of contrast, but we need look no further than social work—can stay within our own milieu —in order to know and comprehend this human phenomenon to the full.

Casework is clearly that branch of social work which carries forward, protects, and lives out in thought and activity the single strand of devotion to the separate, single human self: the worth of the one. Other branches of social work, such as community organization, program making, social action, all by their nature belong to the opposite tendency which places upon the broad program, the external adjustment, the economic solution, the higher value in interest and feeling. Some branches of social work, as yet not so clearly developed (administration, for instance), have not succeeded in clarifying their major identification but flounder in some confusion and problem for this very reason.

The helping person must begin with the devotion to the

psychological at heart, in order to be a helper. In casework, in supervision, in teaching, and occasionally in administration, one feels the dedication to this focus which all the catastrophic happenings in the world cannot dislodge, namely the belief in maintaining life through its expression in person-to-person relationships. Even a lifetime of devotion to this effort to understand in some genuine way the nature of the human self requires a willingness to be satisfied with very little, for mankind has made very slight progress in this direction. But amount of progress is no criterion, nor is any individual in a position to question whether it is or is not enough. In the long run the forward sweep of that affirmation which acknowledges without excessive guilt or apology its dedication to the human spirit in its spontaneous expressions is the dynamic of the caseworker's skill.

To return now to examine this problem in developmental terms, we take once more as a point of departure this 1920 paper of Miss Richmond's already referred to, for in it we find a summation of the experience of preceding decades and a note of bitterness which suggests the intensity of the struggle through which Miss Richmond had maintained her position. In 1920 she writes: "It is only during the last fifteen years that social case work in families has continued to slip from under the domination of the economists. Though case work always demanded a method in sharp contrast to wholesaling, its earlier period was shaped too often by wholesalers. Broad generalizations about relief, about family life, about desertion, widowhood, immigrants, and the rest, served a useful purpose in that pioneer period, but in the succeeding stage of development, case work achieved a more important step forward."[5]

If the dates in this paragraph are examined, it will be seen that Miss Richmond's reference was to the fifteen years between 1905 and 1920, during which "social case work in families" was beginning to establish its own identity. No doubt she knew as she wrote that her own first published work in 1899, *Friendly Visiting Among the Poor,*[6] had played a significant part in the beginning of an epoch in casework development,[7] and had precipitated some of this change away from "wholesaling" and "broad generalizations," of which she spoke.

But the striking fact is that, even in this same "earlier period" to which Miss Richmond refers, there was already ample evidence of the intensity and vigor with which this battle was fought. Even as early as 1886, at the National Conference which took place in that year, Mr. George B. Buzelle, General Secretary of the Bureau of Charities of Brooklyn, was speaking upon the subject "Individuality in the Work of Charity."[8] His was an angry and fervent voice: "We have a vast array of machinery for the production of philanthropic results. . . . And yet the really beneficent results accomplished are painfully insufficient." Continuing, he says: "We may share in plans as wide as the needs of our fellow-men; but if our effort elicit a response, it is the individual who must respond. Through the individual, the wider result must be reached. . . . He must be the principal in action, in his own behalf. We cannot fight his battle for him. He must be the arbiter of his own destiny. He must choose, though he have little discernment. However vacillating he may be, he must decide. He must will, however feeble his will may be."[9]

In the same volume of *Proceedings,* following immediately after Mr. Buzelle's paper, is another entitled "Trampery: Its Causes, Present Aspects and Some Suggested Remedies."[10] It would be hard to imagine a set of circumstances within which the contrast could be more effectively portrayed. In these two articles the approach to the problem is from opposite poles. Both share the same regret that "beneficent results accomplished are painfully insufficient," but the one believes passionately that the objective must be sought through the individual: "He must be the principle in action . . . he must will." The other has no patience with, but only, as later appears so clearly, scorn for, this slow way of working, and searches instead for causes, pursuing them ever more persistently as one cause after another proves inadequate to the task of explaining or eradicating the evil.

Twenty-three years later, in the 1909 *Proceedings of the Conference,* this same theme is once more evident, and again the contrast emerges succinctly in the keynote struck by two individuals who see the problem from opposite vantage points. Mr. Alexander Johnson writes: "In twenty-one years the problem of the poor has passed over from an affair of the individual to one of the neighborhood."

"In 1888," he continues, "preventive philanthropy was just gaining recognition, but the problems of ameliorative relief were the urgent ones. In 1909 constructive effort in benevolence fills the position that preventive work had barely attained at the former period; while the theory of prevention has grown in acceptance until it is a truism to say that poverty is a temporary condition, that it is mainly due to preventable causes, that science has shown us how it may be averted and that benevolence has seized on the method and proposes to put it in practice."[11]

Here Mr. Johnson draws the contrast between that which is "preventive" and that which is "ameliorative," a contrast which was to continue with powerful influence. The contrast became, at times, the vehicle of attack upon casework process. Further, Mr. Johnson's conviction expresses vividly the belief in the efficacy of external, environmental means for the eradication of poverty: science knows the causes, can eliminate them; hence poverty is a temporary condition. What was missing was the understanding and acknowledgment of the equally crucial role played by the individual's own life movement in the use he makes of these environmental factors.

In the same year of the Conference and very likely against the background of the mood and attitude so evident in Mr. Johnson's summing up of the times, Mrs. Mary Simkovitch spoke upon the subject "The Case Work Plane."[12] Says Mrs. Simkovitch, "Preventative work has been considered so largely from the social point of view that the possibilities of its development in what has been called 'case work' i.e., individual effort, have been relatively neglected.

"I think this paper will interest nobody, for I think the modern emphasis is so strongly on preventative work of a social character that case work is secretly if not openly despised. That is one of the reasons why district and family work are conducted with less interest and less capacity than the social preventative work. The general feeling is that case work is a small affair, unimportant, a necessary evil, a depressing piece of business, a practically hopeless job. Everyone's attention is turned the other way."[13]

Mrs. Simkovitch's despair and discouragement are plainly evident, but it is clear that her own attention was not "turned the other way." Moreover, the years which followed were to show that the solution was not so simple as Mr. Johnson had optimistically prophesied, nor so discouraging as Mrs. Simkovitch had pictured.

If time has done anything for us, it has revealed the fallacy in placing so profound a confidence in the illusion of removing "preventable causes" and shows the extent to which this theory obscures the part played by man himself in his own destiny. Actually, this contrast of opposing trends here being examined highlights and focuses one of the most interesting problems with which casework must eventually come to grips: namely, the question to what extent the individual is the victim of external happenings, to what extent he possesses the capacity within himself to choose and determine the outcome. We are now living with the results of extraordinary material benefits provided through law, through program making, and through statesmanship, but still the problem remains, how man himself, the individual, can utilize what is available to his own maximum advantage. Thus this same duality, of external circumstance and inner dynamic, of the mass and the one, continues on in our present experience, as vital as it was in the historical development of social work; perhaps even more vital today, because with the extension of social services the question of what part the individual plays in the use of the service becomes more clearly apparent.

Now we return once more to the point of examining what happened to this same trend in the next developmental phase; what remained in continuity, what yielded to influences of change. One significant fact stands out above all others, namely that, with the coming of the psychiatric and psychoanalytic influence of the 1920's, casework entered upon an accelerated phase of concern with "the special qualities of the individual unit." This concern carried the continuity but at the same time introduced a momentous change in a shift of the center of attention, away from qualities which were environmental and external, toward qualities which were psychological and internal. Interest was greatly heightened by the discovery of man's inner experience, by the powerful desire to explore and understand the emotions and behavior of man.

In retrospect, it is clear to see how Miss Richmond's absorption in the special qualities of the individual was externally focused. The qualities of the individual were sought in facts: in facts painstakingly and finely and precisely gathered, from relatives, neighbors, employers, doctors, lawyers, teachers, and clergymen; from all but from the individual himself, and in every respect excepting this one, there was the utmost regard for him. The theory rested on a search for a solution constructed by the caseworker: the more facts, the more hope that the caseworker could arrive at a sound and valid diagnosis. The more accurate the diagnosis, the greater the likelihood of a workable plan. With a good plan, implemented with sound judgment and a tactful and genuine approach, the goal must surely be reached. As we now know, the one element which of all elements is the most indispensable, the will of the individual himself, was left out of the reckoning. Indeed Miss Richmond had some awareness of this; she referred constantly to her own belief that a change of attitude in the one who was to be helped was the thing which mattered most, but she sought to achieve this change of attitude through direct efforts projected upon the client, frankly and unrestrainedly aimed to effect his change.

It would be hard to conceive of the development of casework without precisely this phase characterized by the fine regard for the external fact, to which Miss Richmond so creatively gave her life's work. In 1917 the fruits of her thought and service came to full expression with the publication of her major work, *Social Diagnosis*.[14] Actually, the publication of this book in 1917 was the end of a period, for already the seeds of the next development in casework, which was to be a psychological development, had begun to take root. In 1918 and 1919, that vigorous interaction between casework and psychiatry and psychoanalysis began to make itself felt.

These developments which came about in casework practice as a result of psychoanalytic influences have been examined with precision, and comprehended in such a way as to become a part of the heritage of social work.[15] A matter of especial interest is how exactly those years in which these influences first made themselves felt can be identified, and how the growth of a professional content falls into clear decades of development. It is possible to see the outlines of the natural and organic time spans of three important decades: the 1920's, the 1930's, and the 1940's, and thus to take hold of and understand as a whole the nature of the evolutionary development in casework thought and practice in these significant thirty years, between 1920 (more accurately, 1918) and 1950. The two chapters which follow correspond to the developmental phases which I have characterized as "The Search for the Therapeutic Factor" and "The Discovery of Function." The development of the third decade is the content of the second part.

But first, in order to give the focus and approach by which this development unfolds, I should like to state the thesis which constitutes, in these pages, the single strand of development to which all detail and factual content are related. It is this: that the important change, above all others, which functional casework embodies, is the shift of the dynamic center for the source of therapeutic results from the helper to the one being helped. From this all other detail of concept, method, process, and content flows. By this statement we do not intend to imply any denial of the determinative role played by the skill of the helper or lack of it; nor of the crucial importance of the helping process in affecting the release of these vital elements in the self. But the quality of this skill does not arise from the caseworker's understanding of the facts and the problem, or from the competence of the diagnosis, or the control by the caseworker of the level upon which the self uses help; nor does it rest upon the accurate delineation of steps of treatment. It arises, instead, out of a primary acknowledgment that the source of understanding is within the self; that here, internally, is located the original upspringing of the impulse toward life, and here lies the control of change and growth.

Today, in appearance at least, there remains a large body of casework practice which describes itself as still located in the same reliance upon knowledge, diagnosis, and treatment that characterized Miss Richmond's method. The only visible difference is the substitution of psychological fact for environmental fact, and therefore to some extent the individual himself plays more part as the source of information. The dominant characteristic of the 1920's was just this emphasis upon the caseworker's knowledge, diagnosis, and judgment—of what was needed, what should be done, and how it was to be accomplished. The new psychological emphasis still consisted of efforts frankly projected to effect change upon another human self.

The origins of functional casework theory and practice lie within this same orbit of influence during the first half of the 1920's. Those who were later to create the concept of function were actively writing, teaching, practicing, within these same early psychoanalytic influences. But gradually there become visible the centers of doubt and the new definition of problem which constituted the dynamic out of which the next development grew; from which eventually the principle of function was forged.

CHAPTER III

THE SEARCH FOR THE
THERAPEUTIC FACTOR

> *Change of mind does
> no good; promises do
> no good; only change
> of feeling will help.*
> JESSIE TAFT, 1927

THESE WERE indeed important and momentous years for casework, this decade between the year 1920 and the year 1930. It was a period of growth for individuals as well as for the profession. The development in casework came about interestingly enough not because of its autonomy as a distinct and separate profession, but because of its relation to a larger, more powerful whole, namely the psychoanalytic movement. Later, in contrast, the decade between 1930 and 1940 (and here I speak of functional casework only) became a period characterized by separation and articulation of difference from psychotherapy, and it was out of this definition of difference that the unique character of casework method evolved. But in this decade of the 1920's the dominant note was still one of unity with another discipline in which the greater strength and creativity were found to reside.

These facts contain more meaning than the bare statement of an·historical reality: they characterize the relation between casework and psychotherapy as a relation in which individuals in one profession (casework) used the help of individuals in another for personal therapy, for help with professional problems, for consultation on cases, for formulation of theory, and even for training in their own skill. This is a different conception of training from that which prevails in the current functional point of view, where the source of training for casework lies within its own profession, through processes of teaching and supervision which maintain the unique character of casework as a separate professional discipline. The comparison between this present-day theory and the historical phase in the 1920's is of exceptional value not only because it illuminates development, but also because it adds immeasurably to current understanding of differences which continue into the present with respect to the origin of the theory, the nature of the curriculum, and the source of help essential in preparing to become a caseworker.

This drawing of a contrast existent in current thought takes us a long way ahead of our story, yet requires mention to sharpen the purpose for tracing these developments. The relation of casework to psychoanalytic influence cannot be understood without realizing this fact of the caseworkers' use of help from psychotherapists. This seems to have been the primary channel of influence, although in addition, and not to be minimized, was the interest of caseworkers in the psychoanalytic literature and the rapid expansion of services which placed the caseworker in a helping role in the same setting with the psychiatrist or analyst, as was true for instance in the child guidance clinic movement. Through the referral of clients to mental hygiene clinics caseworkers were gaining new insight from conferences with psychiatrists. Many discussion groups were led by analysts. Caseworkers were attending classes taught by these exponents of a new point of view. Dr. Taft, in 1925, describes the effect of these influences in this way:

"The linkage between mental hygiene and social case work has been deepened steadily and almost without opposition since the inception of the mental hygiene movement a few years ago. . . . Social case work was starving for a practical human psychology, and had been fed for the most part on academic husks. The doctrines of mental hygiene and the new psychology came as the fulfillment of a long felt need."[1]

In order to understand later developments, it is essential first to examine the substance of casework theory in this decade of the 1920's, when it was still undifferentiated from psychoanalysis and when those who were later to become engaged in the development of the theory of function were still within this same realm of influence. Yet from the beginning, despite all that in the 1920's was so much like the traditional psychonanalytic point of view, the writings of those associated with the Pennsylvania School of Social Work and its field work agencies always showed elements of difference. These centers of difference and questioning attitudes comprised the readiness to make use of exactly that psychological formulation of which Dr. Otto Rank is the author.

What casework took from psychoanalysis in the early part of the decade of the 1920's (besides the heightened interest in the psychological already mentioned) was, first, a new realization that behavior originates in sources of inner need and stress, and represents the effort of the organism to satisfy, release, be free of compelling psychic necessity. This realization that behavior is an expression of the human self in its striving to live accorded to behavior of all kinds new value and new respect. Seen as a symptom of emotional disturbance, all behavior, evil and destructive as well as socially valuable, was accepted as an expression of the strivings of the self. The very use of the words "symptom" and "illness" implied that it occurred through no fault of the individual, with a resultant freeing of the individual, temporarily at least, from responsibility for his own actions, since these actions were a disturbance for which he could not be held accountable. This is one of the points of major divergence between the functional psychology and some other current points of view in casework; functional casework has developed a wholly new relation to the concept of self-responsibility, as we shall later see.

In the 1920's the new attitude toward behavior acclaiming freedom from judgmental bias was stated by Miss Marcus thus: " . . . The case worker can eventually accept any behavior without condemnation once she understands what caused it, and that as soon as she can reconcile the abnormal and anti-social with the normal and social, she is on the road to case work."[2]

Revolutionary as this seemed at the time, it nevertheless reflected a fundamental change occurring throughout social work. The direct result of this change was a throwing off of judgmental standards of approval or condemnation of behavior. Much help must have been given and taken in these times with temporary therapeutic results from this kindly acceptance of the client exactly as he was, including every expression of his behavior. It is important to note again that one of the trends which we are following here reflects the developmental changes in this concept of acceptance; today in functional casework theory and practice its meaning has changed in significant ways. Obviously, this historical phase of acceptance was an inevitable component of evolutionary process, but acceptance becomes a sterile and empty concept when it does not move beyond this point.

A second concept which caseworkers took from psycho-analysts in this period was the concept of the influence of the earliest years of a child's life, particularly of the parental influences during those years. Suddenly the whole matter of parental relationships, mother to child, father to child, father to mother, child to siblings, became of utmost interest. Caseworkers embarked upon an endless search for history, an inevitable result of this concept. On behalf of the child, they sought facts from parents: physical, emotional, and developmental; and on behalf of the adult who came for help for himself, they sought to lead him back into his childhood, there to disentangle memories and associations, in the effort to discover the precise spot where something went awry, where traumatic injury occurred. It becomes increasingly clear how intrinsic to and inescapable a part of this theory it is, to locate total responsibility upon the parents—perhaps blame would be the more accurate word to use. For social work was now embarked upon a new era of accounting for delinquency and failure of any kind by assigning the cause to the early home situation. A parent's natural psychological guilt for too total assumption of responsibility finds an ally in this social point of view. Carried to extremes, it obliterates the child's own separateness and responsibility, and obscures the essential acknowledgment that every individual, even when very young, carries some core of self and feels a measure of accountability for his own actions.

Finally, the third important concept which gained support in this period was the belief in causal determinism, and this belief is but a logical and natural outcome of what has already been described. If the trauma occurred in childhood, if the first five years of the child's life mold his character, then there is no other conclusion than that the solution to the problem must be sought in the past. Returning along the pathway to these early years, one must find the cause and correct it. Here, in this sequence of a causal chain, the past holds the key and wields its power over the present. To make this theory effective, the caseworker must be the interpreter —it is the caseworker who studies, assembles the facts, prepares the diagnosis, prescribes the cure and finally offers it to the client. In short, casework found the answer to its search for the therapeutic factor in just this reliance upon isolating causes in the early developmental experience, believing that the promise of therapeutic results arose from the efficacy of explanation, interpretation, and intellectual understanding. By this means it was hoped the conflicted self would be able to throw off the bondage of the destructive childhood influences.

It is precisely with regard to this question of what it is that accounts for therapeutic results that the paths of two schools of thought in social casework begin to diverge and move in opposite directions. In the discussion which follows I have not attempted to carry into the present that point of view originating in causal determinism, for my interest is in describing the evolution of a new concept regarding the therapeutic factor, one which eventually led to the functional method of helping.

At the head of this chapter is a quotation from a paper written by Dr. Jessie Taft in 1927.[3] This brief but penetrating statement contains the essence of the difference with respect to the source of therapeutic results. The similarity between the thought expressed in this paper written in 1927, and the thought expressed in a paper written by Dr. Taft in 1949, is striking: "We can hardly avoid admitting that the help the patient receives comes not from his reliving of an unhappy past but from the fact that he finds courage to live and feel differently in the present."[4] Yet despite this likeness between the two papers written more than twenty years apart in time, there are also some striking contrasts which illuminate in significant ways the scope and depth of development these concepts of helping have undergone in this same period of time.

The first clear expression of dissatisfaction with the lack of understanding of the therapeutic factor is to be found in a paper written by Dr. Taft and read before the National Conference of Social Work in June of the same year. It is noteworthy that this follows her initial association with Rank. What we find in this statement is not only the dissatisfaction with what is missing, but also an effort to formulate a theory: "No one who was using the office contact as his medium of treatment seemed to be very clear as to just what were the factors in the psychiatric interview which produced therapeutic results, and as far as I know there has never been any attempt to establish a clear cut theory of technique based on conscious knowledge of the relation of the process to therapy or case work. We all fell back on the superior insight which made the material obtained more relevant and the interpretation of it more significant; but the therapy, as far as there was any, remained unanalyzed and uncontrolled."[5] The psychiatric interview to which Dr. Taft refers is her own work as mental hygienist in a children's agency, a kind of helping different from the helping process undertaken by the caseworker. In the same paper she offers this penetrating observation: "In my own work I have become more and more aware that the informational content of the interview matters much less than my attitude and the child's comfort in the relationship temporarily established and I believe that in that direction lies the clue to the therapeutic function of the case worker. . . .

"The point we wish to emphasize is that what gives the office interview its therapeutic value is not a rehearsal of misdeeds or a recounting of old loves or fears; it is rather an immediate feeling experience produced by the temporary security which the relation to the mental hygienist in role of understanding parent affords."[6]

This initial formulation for casework of a theory regarding the therapeutic factor, which still remains authentic today, laid the groundwork for later developments in functional casework. The source of influence in the psychology of Rank is evident.

Both Miss Robinson and Dr. Taft have written of the events and developments, beginning with Dr. Taft's association with Dr. Otto Rank in 1926, that led eventually to the formulation of the functional method of helping.[7] These same developments in the growth of theory can be traced clearly and precisely in their own writings, beginning as early as 1918. The continuity of the development is strikingly clear: elements appear which were present from the beginning and never given up; the sharpening of the problem in one year reveals itself as responsible for the next development in another year; the search continues for ever increasing understanding of the concepts at first but partially comprehended. There is readiness for exactly that psychological point of view and relation to helping which Dr. Rank represented. All of this unfolds from step to step in a sequence in which the later discovery of function appears as a natural outcome. Miss Robinson commented upon this readiness for the point of view represented in Rank's thinking thus: "While the point of view here presented comes to me personally and to many other case workers through the analytic psychology of Dr. Rank it seems only fair to point out at the same time that the very rapidity and thoroughness with which caseworkers have assimilated at least certain parts of this point of view seem to be evidence that their own thinking and experience have been moving along the same direction and find a satisfying expression in this psychology. If this is not true, if this psychology does not express the realities of the case worker's experience with her clients, then it will yield to a more adequate formulation. At the present time it offers the best approach I know to the obscure and subtle problems of the relationship between the worker and the client."[8]

This was written in 1930, in the midst of the developments with which we are here concerned; the forecast that casework will need to formulate its difference from therapy comes to pass in actuality, but not through departure from a psychology the essential elements of which were already complete at the time when Miss Robinson wrote this statement.

Between the years 1918 and 1924 the writings of Dr. Taft, appearing principally as papers in the *Proceedings of the National Conference of Social Work,* reveal many of the same ideas and tendencies that characterized the casework movement as a whole. She was herself not a caseworker, in the precise meaning of that word, but a psychologist, a "Mental Hygienist" to use her exact title. In this role she occupied a unique position in affording connection between the psychoanalyst on the one hand, and the caseworker on the other, and undoubtedly carried within herself these interactions between casework and psychotherapy which we have been discussing. Her papers now constitute an important part of the casework literature reflecting accelerated interest in the psychological aspects of helping. During this period her writings reflect the same belief in the efficacy of the caseworker's direct efforts to effect change. In 1918, in a paper entitled "Supervision of the Feeble-minded in the Community," she wrote: "Such supervision (by the caseworker) would do much to keep the feeble-minded child steadily at work—not only because the worker could come in at a crisis to help adjust difficulties and tide him over a period of discouragement, but because the worker would explain the child to the employer and through her ability to adjust problems as they arose would make the employer willing and able to keep a class of workers who might under ordinary conditions be impossible."[9]

The striking change which has come about in the understanding of helping could nowhere be more precisely illuminated than in this contrast between the present-day concept and the content of this early quotation. In recent years Dr. Taft has commented upon the precipitant which brought this change. The child himself, she says, defeated every effort to keep him "nicely put," and brought about from the helping person the inevitable admission that the child's own will had something to do with the result.

It would be possible to enlarge upon the illustration of that which, at this time, showed likeness between the thinking of those who later developed functional helping, and the thinking of casework as a whole. But we are concerned not so much with these likenesses as with the differences which are already apparent and which remain characteristic throughout the whole development. I have extracted four major factors which seem to me to be present in the writings of Dr. Taft and Miss Robinson during this period from 1918 on; factors which carry forward the continuity in this development. These are: first, an awareness of process which consistently rejected the mechanical; second, an acknowledgment of the complexity of the emotional life which led to the relinquishment of interpretation; third, a realization that the self of the helping person was a matter of primary interest and importance in the whole situation; and, finally, an increasing conviction that the compelling desire to produce change on the outside was at its source the desire to fulfill the strivings for change and growth within the self.

It is of great interest to contemplate the part played by each of these elements in the developments which were ahead. For example, it is hard to conceive how the client could have been accorded his rightful place as the central figure in the helping process, if the projection upon him of the helping person had not first been removed. As a later discussion of understanding will elaborate, the longing to understand the human psychic life is first of all a longing to understand one's own self, and if the helping person is not aware of this, the need to understand is projected upon the one who is helped, in such a way that the latter's own self-initiated movement to develop self-understanding is interfered with. The transformation of the will-to-understand-the-other into the more suitable will-to-understand-the-self, is an inescapable prerequisite to the desirable admission that self-understanding is also the aim for the one being helped.

As early as 1919, in writing of the "Qualifications of the Psychiatric Social Worker," Dr. Taft identifies this problem of the caseworker's interest in her own conflicts. The interest of the student, she says, "is bound to center there until she can work her way out. True she is not much good at casework until she has settled herself, but in my experience, there seems to be no way of avoiding this period of subjective interest among students who are drawn from an imperfect world where most people are unadjusted and unfamiliar with mental hygiene. It seems to me this stage of absorption in the personal application of social psychiatry should be allowed for and the objective direction of attention not be expected until later."[10]

Apart from certain implications arising from choice of words, this basic statement of 1919 is still authentic for casework training. The concept of growth, and of conflict as a natural component of growth, had not yet been fully enough possessed to enable Dr. Taft at this time to disentangle the goal of the training process from its association with "maladjustment." Later, her rather regretful concession that "there is no way to avoid this," because of an "imperfect world," gives way to a positive affirmation of the growth process essential for any individual who hopes to use himself in the role of helping others.[11] In 1920 Miss Robinson related this same idea directly to the immediate problem of training students: "For these entering students the most important and most difficult phase of training is their own adjustment to the problems of social work."[12]

In this same year (1920) and in the same paper, there also appears for the first time another element of paramount importance, whose fundamental meaning has not changed, much as has been the development in fineness of detail and fuller understanding. This element is the realization of the dynamic for learning which resides nowhere else but in the one who is to learn: "In my experience, both in learning and in teaching, I have never found a way of 'getting over' knowledge or technique to a person unless that person had a problem to the solution of which that knowledge or technique was necessary."[13] While this idea was written with the specific content of learning and teaching in mind, it carries equal validity for casework, in opposition to the belief first expressed by Miss Richmond that change was accomplished by "direct action of mind upon mind." It forecasts the later exploration of the reality of the individual's resistance to change initiated from without.

One dominant impression which grows from these papers,

written in the early years of the 1920's, is the constant interplay of opposing ideas, actually in movement within the
compass of one paper. For example, in 1920 Dr. Taft gives a
worker-oriented definition of casework which is certainly on
the side of effecting change by direct methods: "This paper
will assume casework to mean social treatment of a malad-
justed individual involving an attempt to understand his
personality, behavior and social relationships and to assist
him in working out a better social and personal adjustment."[14] But before she has finished the paper, she has gone
beyond this into a vigorous acclaim of the dynamic center
within the individual himself: "We blind ourselves to the
primary importance of the dynamic wish, of the will to live,
or whatever you choose to call the energic basis of human
life,"[15] and she has spoken a convincing word for trying to
understand the child *from himself,* not from the adult's projection upon him.

In bringing to a conclusion these illustrations of the elements that have carried both continuity and change, there
is one other concept to be mentioned. In 1928, Miss Robinson speaks of the importance of spontaneity in the response
of the caseworker. It is, she says, in order to be free "to respond sensitively to the changing emotional needs of the
client" that the worker must be helped toward self-growth.
"The movement in an interview is in flow of feeling and
emotion, registered, of course, by all sorts of overt behavior
changes but so subtly recorded that we have little skill to
read them consciously aright. On the other hand we respond
to them intuitively by that process of feeling with the other
person in the total identification with his feeling state."[16]

Here is the precise statement of the importance of "response" in the casework process, later to become the center
of the concept of understanding and to occupy so important
a position in describing the helping process as it has today.
The word "intuitive" gives a clue to the next development,
for it was out of the inescapable question where the control

of the process lay, that the next movement originated. Also, if we were to try to select but one way to characterize the difference that function introduces, there would be none better than to point to the break-up of this "total identification" by the introduction of form, focus, and partialization, through which the client differentiates his own self from that of the helper.

It is no wonder that Rank's concept of the will, his emphasis upon the present, and his understanding of the dynamics of the helping situation should have found so immediate a response in those already at work upon these problems. In 1924 Dr. Otto Rank came to the United States for the first time, and he returned once again in 1926. It was in the fall of 1926 that Dr. Taft went to Rank for help with her own understanding and skill in helping others. From 1926 until his death in 1939 Rank was actively engaged in therapeutic practice, teaching, lecturing, and writing, and during this entire period he was closely associated with the Pennsylvania School of Social Work. It is not my purpose here to restate these facts of his relation to the School, already so well known, but instead to emphasize two important points. The first is the connection between the problems upon which caseworkers were working in the early 1920's as I have attempted to describe them, and the solution to those problems found in the psychological viewpoint encountered for the first time in Rank's creative work. The second is the acknowledgment of the source of this process of functional casework in Rank's psychology. Here we have been examining the developments which show the separation from therapy of casework, manifesting as it does its own new beginning and its distinct nature and character. Yet this casework method is rooted in the will psychology of Rank, from which it can be said a whole fresh psychology of living, as well as a psychology of therapy, a psychology of learning, and a psychology of casework, have emerged. Dr. Taft later writes of this experience:

"Those few social workers who experienced something quite unlike classical psychoanalysis in their contact with Rank were saved in part from the tendency to put into practice with clients what they themselves had found helpful, by the fact that they were not at all sure what technique had been used with them. It was not anything they could grasp and formulate intellectually. Difference they had certainly experienced and were still experiencing, but they were unable to pin it down to anything definite enough to be turned on the clients. They had learned that help comes from something more than intellectual knowing, that it goes beyond the facts or even the traumas of a life history, that it is a dynamic, present, swift-moving experience with an ending; but what to do with it in case work could not be determined so easily."[17]

It is this expression of "what to do with it in case work" which gives us our direction for examining the next phase in this development. That a completely new and unique concept and process had to be recreated in casework terms is evident, and it was to this that the next decade of 1930 to 1940 was to devote itself.

In the field of casework as a whole this decade was the period of psychoanalytic influence, when casework developed from the stimulus which psychotherapy had to offer. It was a period that saw the development of a comprehensive theory of psychological causation, according to the past the determinative power to shape a man's character. But it saw, as well, the beginnings of another evolutionary process which restored the present experience to its pre-eminent psychological position, and gave recognition to the vitality of the human will. At the same time, there developed a fresh acknowledgment of the strength of the human self and its capacity for creative self-determination. The possibilities of therapeutic value residing in the new experience with a responsible helper, and the importance of response, accurate and immediate, were realized. What was still lacking in casework during this period was the grasp of a factor that could provide the control of the helping process. Out of this problem the search for the form—for the control of the process—led to the discovery of function.

CHAPTER IV

THE DISCOVERY OF FUNCTION

THE PERIOD which we have just been examining is a period of intermingling of casework thought and practice with psychoanalytic influences. In the midst of this accelerated change and movement, casework was seeking its own form and identity. Prior to 1930 it was hardly possible to disentangle what was casework from what was therapy. True there appeared occasional reference to the fact that casework did have, and must in the long run have, just this separate form and distinction as method. But this was still more of a hope than a realization.

In contrast, the decade of the 1930's opened with a distinguished event in casework itself which marks the beginning of a new developmental phase, namely, the publication of Miss Robinson's book, *A Changing Psychology in Social Case Work*. Its effect was to gather together and inform with new creative meaning the developments of the decade just coming to a close. Miss Robinson characterizes her own writing in this way: "In the second part of this study, in using the concept of relationship as a basis for interpretation, I realize that I have gone beyond any articulated philosophy of case work; not, I believe, beyond what is implicit in certain trends of present practice. . . . Another ten years and the process will have moved forward."[1]

Past, present, and future are implicit in this statement: the trends in practice, the author's articulated philosophy which goes beyond any yet attempted, the realization of process yet to be. In this analysis of a changing psychology, a new casework psychology was actually created, given form, substance, and reality. By this clarification of what was known the new problem of what was not yet known became manifest, thus rendering itself accessible to exploration and examination. The search for function was the direct result of a new comprehension of this unsolved problem, a problem which we shall attempt to describe. Its solution came about because Dr. Taft, who was a therapist herself, felt the compelling need, in turning from therapeutic practice to the teaching of casework, to discover, now, not the likenesses but the differences between casework and therapy—the separate, unique, distinguishing characteristics of a method which, while related to others, nevertheless was autonomous.

The effect of Miss Robinson's book upon the field of social casework was powerful and far-reaching. It broke up accustomed ways of thinking and practicing, setting in motion fresh new streams of development. In June, 1931, in a review in *The Family,* Bertha Reynolds wrote: "Some books sink into the pool of oblivion without a ripple. . . . Some are like earthquakes, felt but not comprehended at the time and producing no one knows what changes. One only knows that after their coming nothing is the same again. *A Changing Psychology in Social Case Work* bears the mark of such a book."[2] And so indeed it has been. Miss Reynolds adds, "It produces fear, consternation, wonder, deep delight. It cannot be dismissed lightly even though one's fundamental disagreement prompts one to set it aside."

The fear of which Miss Reynolds speaks is an altogether natural and inevitable fear, one which had to be grappled with immediately. It could not be overcome by denying that it existed or that this was a deeply penetrating impact opening up an awareness of the responsibility of the caseworker which could no longer be evaded. Miss Robinson herself takes hold of this whole problem again in a paper[3] read at the National Conference of Social Work in Milwaukee in June, 1931, approximately six months after her book appeared from the press. While the title of this paper interestingly enough is "Psychoanalytic Contributions to Social Case-Work Treatment," the substance of its discussion develops the unique nature of casework, just now beginning to find what is its own. Consequently, in order to understand accurately the significance of these developments, the Milwaukee paper must be considered along with *A Changing Psychology in Social Case Work*.

One would think it difficult to select from so much rich content, in so significant a book, any one thing to which to point and say, this was the most significant of all—and yet actually that is not the case. For it was in the new understanding of relationship and its meaning and use both in natural life experience and in casework process that the dynamic for new development lay. In the decade of the 1920's this was spoken of as "transference," a psychoanalytic term, and used by caseworkers with timidity. In 1924 Dr. Taft had written an article on the "use of transference in the office interview";[4] but by office interview she was thinking not of the usual practice in casework, but of a very special treatment process carried on by herself as a mental hygienist in the setting of a casework agency. The transference was the emotional quality aroused in the patient through the very therapeutic experience itself, but for some practitioners its justification lay more in the purpose which it served to accomplish free association with the past. Enough has already been said in this discussion to indicate that, in the different developments which we are here tracing, the "transference" (and in functional helping this word has long since passed out of use) was suddenly realized to be the very substance of the present experience out of which therapeutic results eventuated.

It was with this concept that Miss Robinson was engaged, when she took hold of its meaning for casework practice: "The term 'transfer' is too directly borrowed from psychiatric terminology and leaves the case worker again with a dependence upon another profession and a confused sense of likeness at this point instead of forcing her to analyze her own process in its unique difference from every other professional venture.

"The word 'relationship' which I have chosen here implies interaction and continuity. Further than this it remains to be defined by whatever distinguishing characteristics we can find as we examine the use of this relationship on the part of the client and on the part of the case worker."[5]

The word relationship is still indispensable in present-day thinking and practice. In this discussion of choice in casework process I have made use of it, adding to it another indispensable word, engagement, one which carries some suggestion of the interaction of which Miss Robinson speaks above, and in addition the immediacy of response which constitutes so important a part of the process.

The key point which was absent from Miss Robinson's book, with which she already begins to deal in her Milwaukee paper, was any indication of where the control of this process lay. Her own thinking and writing had gone the whole way in admitting, describing, capitulating to, the primary place occupied by the client in this process. It was precisely this capacity on the part of the helping person to enable the client to feel his own strivings and to define himself in his own terms that afforded the key to the new relationship. The norm, the outer value imposed upon him as a standard and goal with educational intent was gone, and with it control; for whatever else one might say about the worker-conceived treatment plan, it did at least constitute a charted direction, and when this was given up, the absence of purpose, form, and direction in casework process became apparent.

This is indeed a dilemma, for having granted so much control in the hands of the client, where lies any reasonable or necessary control of the process itself? Obviously if the caseworker does indeed feel with the client in identification, as was the essential first step, then what is to prevent both caseworker and client from sinking into the quicksand of the client's confusion and immobility, resulting in surrender to the magnitude of his insoluble problem? That there must be control is evident. And that some of this control must be in the hands of the caseworker is also evident. Since it can no longer be control of the client by the caseworker, then once more it is asked, where is it and what is it? From the core of this dilemma emerged the growth of the solution: the new understanding of control of the process, of control of the elements of the situation in which help takes place; all of this being made possible in new ways because of the difference which function introduces. The first problem for students today is to acknowledge the powerful control which they exercise by virtue of one fact and one fact alone, that of presuming to be a helping person. From this realization the development of the student moves from control of the client to no control at all; then to assumption of the responsibility for the control of the process and of the immediate situation in its form and time.

The precise difference between Miss Robinson's thinking in 1930 and 1940 is illuminated by two quotations which reflect this contrast. In 1930: "First I would make a sharp distinction between the goals of psychoanalytic and of case-work therapy in the extent of the change they hope to effect. A psychoanalytic process disturbs the patient's whole adjustment. In it his most fundamental relationship patterns are utilized and to some extent modified. A new balance grows out of the readjustment experience. In a case-work process, on the other hand, the case-worker may change any aspect of the environment to relieve pressure on the client or to permit him greater opportunity, or she may attempt to change the client's use of a particular aspect of his environment. In doing this, she enters into a relationship with the client which he will use in a characteristic way and in which he will display his fundamental relationship patterns. It seems essential that the case-worker should understand these patterns, but

I would suggest that it is not the function of the case-worker to change these patterns in any radical way. In analysis, a patient is learning to handle his own fundamental problems and the conflicts in himself; in case-work a client is learning to handle a particular problem usually outside himself, in its projection on to the environment."[6]

The understanding of the extent to which in casework, in distinction from therapy, the client's problem is worked out and lived out through projection on the outer reality, is already present in this quotation. This point continues into the newer development; the greatest change in concept comes about in full recognition that the caseworker cannot control the depth of the use of help nor the fundamental nature of the change produced in the process. This is the crucial point apparent in Miss Robinson's writing in 1940: "The word 'partial' has often been used to distinguish change accomplished with case-work help from therapeutic change. True, the definition of agency service and the client's own focus of his problem inevitably and rightly limit and place the problem in partial terms. But no definition and no particularization on the part of the agency can interfere with a client's necessity to place total value on the partial service. Furthermore, when the process of change is felt as inner movement in the self, the client truly risks a total change. This fear of being overwhelmed by his own unleashed forces and invaded by another who has the control, cannot be avoided. It may be reduced by conditions set before him, requiring the breakup of his activity into parts with which he can deal, but somewhere he must take in the shock of the realization of change. This shock involves the whole self for at least an instant in time. It is bearable and therapeutic, not because it is partialized, but because it is met honestly without evasion by a self that has the courage and the organization to meet it sincerely. For this reason I would say that the caseworker as well as the client must use her whole self if she meets her client's need."[7]

The clear evidence of development in understanding of the problem of control in a helping process is strikingly apparent in comparing these two statements, each related to the same theoretical question. Whereas in 1930 Miss Robinson attempted to differentiate casework from therapy in terms of the nature of change—fundamental or otherwise— in 1940 she has come to the opposite realization, that the caseworker cannot control or avoid the client's risk of total change. "This shock involves the whole self for at least an instant in time." And the use of the caseworker's whole self is required. The form within which this occurs is comprised of the function and structure of the agency, constituting the outer reality upon which he projects his inner conflict.

But this momentary illumination of the contrast in time takes us once again far ahead of the sequential story, for what Miss Robinson writes in 1940 is the result of a developmental process during the ten years which separate the two periods of writing.

In 1934 Dr. Taft joined the faculty of the Pennsylvania School of Social Work, and in so doing she gave up a practice as a therapist and an especially focused interest in casework with children. The latter was not "given up" in any sense other than through its integration now with the interest in all other casework services implicit in the task of taking on the function of a casework teacher. But the actual evolution of the concept of function took place primarily in the field of casework with children in foster care, quite naturally, because of Dr. Taft's original and continuing interest in that field. I have already made mention in passing of a fact that I wish now to re-emphasize because of its striking significance. Dr. Taft, who was most instrumental in the discovery of function,[8] and who is today the most vigorous proponent of the theory of distinction between casework and therapy, is herself the person in social work who of all persons had the most direct connection with therapy, as therapist herself, as translater of Rank's books, as writer of an important book on child therapy, *The Dynamics of Therapy in a Controlled Relationship*.[9] If one believes in the compelling influence of an unsolved problem when it encounters readiness in a person to tackle a problem, then here is a precise illustration. For just because of her close identification with psychotherapy, Dr. Taft was impelled to discover the difference, to separate from that which was so dominantly therapeutic, and to find what was unique for casework in order to understand and teach it. And by so doing she made a lasting contribution to the field.

The concept of function was fully developed by the year 1937, when the first volume of the series of Journals of the Pennsylvania School of Social Work, entitled *The Relation of Function to Process*,[10] appeared. Edited by Dr. Taft, it contains her fundamental statement of function which has remained without modification its authentic definition. Today there is not a word of it that one would wish to change. Its meaning is so whole, so complete, yet so compressed, that even for those who believe they understand it fully, there never is a time of rereading but what the understanding of what is written there moves to another level. Simultaneously, in the years when this point of view was being evolved, Dr. Taft was also engaged in major publications, bringing to fruition her own thinking and experience in therapeutic and psychological terms. In rapid succession there appeared, first, in 1932, the important paper on "Time"[11] read before the National Conference of Social Work (a paper which later became the first chapter of a book); in 1933, *The Dynamics of Therapy in a Controlled Relationship*, already referred to; and in 1936 the English translations of and introductions to *Will Therapy*[12] and *Truth and Reality*.[13] It is as if at once two parallel tendencies had been contained in one person, the one an ending phase, possessed in this amazingly productive writing in psychological content; and the other, a new tendency in a beginning phase, of which "The Relation of Function to Process" was the first written expression.

In the Preface to the Journal, *The Relation of Function to Process*, Miss Robinson states: "The problem of the relation of function to process in social case work has been the focus of study and experiment in the work of the case work faculty of the Pennsylvania School of Social Work" for a period of some four years (roughly, from 1933 to 1937). The two volumes of the Journal which followed (in 1938 and 1939) give additional evidence of the great activity in thought and practice which was going on at the school during this period. One other major event in the same development was the publication of the first book on supervisory process, *Supervision in Social Case Work*,[14] which not only added rich detail to the concept of function but also created a new concept of process in a function other than casework. In her most recent publication, *The Dynamics of Supervision under Functional Controls*, Miss Robinson carries forward the concept and method first stated some fifteen years previously and clarifies the universal concepts in which all processes of helping are rooted, at the same time that the distinctive and unique differences inherent in each function are recognized.

This chapter has undertaken to trace the events and publications through which a fundamental change was expressed, a change which came about as a result of the discovery of function and its creative utilization. The problem in 1930 was one of discovering where the control of the process lay; what distinguished casework helping from psychotherapy. In 1930 it was still believed that the caseworker somehow controlled the depth of the client's use of help and the extent and quality of the internal change which he experienced. The importance of the external reality factors of agency and client problem was fully acknowledged but not yet with clear understanding of where the significance of the outer reality lay. From this awareness of problem, explored and worked upon in the teaching process, in the supervisory process, in casework process in school and agency, it at last became clear that form bears a fundamental relation to the process; that the concrete reality of the helping situation carries the true projection of the deepest conflict of the self; and that help upon a practical, tangible life problem affords the potentiality for help which touches the core of the self and sets in motion an authentic process of growth.

This compressed summary has touched upon the question, what was the fundamental difference which function introduced? The question cannot be answered historically or in summary, but only by the full presentation of the functional process of giving and taking help. The whole of Part II of this book will be devoted to the exploration of the nature of this process.

P A R T I I

CHOICE IN CASEWORK PROCESS

The ego needs the Thou in
order to become a Self. . . .
OTTO RANK

CHAPTER V

STATEMENT OF THE PROBLEM: THE ULTIMATE SINGLE NATURE OF CHOICE

THE VITAL problem of choice, as it manifests itself in the casework process, arises, interestingly enough, from the very center of the most significant development in casework practice in recent times. This development has already been described in the preceding chapters as the evolution of the full willingness to concede to the one who seeks help the central role in the process; to yield to him the place of "chief actor," to use Rank's words; to see him as the dynamic center of vital forces, imbued with selfhood which carries the impulse and will to determine its own self-direction. This concept lies at the very heart of functional casework and is intimately and inextricably related to every other concept in this casework theory.

Over the years, as new light has been cast upon the client as the central, active figure in a process in which he uses help, various structures in agency setting have been developed in order to focus upon and further the client's choice and responsibility. The most ordinary, most tangible, most seemingly procedural piece of agency way of working can be recognized as an outgrowth of a concept whose roots are deeply psychological. In fact, the inevitability of these very structures as the evidence of the concept of which we here speak is strikingly apparent. The client comes to the social agency which he chooses, to its office, to apply for its services. His interviews take place in the office of the agency, at a designated place, at a regular time. To him is communicated, in a process of initial exploration of whether he wishes to use this service, as much as is communicable regarding the manner in which this particular agency offers its help, in order that he can discover whether this service is for him. By these means and numerous others similar in character, the client's necessity and right to find his own way into the use of this service, on some shred of his own momentum, is safeguarded. The will of a social agency which does not have these structures, or is careless about them, is a powerful unrestrained force, no matter how benevolently intended, that can paralyze into immobility the unstable, unsure self of a troubled person, and sweep him into entanglement with an agency service long before he has any self-initiated movement.

These agency structures—tangible, concrete evidences of a fundamental recognition of the client's autonomy—express the unshakable belief of casework in the concept of freedom of choice. It is the client who must choose whether he wishes to use the help of this agency on the terms on which he finds it; he is the one to whom is left both the necessity and the capacity for disentangling a host of reality problems through which and in spite of which he must act in order to live. No matter how persistently he tries to transfer to the caseworker the burden of telling him what to do, he discovers in the long run how utterly impossible this is. The caseworker, as well, relearns this lesson from every client he helps.

To this human truth, the relation of the caseworker can only be described adequately as a capitulation, a yielding to the way life is, and the way man is made. Words such as "permitting the client to participate," or even the words I have used above, "to concede to the one who seeks help the central role in the process," all carry a serious flaw, in that they imply a possession in the hands of the caseworker which can be conferred or withheld, given or not given, whereas there is no way to escape the incontrovertible fact (and how glad we can be for it!) that only the self can and does control whether it will or will not use help; whether it can or cannot admit another into the realm of innermost conflict and make effective use of the helping person for this purpose.

This belief in the client's freedom of choice in the practice of many caseworkers has been interpreted to be dependent upon the necessity for actual reality choices. If these are not open to him in his situation the casework agency usually feels obligated to provide opportunities for choice in the actual environment. On the other hand, in recent casework practice we have been faced by the arresting fact that help is possible, and not only possible, but profoundly effective, in situations where there appear to be no conceivable reality choices. Now, suddenly, there is a clash, an encounter, between an idea on the one hand and actual experience on the other, a contradiction which cannot be immediately reconciled. Against the background of a mounting desire for greater reality choices, often of an economic, social, and environmental nature, there comes with the force of a new beginning the impact of an actual fact: that help can be given even when these reality choices are seemingly absent. More and more it becomes apparent that even when the necessity for the use of help arises initially through outer compulsion, and even when the person of the prospective client is removed by force from one place to another, even then, help can be offered and utilized in most striking fashion. From this there emerges only one possible observation and conclusion, namely, that choice among a multiplicity of reality factors does not play the crucial role sometimes assigned to it. Hence we are faced with the necessity of examining anew the psychological meaning of choice.

For this purpose it is valuable to look again at the specific casework services that have contributed to this point of view. In respect to the problem of choice these services at first glance seem to be so different in the manner in which they begin, that one would wonder how any common base of method could apply to both at once. On the one hand, there is the group of services characterized as "protective" in nature originating on account of neglect of children, or because of behavior which carries the offending individual into court. All of these services begin involuntarily, and it is out of precisely this involuntary beginning that some of the impetus for examining the question of choice arises. On the other hand, there is the service of so-called pure counseling, where the reality factors of the concrete service are absent, where the request for help is as voluntary as it can conceivably be, and yet where it is evident again and again, in unmistakable terms, that another kind of choice must be remade at some point in the beginning process, despite the appearance of an initial desire for help which brings the seeker after help to the agency. Still another service which has contributed immeasurably to this opening up of the reexamination of the concept of choice is the casework service located at the point of admission to the mental hospital. Here we have the compelling reality that the patient has come, in many instances, against his will, that it is decided by others that he shall come, that he does not and cannot admit the fact that he is sick, and that minor reality choices which may be open to him fade into insignificance in the face of the one inescapable fact that he has been committed as a sick person to a mental hospital.

Here, then, is the situation as it now exists. Functional casework has moved through creative impetus into situations which no one would have ventured to predict could hold any potentiality for effective helping. The administrators, supervisors, and caseworkers who have been willing to undertake these seemingly impossible tasks have gathered into their hands both the potential and the obstacle, and have demonstrated that something can be created to give help in any situation, provided there is willingness to take the situation as it is and create from the given, the fixed, the unchangeable circumstance.

But the answer to this problem cannot be so readily found in any facile statement that a helping situation can always be created in any situation, no matter how discouraging, so long as the factors as they are found are accepted and used creatively. Something else, of utmost importance, must also be present, in order to afford the potential for effective casework help. What is this something else, that can account for the contradictory evidence of our experience? This is the challenging question to which the present discussion leads us.

The key to the exploration is perhaps to be found in the very beginnings of functional casework, and if we look there we come inevitably to examine once more the field of child placement which played so important a role in providing the casework experience in which the concept of function was developed. In this field it became apparent very soon that the child who was to be placed in foster care had no conceivable reality choice in the matter. It was his parent who initiated and carried through this move, and the child who could do no other than let himself be placed, physically at least, so that he found himself in a family of unchosen strangers, in the care of an agency of frightening proportions, and was required to accustom himself to a separation thrust upon him by external force. Under the circumstances he had only one escape, which was to refuse the placement psychologically by any behavior which served as an outlet for the rebellion against the violence done him, contrary to his own readiness. Even a baby spits his food, tenses his body, refuses comfort, and rejects in every psychological way known to humankind the indignity and affront of an alien will imposed upon his own.

The form and substance of child placement changed when the concept of the child's own will entered the realm of helping. For now it was suddenly clear that even though the child had no reality choice with respect to whether he would or would not be placed, physically, he did have, and retained in a way that no one could take away from him, the choice to refuse the placement psychologically. Even though he had no choice of foster parents, he did retain the choice of whether he would or would not take them on as adults to whom he could find a relationship in his childhood needs, emotional and biological. Once this fact was faced squarely, that the child had it in him to refuse placement, no matter how carefully the home was selected or how meticulously he was placed, and when this fact was capitulated to in thought and feeling, then there opened up the promising, fruitful pursuit of the way to create the situation in which the child could discover his own self-created movement. In a word, it was discovered that the casework aim should be to find the way to help the child become related newly and constructively to the inevitable reality factors, at the same time that there was available to him the support of an agency and a caseworker who knew, astonishingly, how to help him bring about his own separation in ways that could transform the experience into a self-willed movement.

From these origins in the child placement field, this electrifying psychological truth moved rapidly into other areas of helping, and soon became sturdily established as a part of the generic whole which forms the common ground in which every functional helping process is rooted. At the same time, when this truth is incorporated into other casework services, especially those dealing with adults, it is evident that an opposite swing has developed, toward more and more emphasis upon the necessity for the reality of the choice. This tendency seeems to arise not so much because of any abandonment of the original principle, but more because of the great difficulty and complexity of maintaining the level of pure psychological movement, and also because of the guilt inherent in holding so unswervingly to the conviction that there is, in the long run, only one single choice which matters in this process of helping. Twenty years of experience give functional casework the right to say that as helping persons we cannot afford to allow ourselves to be misled by the attractive lure of the reality choice. Its attraction seems to lie in an ideology through which escape is sought from the guilt that the helping person inevitably carries.

Statement of the Problem

It seems necessary now to restate the meaning of the single nature of choice. No matter what the service, no matter how it begins, whether voluntarily or otherwise, no matter how much or how little external pressure has been exerted upon the person to get him to the source of help, there is but one crucial moment of time that matters, and this is the moment in which the self chooses between growth or refusal of growth, life or the negation of life; when the organism, in short, chooses to live and turns its energies from the negative fight against what is, to the vibrant immediacy of what it can do, no matter. This is the moment in time that occurs in every process of help, irrespective of difference of function. And while I speak of it here as a "moment" of time, I mean as well a moment which recurs again and again, never to be wholly settled or determined, but in constant process of becoming, as is the life process itself.

While this sounds like a momentous moment, an event of major importance, as indeed it is, its fascinating other-sidedness lodges in the fact that the smallest, most ordinary, most inconsequential actions on the part of the self in the process of which we speak, can carry the meaning of this turning point. This is the mysterious and enchanting way that life is, which provides a unity and connection between the commonplace and the profound.

If caseworkers truly incorporate this concept into themselves as a genuine part of the professional self in helping, then an unrealized potential for helping opens up. In a later chapter we shall be examining in more detail the true significance of content in the pure psychological movement of growth, as intensified in the helping process. But now it is enough to view in its full and true significance the one, single, unadulterated stream of knowing and understanding that comprehends this pre-eminent reality, so essential a part of the make-up of the helping person.

After the whole discussion of casework process has been introduced via the projection of the dominant idea of the new level on which the one choice actually resides, and this has been spoken of as growth or the refusal of growth, an inevitable question and objection begins to take form to challenge the writer upon this subject. Why should growth have anything to do with so concrete a request for help as, say, a request for a housekeeper, a request for child placement, a request for financial help, a request for assistance in becoming established as a new American? Certainly no client who comes to an agency with any of these requests ever comes, by any stretch of the imagination, asking for an inner experience of growth. He approaches this intent more nearly when he seeks out a child guidance clinic, or a psychiatrist, or marital counseling; or he may have some idea of this necessity once he admits, as a patient in a mental hospital, that he is sick. But even in these services, as we know all too well, he soon reveals his expectation that the change he desires will be produced by the other, by external means, or by change in the environment, and he does not know the necessity for inner change even under these optimum circumstances, but has to discover it anew in each situation.

If this be true, how can we possibly speak of choosing help, how can we possibly feel comfortable in offering the kind of service that the social agency offers, when we know so well that the client cannot choose it because he cannot know that it is like this? This is the problem which will be described and worked upon in the following chapter, which deals with the client's initial movement toward the social agency as the first tangible expression of his exercise of choice.

CHAPTER VI

THE CLIENT'S INITIAL MOVEMENT
TOWARD THE SOCIAL AGENCY

> ... *The patient's ap-*
> *peal for help is the*
> *beginning of the*
> *process of healing.*
> OTTO RANK

THE HISTORY of functional casework abounds in illustration of the manner in which a sudden illumination of
understanding occurs and new areas of potentiality for helping open up when a single new concept penetrates current
thought and practice. Such a concept is the one expressed in
the quotation from Rank at the beginning of this chapter,[1]
and the same thought appears frequently in casework literature because of the meaning it has had for caseworkers. Its
apparent simplicity and natural rightness account for the
speed with which it was put into use, yet just this simplicity
creates at the same time an illusion that this fundamental
concept is easily understood and immediately put to the
client's use. In actuality, it is an extremely complex concept
and one which is peculiarly susceptible to stereotype because
of its illusory simplicity.

Stated briefly, the problem with respect to this concept—
a problem which we can now see more clearly after twenty
years of experience with its use—arises from the assumption,
too hastily arrived at, that the client's initial appeal to the
agency is in fact and in substance a genuine appeal for help,
when in actuality it is never such, nor can it be, no matter
how abundant the evidence that he has given the matter
careful thought and has chosen of his own volition to move

toward the source of help. Not until he has experienced in actuality a genuine piece of what this help is like can he have any reliable basis for choosing, and even then, at every point of crisis in the process, he must choose anew either to go deeper or to take himself out. The beginning for each one who moves toward the source of help is intricately complicated by all manner of circumstances which serve to rationalize and justify the request. If there is any one way of characterizing the function of the helping person at this point, it is this: to help the applicant disentangle his own will to seek and find and use help from all the other wills and pressures and external forces that operate upon him so powerfully. This process of disentanglement he cannot accomplish alone, for if he could, he would hardly need to come for help in the first place. It is this very concrete need which he brings at the beginning, apart from his reality problem, that constitutes the very essence of the first brief experience in using the agency's help and that gives the basis for the emergence of the decision—his own and that of the agency—to begin again, this time with intention to embark upon an authentic and thoroughgoing use of the service that the agency has to offer.

It is my own belief that this process of disentanglement of the will from all the other pressures, this initial period of exploration for the purpose of discovering if help is indeed wanted and can be used, requires the time form of at least three interviews; that it must have a definite and known terminal point, with a decision clearly arrived at. This decision grows out of a realization that a fragment of movement has taken place within a process complete and whole, in spite of its brevity and limitation. One can know with assurance that the client can use help because he has in fact already done so.

In order to understand the problem more accurately, it is necessary to restate and incorporate into this discussion a comparison of two points of view, each of which gives rise to a different series of consequences in a helping process. If the caseworker operates diagnostically, with the belief that he can decide (with more or less factual knowledge) what the nature of the client's problem is, what kind and what level of treatment it requires, and whether or not the client has come to the right agency, then this initial phase is predominantly oriented to fact and to a *prior* decision. From this point of view stems the common belief that it is possible to know in advance to which social agency a client should be referred and that it is possible for agencies to establish lines of distinction for the purpose of deciding the proper and suitable service to which the client should be referred. From this belief many practices originate, such as the endeavor to ascertain from the character of the reality problem and from the degree of apparent emotional disturbance whether the applicant requires a psychiatrist, a family agency, a child placement agency, or public assistance. If the question is honestly faced, one can see how doomed to failure this endeavor is, how fraught with frustration for caseworkers it has always been, and how flagrantly disregardful it is of the client's own choice of a source of help.

In functional casework the beginning stage of the process rests upon concepts diametrically opposite from those just stated. The functional caseworker begins with the belief that it is the client who knows, and that he can be helped to reach this essential self-knowledge in a way that is self-determined. He does not bring this knowledge in any accessible form when he first comes to the agency, but the very application process itself is designed to enable it to come into his possession. With just this much in the way of belief, the helping person has already given substance and meaning to the generalization that intends to "respect the individual," for the most important part of such respect is that it should never lose sight of the fact that the source of healing is within the individual, if he can be helped to reach it; that he alone can uncover and know the problem; and that in the last analysis it is he who holds the ultimate power to use or not use help, he who determines the level upon which he will use it.

Thus far, every word which has been written will be recognized and affirmed by functional helping persons as known and familiar territory. The question then is, wherein lies the problem? Why is this so difficult to accomplish and from what source come the obstacles which at times seem to stand in our way? The difficulty arises because here, as everywhere in helping, the caseworker must carry simultaneously the two-sided character of the experience of choosing, the contradiction, which is the essence of choice itself, until it has been taken back and repossessed by the one who seeks help. Specifically, as related to the particular aspect of the beginning phase which we are discussing here, it is not enough to know that the client's "appeal for help is the beginning of the process of healing." There must also be held in constant relation to this fact its opposite, namely that the initial move toward the source of help is not yet a true choice, and that only out of the process itself comes this new movement, the moment which we recognize as the authentic inner affirmation of the impulse toward life. Students of casework know this movement internally from their own experience. No matter how careful the preparation to come into training, no matter how painstaking and thorough the plan, nothing that happens in advance ever approximates or in any way substitutes for the inescapable choice which must take place, once one is genuinely in the learning process. Knowing this for themselves, students know it also on behalf of their clients.

Some very concrete and particular aspects of this problem require examination, and it is the purpose of the remainder of this chapter to consider a few of these specifics in relation to the general statement of the problem as it has been here presented.

There was a time, in the decade between 1930 and 1940, when conviction regarding the value of explanation to the applicant was at its height. The intention of this explanation was to encompass, insofar as possible, all the conditions implicit in the use of the service: the requirements, the policies, the limitations, the obligations which went with taking what the agency had to offer. The purpose underlying this effort was in line with what we are here discussing. It grew out of a desire to help the applicant choose the service in a more responsible way, in order that he could truly know what he let himself in for if he took something from the agency, either in the way of material benefit or psychological help. This trend toward fuller explanation seems to have arisen as a reaction against a repudiated approach whereby the client was far too rapidly "taken in" without any concrete knowledge upon which to base a decision. But it also indicates a trend toward a new goal, namely, to offer to the client the opportunity for a clear and responsible choice. The locale of much of this explanatory trend was in the public social services, where it found swift compatibility with the legal necessity for utilizing the content of the law and policy of the public agency. However there was also a similar tendency in other functional agencies, always directed toward enabling the applicant to make a reality choice with greater self-responsibility.

As happens inevitably in any development, this reliance upon the efficacy of explanation overreached itself. Too great reliance on explanation tended to obscure the true nature of the individual's relation to a beginning process of using help. The other side of this praiseworthy intention to facilitate choice by means of explanation is the reluctant admission that no one can hear what he is not ready to hear, nor understand that which is wholly outside of himself; explanation can become only an additional deadening weight when it is projected upon the one who is unready.

This realization forced the caseworker to seek for some wholly fresh and creative use of "explanation" in order that the client could in truth know what constitutes choice in the experience of using help. This "knowing" is altogether different from a logical comprehension of the factors, the facts, and the conditions of this situation, as the caseworker knows them.

As the caseworker listens to the client in the application process, the appearance of the particulars in the content of the interviews seems to occur in some natural timing of the client's. The more the helper learns to deepen his own awareness of the other in the interview, the more precise will be his hearing of and his response to those moments of inquiring readiness on the part of the applicant. The characteristic tendency of the inexperienced caseworker is to respond to a question with a factual answer, when often there really is no answer, or when, if an answer were given, it would be rejected by the one who asked for it. If one drops out of attention momentarily the specific content of the question directly put by the client, then it is possible to acknowledge the value of the question to the asker: it may be as the conveyor of apprehension; of doubt as to whether the helping person can really help; of defiance of the conditions which he already senses; of guilt for having come at all; of challenge to the strength of the worker, testing out whether this person has the strength required.

It is always very difficult to put into words the basis on which the caseworker knows whether or not a particular individual in need of help can use the help which the agency has to offer; at the same time in actual experience there has developed a reliable criterion. In essence the conviction forms from having realized that a genuine part of the person seeking help is accessible to, and can be reached by, relationship to the other person. It grows from an awareness that some new element from the immediate situation has been taken in by the client, internalized, and related to in a new way. Every concrete piece of the structure of the agency is an element of this nature. As the client meets these pieces of structure, the fundamental question is: can this person be receptive to this externally imposed condition, in such a way that, instead of pitting his strength against it, he takes it into his possession and utilizes it constructively? In an application process which eventuates in no movement, the client remains solidly fixed in opposition: opposition to these conditions and to the caseworker's way of working, which remains alien and external to his own fixed pattern. He continues to locate responsibility upon all but himself. What the caseworker eventually must learn to recognize with sureness and precision is the moment of yielding in the one seeking help, when the first admission of fault, or flaw, or shortcoming, or self-responsibility—whatever one calls it—suddenly appears and marks the beginning of the capacity to effect some change in the situation through realization of the necessity for change in the self. It is this change, however slight, which can and does happen in the application process, as it must happen again and again in the later continuous process of help.

In short, what we are saying here is that the application process, in certain essential ways, is exactly like the continuous helping process, and that unless it is distinctly and accurately so, the chances are the client will never move into effective use of the agency's service because he has never as yet chosen it from his own self-initiated movement. We are speaking here of a total process which begins at the moment of initial application; which reaches a momentary and partial ending after a time-limited period of three or four interviews; which moves into a new beginning, often with a different caseworker, and thus proceeds into a more lengthy and substantial process, also limited in time. Within that early period, when the reality choice is one of whether to go on with the casework service or to terminate it, the same fundamental dynamics of movement occur. That there are differences in the content and depth of the application movement from the longer helping process goes without saying. But first, before knowing what those differences are, the necessity to affirm the likeness is paramount.

Nature of Choice in Casework Process

In this initial relationship between the one who seeks help and the caseworker who represents the agency service there comes about a kind of togetherness, a unity, a feeling of understanding, that is commonly spoken of in psychological terms as identification. Were it not for this, the whole situation would be barren and without life, and nothing would ever come of it. Not only in the initial phase, but throughout the process which we are here examining, the concept of identification plays an important part, and it is to this that we turn next as we move now more deeply into the consideration of the nature of choice in casework process.

CHAPTER VII

THE QUALITY OF THE CASEWORKER'S IDENTIFICATION

T HE PROBLEM of taking hold of this interesting word "identification" is essentially one arising on account of the change occurring in the quality of identification as the process advances. What can be said regarding the nature of identification in the initial phase of a helping process is quite different from what can be said of it in the concluding phase.

Further, the problem of understanding the nature of identification is complicated by the fact that its quality changes drastically with the development of the caseworker's skill. What we strive so hard to help a beginning caseworker achieve in identification with the client when he is first learning to help is of quite another order from the quality of identification manifest in skillful helping. Yet the very contrast in time, first encountered as a problem, holds the key to understanding, for in the comparison between identification in beginning and ending of process, in inexperienced and experienced helper, lies the opportunity for discovering the nature of this phenomenon which plays such a major role in the relationship of helper to person seeking help.

Still another problem arises from the fact that when we really come to grips with the meaning of identification, we find that our language often states the reverse of what is actually the case, and that we have not yet developed enough precision in thought and speech to convey the important and fine distinctions which have developed over a period of time and do actually exist in practice. I refer here again to the quotation from Miss Robinson's 1928 National Conference paper (which I have already utilized in the discussion of the development of functional casework) to recall the beginning of one continuous line of development with respect to just this change in the concept of identification. In 1928 Miss Robinson spoke of the caseworker's "total identification with his (the client's) feeling state,"[1] and it was precisely this totality of identification which had to give way to admit the recognition of the separation aspect in relationship which is an equally powerful factor.

When the student is just beginning in this process of learning casework, the problem is one of helping him find a way, any way that is natural to him, to identify with the different self of the client. In contrast to this, what we discover when we examine a fine and effective piece of helping is that it is not the caseworker who has identified with the client but the client who has discovered ways to identify with the caseworker—actually, more accurately stated, with the function which is manifest in the caseworker in every step of the process. Hence it seems more accurate to state that the caseworker identifies with his function (not with the client)—this is the primary and elementary origin of identification. It constitutes the steady, unchanging part of a process that in other respects is highly mobile, granting more mobility to the client, to the one seeking help on account of this form. The existent difference between helper and client must be bridged through the client's movement—toward the uniting with the source of help, through his own discovery of partialized reality with which he can identify. If this is so, if it is indeed the client who must create the identification, then this raises a question whether it is ever accurate to speak of the caseworker's identification with the client, when in actual experience such identification can often engulf the client in such a way that he cannot separate enough to present himself in his own terms.

This is the gist of the problem regarding identification and is the approach by which this chapter then considers the question, how can the client thus identify? What does he find in the caseworker sufficiently like himself with which to unite? What brings him back to seek more of what he has already found in prior interviews? If, as we would certainly agree, this immobility of the caseworker which comes about through identification with function is not a refusal, but a highly sensitive response to the client's movement, then how can we describe the situation in order to understand it more effectively?

When a genuine process of helping moves into its ending phase, there can never be any doubt that something of value has transpired between two people. What this is, can, momentarily at least, be spoken of as identification, at the risk, however, of a great oversimplification. There is no mistaking the fact that out of a helping process there eventuates, in slow growth, an experience in which there is a heightened sense of life: as if here, in this moment of time, has been manifest an expression of movement and change like a veritable piece of life itself. What this is, is almost inexplicable, known in immediate experience, and willingly left to be so. It is as if the experience is whole and complete in itself—it needs no tangible proof of outcome to demonstrate its worth. Every person functionally trained, who has in the course of that training been both a helper and one using help, knows, with quickened sense of affirmation, the quality of this ending relationship.

But at the beginning, when client and caseworker first come together, there is no identification whatsoever between these two people. This seems at first glance a most stark and unqualified assertion, yet a moment's pause to look at the beginning situation in its true terms reveals the extent to which this is indeed a fact. The obvious differences instantly apparent in appearance, in manner of living, in life experience, in the very fact that the one is a helper and the other not, are very great indeed. For the young caseworker who is just learning the initial steps of becoming a helping person, the problem is one of finding some way to relate to differences so compelling, for no helping is possible until this happens. Older, more experienced caseworkers, who come into training with attitudes more organized and developed, present in many respects just as keen a problem, but it is likely to be less apparent because disguised as its opposite. An excessive identification with the generalized problem of human deprivation and want is at bottom still but another expression of absence of relationship to the individual. This attitude projects upon him a number of assumptions which operate to his disadvantage because he is prevented from defining his need in his own terms.

Thus, in getting into this problem of identification we are confronted with the necessity of facing squarely the absence of any natural base for identification between two people who now meet for the first time in the setting of a social agency: the one in the role of representative of a helping function, the other in the still undefined position of one who searches for something, as yet not known. One might well ask what it can be which starts this process in motion, what can possibly create the beginning of a relationship from which authentic help may come.

The answer is to be found, in a preliminary manner of speaking, in the realization that only in the willingness to help, manifest in the function of the agency, does the dynamic lie for the initial, original upspringing of identification. It is a matter of paramount importance, which merits careful examination to determine of what this initial identification consists. Within the helping person the function of his agency becomes manifest; in his thought and activity and response, the entity and existence of his function expresses itself. This function is comprised, first of all, of a positive, affirmative desire and willingness to help. Here it stands foursquare, neither timidly nor indifferently, but positively, as living evidence that to this place persons come for help and here help can be given, authentically and substantially. The willingness to help takes on dimension and proportion, form and structure, through a place, a person, equipment, status, and institutionalization, all of which are there, sturdily and reliably, when the individual seeks them out. Familiar and obvious as this may sound, it yet needs stating and restating in order to deepen and possess the full meaning of this willingness. With this willingness the client finds identification if he is at all capable of using help.

The function of which we speak is comprised of many other facets in addition to the primary element of agency-centered willingness to help. There is also a willingness that belongs to the self of the caseworker. There can be no question that the desire to help, enlivened by impulsive elements which strive for creative expression and have chosen this way, in being a caseworker, is of most important value to the one being helped. At times the desire to help is felt so powerfully that it inevitably calls forth a countertendency within the caseworker to restrain and deny, to hold back, to control and refashion this energetic expression. The will to help is a powerful will assertion, and like all will phenomena is bound to arouse denial as its customary accompaniment. It cannot be left unsaid, either, that the projection of the will to help, which we shall be examining more fully in the next chapter, can indeed become pure projection and thus obliterate the self of the client; but this natural fear of the desire to help must not be so great as to interfere with its essential use, for it is an indispensable element in the ability to help.

It happens so frequently as to be suggestive of a universal tendency, that the client at some point early in the process will ask, "Can you really help me?" and the caseworker, in his newness and also in his desire to acknowledge the degree to which the outcome is in the client's hands, may sometimes say, "I do not know, it depends upon you," adding, perhaps a little apologetically, "We have been able to help others." I have never known it to fail that at some point of time in every casework class this very situation appears in a recorded interview, and then it affords a significant point in learning. For now the caseworker examines it to discover that what the client needs from him is the sure knowledge that he can help, the only question being whether the client can use it. No better illustration of the process of differentiation, partialized and concrete, could be found than this. Here the caseworker has the opportunity to separate himself from the client's doubt, sifting it into true components, letting him discover that the doubt is not a generalized vapor which envelopes all—the caseworker, the agency, and himself—but is in fact a limited doubt. What use can he make of it? The knowledge that help is here, and that this caseworker knows how to give it, is the steady unchanging factor, which cannot be drawn into the ambivalence and doubt the client brings. But it is a great deal to ask of a learning caseworker, or even of a very experienced one for that matter, to feel an at-oneness with his function, his skill, his strength, that will enable him to contain comfortably so audacious a statement. Actually the excess of the opposite is justifiably feared, for if the client senses, as he is bound to do, an overemphasized will, "I *can* help," he in turn will be challenged to a will assertion to prove it is not so. This kind of search for delicate balance is a familiar experience in learning the helping skill.

Now we approach the core of the problem of identification, in reflecting upon the question, what is it, indeed, which the seeker after help feels in the caseworker from the very moment when he first begins to work with him upon a problem? How can this be described, and what are some of the common misconceptions with which it can be contrasted? Phrases commonly used such as "respect for," "leave him free to," "understanding of," "staying with him in feeling," are useful but leave much to be explored if we are to understand the nature of this quality.

It is by no means an infrequent occurrence that a client says to a caseworker, even in an early burst of feeling, "This is different from anything I have ever known," and he is

right when he says this, for it *is* different. The emotion which gives rise to this exclamation is an appreciative emotion, an expression of surprise, of gratitude, and, in the very act of being said, is evidence of a new-found momentary release as the impulse comes through to this new expression. His accurate observation of difference is not in this instance a separation; on the contrary, it is a sudden uniting, an immediate awareness of having found that which has meaning for him. This is one of the seeming contradictions in helping, that he has united with the difference, yet it is a contradiction which heightens understanding; one of those many paradoxes, the core of which yields the meaning we seek.

For the problem we have to understand here is how the psychologically oriented caseworker, the more or less self-conscious, developed, and creative self of the helping person, can make so immediate a connection with the relatively un-self-conscious, nonpsychologically oriented person. This problem is even more evident when one thinks of the highly developed nature of the functional orientation of the caseworker. What, then, is this sudden sense of uniting, of togetherness, of wholeness with another felt by the one who seeks help, which we cannot dismiss as an accidental happening but acknowledge as a matter of supreme importance, without which no helping process can eventuate, cannot in fact even begin?

There is no way to account for this except through recognition of the fundamental connection between accurate and authentic psychological knowledge and the commonplace forms of various and multitudinous expressions of living. Beyond proof one knows there is somewhere an underlying stream which unifies experience, which holds together in some wholly incomprehensible manner the extremes of experience, so that the most enduring art forms make connection with the homeliest expressions of living, and the constantly evolving individuation of the creative person becomes at the same time accessible to the mass. One must believe at bottom that the universe makes itself manifest in every human individual, and the answer lies in finding this connection with the universal at the same time that the uniquely individual is affirmed. This awareness can never be in logical terms and must at times be deeply intuitive, but experience confirms it incontrovertibly.

This highly philosophical observation may seem a far cry from the practical situation of the caseworker and the client. Actually it is not, as I hope to show by describing some of the concrete components of the "knowing" which the caseworker achieves through psychological training, through which, in this same process of differentiation, ever greater individuation and enlargement of the professional helping self takes place.

At the moment of time under consideration here, namely, in the very beginning of the helping process (and presuming always in this discussion a developed, reliable skill), there is no mistaking the fact that the client finds something to which he returns and of which he can make ever-deepening use. In the caseworker he finds a willingness to help, a belief that he can help, and an identification with the function which gives him dimension and proportion in his functional capacity. It is this very difference between the functional relationship and the natural, personal relationships of living, which the client senses. Interestingly enough, it is not absence of feeling to which he reacts, for he finds feeling as real and spontaneous as ordinary living provides—in fact to an even greater degree for the very reason that it has form and purpose and structure.

In the form and texture of this function of which we here speak, there is present an attitude on the part of the helping person for which the word consideration is admirably suited. There is consideration for him as a person and for the problem he brings. It is a consideration which encompasses a special form of attention and interest, a deepened and matured attention and interest, which unreservedly regards him as the center of this hour and place. More than any-

thing, it is a fundamental regard for the freshness and newness and uniqueness of the human experience he brings; a
regard for him at first as a live being, even though at this
very early time the helping person can know so little what
he is like in actuality. But even when he knows the uniqueness of the client so little, he relates to him immediately on
a level which includes more than reaction to the impact of
the obvious outer expressions of himself: his movements, his
hesitations, his compelling necessity to explain himself. The
helping person relates therefore differently from the way
that ordinary living provides, since he relates to another level
of the self which the client brings. Perhaps this can be described as a kind of sensitized waiting and a slow readiness
to feel the client's timing; in short, to feel responsive to this
other self as different from one's own self, capable of being
understood only through its own expressions, not through
imposition of one's own interpretation of what he is like.

Some of this consideration undoubtedly comes about
through the concentration of focus upon the problem which
the client brings, for that is what he has come for, that is
what the caseworker is there for, and as soon as he begins to
project any piece of this problem, and thus projects even the
smallest, most tentative piece of the self upon the caseworker,
he can in turn immediately identify again with that piece of
himself already put out upon the helper. This highly complicated process which we are attempting to explore can and
at times does begin immediately, be it ever so slightly, though
certainly in no manner comparable with the way in which
this constant projection and identification goes on in a developing process.

Highly important to the understanding of the caseworker's
consideration in the initial phase of the helping process is
the recognition of the degree to which the will of the helping
person is contained within the self, not projected outward
upon the other. The word containment is the only one I can
find which seems to approach the description of the differ-

ence between this and the active will which goes out at once in effort to change the other person. Indeed, the will to help is present, but it is a contained will. It may be described as a composite standing-for, an affirmation of, the belief that human beings are capable of change and discovery of new strength and capable of the use of that strength for the solution of tangible life problems. The distinction readily apparent between the quality of the developed, functional skill of the helping person, and the natural tendency of the impulse to operate to effect direct change in the other, is a distinction made manifest in this very difference between the will which is contained and the will which is propelled outward.

In short, it is unquestionably true that one of the facets of difference which the client feels in a helping process is a new freedom for his own will in relationship to another; and this, strangely enough, because of heightened awareness of the boundaries beyond which his will cannot go. All of our language which strives so indefatigably to describe the manner in which he is helped "to discover" whether this concrete service is something he can use is the tangible expression of this mobile process, in which the client's self is left room to move toward ever greater discovery of its own desire, direction, nature, and capacity, but always in relation to a form, a given, which does not and cannot move.

He feels as well the fright arising from this very situation in which he is so unmistakably the center. The relation of two people, in an office quietly set apart for his purpose, where he feels the expectation that from him alone can come the key to the problem, gives rise to mounting tension. This is indeed a frightening situation from which he must inevitably feel the impulse to escape; but this impulse is interlaced with an impulse, as well, to live this out, to go further, to discover what is this sudden sense of self which he feels. The limitation of language precludes the possibility of describing simultaneously two sides of the same feeling, for

here, as in so many similar circumstances, it is not a matter of awareness of one side alone, but of the other side as well, and where only the constant maintenance of the duality of the situation can afford the milieu in which movement can take place.

Psychologically speaking, function holds the very essence of this ambivalence, and holds it for the one using help while he flounders first this way, then that, in movements which are now away from, now toward, the source of help. This ambivalence in reality terms is but a reflection of the two-sidedness of the conflict within the self, the very conflict to which he must eventually find access if he is to do anything new in this situation. At first, and almost universally is this true, he unburdens upon the caseworker the picture of the trouble he is in, a picture colored and intensified by the fact that he has been preparing himself to come to this agency. His reverie in advance is the kind of reverie that we all know when we ready ourselves for an encounter: he argues, he explains, he justifies, he excuses, and he usually has a temporary and hasty solution. The caseworker includes this in a larger whole, one which feels the mounting tension of his coming, which feels his dire necessity to tell it the way he has thought it out before he came, which feels at the same time how inevitably he fails to say it just the way he wants. At least two additional factors of major importance the caseworker knows: that his compelling necessity will be to locate the responsibility for the problem entirely upon the outside, and, secondly, that he will conceivably exaggerate the problem because of his intense need to project it upon the other, in fear that the helping person will not understand it truly, as he does not himself. Within his function, within himself, within his agency concept, the caseworker can respond to the intensity of his feeling while withholding himself from engulfment in the overwhelming impact of what great misadventure he has had, for it is this very engulfment and its totality with which he most needs help. If the caseworker goes into it with the client he fails to give him just the help that he needs.

It is this accretion of sympathy which is the snare and pit-fall of the helping person. All too often the reality suffering is indeed so great, the misfortunes which befall so unbeliev-ably weighty, the combination of deprivations and accidents so overwhelming, that it is a wonder the client can feel any-thing except complete defeat. But the caseworker does in-deed know this: that if this human self is to find any shred of capacity to cope with what has happened to him, he must also be able to find the germ of a sense of self-responsibility. For it is too obvious to escape notice that despite the pre-ponderance of excuse, of rationalization, of blame located upon the outside, at bottom he feels his own part, and feels it with inevitable guilt. What he craves above all else, yet does not reach in accessible form, is the recognition that he is not the victim of circumstance but a responsible agent even with respect to acts and attitudes which he finds blame-worthy. Only the necessity of fighting the helping person, to impose his own will in opposition to the pressure which he feels externally, will interfere with his sure movement to reach this admission and to give it, as a genuine piece of the self.

Later, in far more detail than is possible here, the whole concept of self-responsibility as it expresses itself in func-tional casework will be examined with more care. Now it is enough to mention it in order to include it within the scope of this condensed exploration of the nature and meaning of the function the helping person contains. It is a function which comprehends the opposites of self-responsibility and external inevitability; which knows the universal tendency to come for help bearing the compelling necessity to say: see what has "happened" to me; which accepts this, but does so within a larger whole containing as well the knowledge that location of responsibility must move from outer to inner, if growth is to be the outcome.

The Quality of Identification

Sympathy is an emotion that gives meaning to natural human situations, but it is not very well understood with respect to its part in professional relationships. What is at least clear, is that the nature of the positive feeling present in the helping situation is of a different quality and upon another level. On occasion, however, the emotion stirred in the caseworker is more of the quality of sympathy than otherwise, static as an emotion on that account. Sometimes, along the pathway of learning how to help, even this emotion, when it is real, is welcomed as a thoroughly valid and authentic expression of feeling, but in and by itself it engulfs the caseworker in the client's problem, and the only resultant change is that there are two involved instead of one. I do not mean to belittle the moments of helping which seem to eventuate from nothing more than a kindly reception of a troubled story, an experience psychologically comprehensible as the relief which arises from momentarily uniting with another, thus softening the feeling and liberating the armored will. It is true that wonders can happen from just this very instantaneous unity which causes the fear to subside. But it need hardly be added that no genuine beginning of a self-movement toward growth eventuates from this sterile uniting in sympathetic feeling. Actually, sympathy soon deteriorates into feeling-sorry-for, and being-felt-sorry-for is closely akin to being-looked-down-upon, and therefore soon is felt as an affront.

The movement in learning to help is characterized, first, by an awakening capacity on the part of the student to feel for the self of the other, and any kind of real feeling—concern, sympathy, anguish—is welcome and indispensable evidence of change. This capacity must develop into a slowly growing ability to contain the two sides of the immediate situation, that is, the feeling for the person he is, and also the feeling for the better self which he might be but is not. Of all the aspects of this helping function with which the caseworker holds her identification in the early contact with the client, perhaps none accounts more meaningfully for the fact that the client knows there is something here and returns to it. In nonconceptual, nontheoretical, nonconscious terms, intuitively and immediately he knows this enlargement even though he cannot yet own it or possess it for himself. Toward this expansion the self stretches and reaches, beyond its known limits.

In concluding this chapter, we come back once more to look again at the nature of the caseworker's identification, and see it as primarily an identification with his function. In order to avoid the surface connotations which these words sometimes imply, this discussion has sought to put detail and content into the nature of that function which is informed with meaning through the caseworker. What is described here could never be spoken of as an "objective" attitude, excepting only as it remains centered upon the "object," in this case a living human self. On the contrary, it is a vital, dynamic experience, in which the fear of feeling and emotion is contained within form and thus loses its power to obstruct expression and movement. The whole development from undisciplined human being to disciplined professional helper can be described in part as a process of becoming aware of one's own emotions more accurately and immediately in order to respond precisely and genuinely to those of the other. The opposite of this is the fallacious but commonly held ideal of the caseworker as one who is objective, "free" of prejudice, "free" of judgmental attitude. Actually, the more the self grows, the more it is full of emotion, the more sensitively it responds, the more spontaneous it becomes. It is a matter of affirming, containing, recreating, the self, courageously and spontaneously, in order to learn to help.

In the next chapter we shall once more take hold of one facet of this problem, namely, the will to help as it manifests itself in the caseworker, and examine its nature as it expresses itself in the helping process.

CHAPTER VIII

THE WILL TO HELP

WHAT IS the nature of this will to help and how can it become either an effective dynamic or an equally effective obstacle to any constructive movement on the part of the client? These are the questions which must be explored, for the will to help is, in all certainty, a very powerful force, little understood and very often denied; feared because of its strength and the responsibility which it places upon the helping person.

Once again there seems to be value in examining this problem through the comparison of different points in time, as revealed first in the natural self of the casework student seeking training, then in the developing self in learning, and finally in the mature self of the experienced caseworker. For in these three points of time, which correspond to the natural eventuation of a growth movement, are to be found the authentic outlines of the maturing will to help as it eventually manifests itself in the skillful caseworker.

This brings us inevitably to the interesting question of the motivation which brings any individual into casework, into the choice of a helping profession, and into the difficult and painful process of self-development which any ability to help demands. Only a very deep devotion to the intrinsic worth both of the own self and the other can account for undertaking a task so demanding and so fraught with pain and pleasure alike.

When the original and most accessible motivation which brings a caseworker into training is first expressed, it contains often a considerable emphasis upon the desire to contribute to the well-being of the world. Usually the individual describes some point of impact when the realization of human suffering, material and emotional, was first felt, and not infrequently he can identify some actual event in his personal or professional experience which set into motion the incipient desire to change the situation as he finds it. The preponderant characteristic of this early expression of desire to help is a desire to change the outside, not only the environment but human beings as well, for it is likely that the average caseworker who comes into training with any experience (and even the young inexperienced student who has been stirred through college courses devoted to social and economic issues) sees not only the potentiality for change in the environment, but also the promise of change within the individual human self. Whichever way he looks at it, whether in terms of the broad sweep of human progress, or centered in the single individual, it is the effectuation of change upon the outer reality that constitutes the drive out of which the interest arises. When he comes into training, in contrast, he discovers that the center of change is within himself.

Furthermore, combined with this desire to be active on behalf of human welfare, there is usually an equally powerful expression of interest in understanding human behavior; in fact the latter seems to become the next step into which any discussion of the question, "What brings you into training?" inevitably leads. There is no escaping the realization of the universality of this craving to understand the way human beings are, what they do, and why they do it. The association between the thought of being able to help and the necessity to understand human behavior is clear and direct.

But now, what is here described is soon discovered to be merely the surface manifestation of a motivation deeper in origin and more complex in nature than is apparent at first glance. Under favorable conditions not very much time is required in the training process before the learning self finds new ways to admit, "I want something for myself," and "It is my self that I crave to understand." These two admissions, felt at first as too self-centered, and needing to be denied on account of the guilt aroused, are suddenly acknowledged as authentic parts of the self that can be accepted and included and to some degree satisfied. In this very realization an important part of the training movement of the student eventuates.

In order to go into this problem even more penetratingly, it is necessary to consider as well the creative strivings of the individual who comes into casework, strivings to use the self more effectively, to find channels of expression that satisfy; to live out whatever of capability and potentiality is felt to reside within the recesses of its being. Perhaps "creative" seems too pretentious a word for these common, universal strivings, reserved as it is for characterizing the higher forms of art. Yet there is no other word which seems to carry this same meaning, when one undertakes to speak of the kind of creative expression which is actually life experience itself. At the heart of Rank's psychology lies the belief that life experience is and can be creative, and that the striving for growth and individuation is in itself an expression of the creative impulse. The same thought has been philosophically comprehended in recent times by Bergson, Dewey, and others. The individual who selects casework as a profession is likely to be one with more than average awareness of himself and his difference, and more interest in, and sensitivity to, experience. The striving for creative expression brings him into a helping function, where he does indeed discover, if he develops any skill at all, that in this medium it is possible to find form and use of himself to the extent of his capacity. L. P. Jacks calls it "skill-hunger": "Man is a skill-hungry animal, hungry for skill in his body, hungry for skill in his mind, and never satisfied until that skill-hunger is appeased."[1]

Thus we begin to identify some of the important elements

of the will-impulse combination which brings the individual into the choice of a helping profession: desire for skill, striving to understand the self, pressure to live out the endowments of the self, and a compelling will to change, to recreate, to make over the outer reality in which he lives. These now stand at the threshold of new understanding, to be seen either as the static, resisted, denied elements in helping, or the accepted, affirmed, and therefore constructively used elements in this so fine and precise a task.

When the desire to help in its unformed, natural, undeveloped state is given free rein in social work, it becomes a powerful projection of unassimilated and unrecognized pressures within the self of the would-be helper. Under these circumstances the client becomes an object—an animate one, to be sure, but an object nonetheless—to be observed, studied, interpreted, and diagnosed. The longing to understand one's own self thus seeks the answer through the effort to understand the other. The tremendous dynamic of the will to change seeks its satisfaction by way of the mounting desire to produce change externally. Parts of the self felt as problem are seen in the other. The inner stresses and conflicts which are the natural substance of any life process are mirrored everywhere in the environment, and the impulse to effect change begins to operate with this compelling drive.

Beneath this activity, propelled outward upon the client, lies a theory which is in itself a powerful projection. It is a theory with respect to the method of producing change in the one who seeks the caseworker's help. According to this theory, the change happens as a result of the caseworker's understanding: of causation, of the client's problem, of the solution. Centrifugally, diagnosis originates and continues to be centered in the caseworker, even while it is directed outward with purpose. It can be successful only if the client takes it over organically and makes it his own. It is hard to see how this can ever happen, knowing the inevitable reaction of the will to projected pressure of this kind. More likely the truth is the client fights to the last inch the imposition upon him of another's interpretation of where his problem lies, what its nature is, how it came to be the way it is, and where its solution can be found. Sometimes, in fact, the necessity to fight is so great that the very energy thereby generated motivates him to produce some change in his situation in order to escape and by this means he uncovers new sources for self-responsibility. But this is a far cry from a reliable way of helping because the change springs from opposition and does not necessarily become a part of the self.

Against the background of this contrast it is possible to comprehend and examine, in its sharp difference, the process of development which the powerful will to change the outside, as it first appears in the natural self of the student, can undergo in a true process of inner growth. The desire to understand the mysterious and alluring realm of psychic phenomena, constituting as it does the primary desire to understand the self, is admitted, acknowledged for what it is, and accepted in the sense that it is confirmed positively, not negatively as something evil which ought not to be. It is, which is enough. Gradually, but from the very outset, the functional training process supports and encourages this willingness to understand the self, and uses every facet of the immediate experience, commonplace and momentous alike, to deepen and enrich the comprehension of the self in all its impulsive and willful and self-striving assertions. Once this desire to understand the self begins to be satisfied, as it cannot ever wholly be, but only relatively speaking within the possibility of the present experience, the projection upon the outside becomes amenable to a gradual return and taking back into the self where it belongs. The creative urges for change also become transformed into a will to have the change occur internally, now felt less compulsively, with less determination, with less of a preformulated goal; and the sense of mounting inner strength, as well as outer strength in the help available to the one learning casework, frees the willingness to live out a process, step by step, day by day.

To express this change in the self we resort once more to the use of the word containment. Strength becomes contained, and through its containment enlarges. Bit by bit the artificial strength heretofore clung to as essential, serving as an armor intended to afford invulnerability against the onslaught of life reality, is given up for the enhanced awareness that man is indeed a vulnerable creature who lives in fear and danger and change and flux. It becomes evident that if one can but know this life reality, can go with it and live out its very precariousness in change and process, then truly, and only then, can life find genuine expression.

Now, too, the powerful will to create, to change the material things of the environment, is no longer rejected as evil, but takes its rightful place as a part of the creative urge itself. And through this realization, the growth process finds new impetus.

If the will to help can become contained and affirmed within the self, it no longer drives out upon the client in sheer projection. Since it does not threaten him, the client can move toward it, to discover what is there which he can use. This strength in the helping person, which we have characterized as an inner strength, is immediately felt to be different from the kind of strength which depends upon knowledge about the other or resorts to a complex and elaborate system of causal explanation. In relation to this inner strength, the individual who seeks to use it becomes more aware of his own, in comparison and contrast, in awareness of difference, in sense of likeness, in give and take and engagement with another human being. He knows the character of his own will through engagement with the will of another, when the focus remains always devoted to enhancement of his own understanding.

Yet another related concept becomes illuminated at this point, the importance of which it would be impossible to

exaggerate. At bottom, as the substratum of every effort to
help, is the solid belief that only the client can know himself
from himself, and that any understanding worth its name is
self-understanding. To be sure, the individual client can be
known by another from the way he is in a relationship, the
way he acts, speaks, responds, moves, resists; by the admix-
ture of will, impulse, fear, and guilt which manifests itself
under these particular circumstances, but in the last analysis this knowledge is partial and transitory. The caseworker
in the training process knows this for himself in the help he
has used: the goal is self-understanding, and the only accept-
able truth is the inner truth of the own self. What the helping person puts in to facilitate this understanding in terms of
acceptance, immediate response, awareness of past and present, in terms of psychological movement, are all particulars
of the same problem which we shall examine in more detail
later. But taken all in all, one always returns to this first
elemental affirmation, that the self can only understand
through an immediate experience and new comprehension of
itself. That one can be helped toward this goal in substantial and responsible ways is the conviction out of which any
person undertakes to help. Here we describe once more a
duality, a two-sidedness of self and other, which the restrictions of language cannot altogether convey simultaneously,
but which fortunately the helper can contain in immediate
awareness in simultaneous juxtaposition.

In bringing this chapter to a conclusion, it is necessary to
refer to one other fundamental factor in the will to help, and
this can only be mentioned, since it requires fuller development in order to do it justice. This factor is the essential engagement of the will of the client in order to effectuate any
helping movement. Even experienced helping persons back
away from the full realization of the extent to which two
wills are engaged in the helping process. The reason for this
is not hard to find. What the helping person aims to avoid at
all costs is the kind of will struggle which sharpens to that

ultimate point of encounter between two powerful forces—the one in the helping person, the other in the client—the outcome of which can only be defeat, no matter which will triumphs. In this situation, the client can use his whole strength only in refusal pitted against force; stated in pure psychological terms, in counter-will in opposition to the powerful will which he meets in the caseworker. This occurs even when the content of the caseworker's powerful will is composed solely of benevolent intentions.

Yet this fear of the will struggle, if the fear is excessive, restrains the caseworker from that very encounter with the client which is indispensable and which the client will surely seek dynamically if anything in the process has touched him. The fear on the part of the helper is unavoidable; it is a reality that exists and cannot be changed. What can change is the caseworker's relation to the reality.

The connection between will and fear is direct and immediate. Will is a means for conquering fear, and at the moments of keenest will assertion—sheer will stripped of feeling—fear is not felt or is felt as under control. Let the fear well up and it threatens to take possession of the self. In helping, it can be accepted as axiomatic that the greater the fear, the more the will sharpens. This continues to be true for the client, although in the process of using help it too can be modified. But for the caseworker the training process precipitates change with respect to the will-fear connection. Where there is genuine psychological growth there is increasing capacity to feel the fear with resultant decrease in the necessity for will to control. The functional helping situation is set up with a structure designed to permit the client's fear to be released and felt, something which ordinary life seldom affords and which he can hardly venture alone without risk of loss of life. Actually the self can choose to feel the emotion, even of fear, and thus be the possessor of the emotion, rather than the other way round: the emotion possessing the self.

For the helping person, the answer to this problem of the

accentuation of will by fear is to be found in the change which occurs in the growth process. The fear is contained within a larger whole comprised of self-awareness, which includes the awakening realization of the constructive, life-producing aspects of the human will. When the convincing evidence that emotion felt and acknowledged does not engulf and destroy, but frees and creates, has been experienced again and again, the fear of the emotion actually diminishes.

It is to a deepening comprehension of this process that the following chapters are devoted.

CHAPTER IX

THE MEANING OF ACCEPTANCE IN THE CASEWORKER'S RESPONSE

THE EXAMINATION of the will to help has served to concentrate attention upon but one of many aspects which might be assembled to construct an answer to the question, "What is a caseworker made of?" We have just seen how one must acknowledge that a caseworker is possessed of strength, and, having strength, has a will, and having will has an urge to create, that is, to change what is, in the image of one's own idea or conception. And we have said that, in order to avoid the devastating effect upon the client of sheer projection of this will to change, the impulse-will organization of the would-be helping person must undergo a development and growth, in the process of which the projection is taken back from its exaggerated location upon the other, to ever greater containment within the self. This resulting containment is quite a different matter from a contrived control of strength through a decision of the will; is in fact just its opposite, since a denial of its existence or a repression of its strength constitutes a flaw which interferes with any effective effort to help.

It is on account of this very sense of strength and creativity in the helping person, manifesting itself more deeply and more powerfully than is ordinarily the case with the average person, that it is possible to understand its opposing tendency, namely, the need to deny that this strength does in fact exist. At times one sees the profession of social work painting a picture of its individual practitioner as a person who is essentially non-judgmental, non-moralistic, unprejudiced,

The Meaning of Acceptance

and pre-eminently objective; free of any reactions of surprise, shock, blame; unencumbered by standards of value, or criteria of right and wrong. The caseworker, it is said in a wholly false use of the word, "accepts" the client as he is, with implication thus of a most misleading use of a very useful and indispensable word. For acceptance is indeed a word full of movement and life provided it is imbued with the concept of constructive acceptance; but it is a word which can also be used destructively when called upon to justify a static acceptance of the client's immobilized self, and this comes about through excessive identification with his misery, or fallacious excusing of his behavior. This contrast between the two possible uses of the word constitutes the focus in this chapter: how to undertake to comprehend the difficult and fine distinction between acceptance that is sterile and acceptance that constitutes a dynamic in the caseworker's attitude.

One might well ask, too, what it is that happens to all the prejudices, the morals, the ethics, the standards of behavior, and the feeling reactions which the caseworker certainly shares in common with all humanity and clearly cannot dispose of by throwing them away, merely by an act of will. If one were satisfied with the picture of the objective social worker described in the paragraph above, one would indeed be satisfied with a human being who had lost all humanity and all self; and a deadly thing it would be! Instead, it is apparent that just the opposite must be true, if we accept the fundamental thesis, as this whole discussion does, that the caseworker should be a person of some unique endowment who undergoes greater than average self-growth and individuation in the process of preparing himself to become a helper. Then, clearly, this person who has consciously chosen development becomes a person with more will, more creativity, more and richer emotion, freer impulse, finer discrimination, more mature values, and a greater desire to use all of these in some more freely experienced existence. What a strange thing it is, this necessity at times to repudiate these parts of the self, or at least to compartmentalize, so that the client is deprived of the very thing that alone can make helping worthwhile, namely, the use of the whole strength of the helping person.

It is a fundamental concept in functional helping, and a fundamental tenet of functional training, that the learning self must be enabled to discover and release and utilize more and more of its growth potential, and, through use, to facilitate integration. But while this is fully understood and acknowledged, it is by no means an easy matter to draw the distinction between acceptance as descriptive of an attitude of the helping person which includes and utilizes all that he is and thinks and feels, and acceptance which denies and obliterates these same living currents of the self.

For if now, without stint or reservation, we are to come to grips with this problem of the meaning of acceptance, we are confronted once more with an inescapable starting point located nowhere else but in the helping person himself. We can begin to understand acceptance through some consideration of its meaning in relation to the own self, since we speak of the process of growth as comprising a process of acceptance of the self. Through this acceptance, the helping person in turn is enabled more effectively to accept the self of the other, and then to help the other to accept himself more fully, thus gaining more capacity for coping with reality. These are the essential facets of acceptance which play back and forth in interaction upon one another, and none of them can be omitted from a consideration of the meaning of this concept.

At first the characteristic mood of the beginning student in arriving momentarily at acceptance of the self is one of relief, as if now the necessitous struggle to become different, to be hospitable toward strivings for change, can, temporarily at least, be given up. The inner conflict of the self (and by this we mean not the extreme conflict of the neurotic but the common, usual conflict of any ordinary life process) is bene-

ficently put to rest, and the self becomes whole in some new sense of "I." At this stage the self must struggle anew between the forces which strive to maintain the status quo, holding on to the past and to the old self, and the forces which strive for change and development. Soon it is all too plain that acceptance of the self is no complacent, relaxing settling down with the way things are.

For, in essence, the gist of acceptance of the self resides in an unfolding willingness to permit the denials to drop away, and not only this (somewhat passively stated as "letting drop away"), but also a fresh active acceptance of the desire to be aware, in the moment, of the true feelings and the true circumstance, no matter what they may reveal. Less and less does the proud self need to create an illusion in order to mask the true situation, and more and more does it place higher value upon the authentic and accurate awareness of the passing moment. Indeed, this is but a description of an ever continuing process, once more calling for the reminder that it is never thus completed or achieved, but always in process of becoming.

In the most general terms one can say it is a matter of accepting one's self as human, which, strangely enough, most human beings find it extremely difficult to do, and even those who believe they do are often enough only caught in other deluding denials. At each new point of acceptance of the self, as within a newly created vortex of energy and life, there is set in motion once again a new process of deepening acceptance. It is possible to describe what comprises some of these centers of acceptance.

To accept one's self means to realize the nature and extent of the impulsive elements and the degree to which, in the creative person, the impulsive elements become ever more rich and more powerful. A change begins to take place when the older attitude which so deeply feared the impulse is given up, and the self is freed from the struggle in which it was forever engaged, striving to restrain or repress this ever upsurging original life. The more the impulse is fought, resisted, denied, the less the whole self can be free or integrated, for it can easily be seen how much strength must go into this conflict. With the awakening recognition of the impulse as life-giving, life-creating, there comes immediately an inevitable fear, not to be explained away or otherwise got rid of. The only question is, can the fear be encompassed and contained and utilized constructively. There comes, as well, a crescendo of desire to release the impulse: freed from the constricting nature of fear, affirmed as right, even wondrously viewed as the stuff of living itself, the forward urge is to live out the impulse. Here it is spontaneity alone which matters, and the self is stirred with an intense desire to live, to give out, to spend itself to the utmost. Yet still another stage, if the development proceeds and comes to full fruition, is that in which there is new unity of impulse with will, in which the impulse feels its spontaneity, but springs now out of sturdy roots; when freedom comes not from license or lack of form, but through that form of self which is only to be achieved through a long, slow process of growth. For now the impulse becomes contained in the service of the whole self, and the creative will molds it and gives it direction. There is new readiness to capitulate to the compelling truth that formless spending of the self is but of transient meaning and never seems to hold the answer to the search; that only in form, in function, in a discipline sometimes felt to be as rigid and unyielding as any outer limit, can true creative expression be found.

To accept one's self means, as well, to acknowledge the own will, and this, in turn, means the acknowledgment of many concrete partial expressions of the total will. It means to acknowledge within the self a high degree of self-responsibility: no longer can it be a question of "what happened to me," but what I myself created through a utilization of external circumstance and inner willing. All of the so-persistent, so-continuous, so-deluding denials of the will expressions

of the human self begin to drop away, and a new awareness of inner strength grows. This is bound to be fraught with both exhilaration and anxiety, for it means both the release of energy and the admission of self-responsibility. It is an electrifying moment when the self first admits, and then acclaims, a sense of "I." I think, I feel, I will, I am of worth, a part of an existing whole. I am responsible, says the new self; I am not a mere product of all that has happened to me in the past, nor of the blind instincts which rule me from the mysterious, labyrinthian recesses of a hidden unconscious. Over this moment I hold some potential for choosing and directing my own destiny. This is the meaning, be it ever so partially stated, of acceptance of the self.

Further, to accept one's self means to admit into the realm of respectability—not merely tolerated, but welcomed—the determinative role played in life by the emotions. To accept one's self as human means to acknowledge and go with this primary fact, that man is made of emotion; and the wonder is that he has had to be so fearful of it, so guilty for it, so denying of it. The acceptance of the emotion is the key to the opening of more acceptance of the self, and opens as well the possibility for seeing what is so unmistakably there before us if we would but see it, how the emotion and the intellect are not separate faculties but in constant interplay and interaction one upon the other.

To accept one's self means to admit for one's self that the ideal of goodness in one-sided isolation is a false and sterile ideal because it denies the whole reality of life. The nature of man is such that he contains within himself two equally powerful forces: one positive, one negative; one constructive, one destructive; one loving, one hating. This two-sidedness of the self is what demands acceptance. There are times when the helping person knows beyond doubt that what the client craves is to be felt really and accurately, bad as well as good; when, in fact, he seems to want above all else that the other know the less admirable side of himself as well as the admirable; as if the most important thing of all is to be known as the true self and not under any false colors. It is just this being known more sensitively and finely, in the helping process, that constitutes its difference from ordinary life experience.

To accept one's self is to realize that the human being reacts with pain and distress at the awareness of difference. One of our most cherished statements becomes our greatest delusion: much, much too soon the self ventures to say, I have learned to "accept difference." Often this is but a phase in a process, for it can also represent a plateau upon which the person remains fixed and caught in some faulty, conceptual, fabricated attitude and speech which *seems* to accept difference, when what truly occurs is a projection of a piece of the self upon the other and a resultant denial that difference exists. One cannot ever say merely that the self accepts difference and, by saying this, have understood its meaning.

Difference between the self and the other creates fear and guilt, and arouses comparisons in terms of better and worse, and reactions of thinking, "It ought to be different from what it is." We speak of a highly complicated matter, and a very slow growth, related primarily to the self, when we speak of acceptance of difference. Accepting one's own difference is something other than a matter of becoming more courageous about one's opinions. Of all things, it is least of all opinion, where one commonly thinks of it first. Neither is it a flamboyant tendency to dress bizarrely, to live unconventionally, to speak shockingly, as sometimes this "affirmation of one's own difference" is interpreted to mean; even though, too, at times the temporary expression of discovering difference comes out in these dramatic terms.

Now we come as well to the other side of "difference," also a part of the acceptance of the self: that is, an equally strong craving for likeness and unity. In fact, it is wholly

The Meaning of Acceptance

suitable to bring to a close a discussion of acceptance in an effort to understand the uniting tendencies in the self, and how these tendencies lend themselves to the use of another in that special instance of the helping role. Essentially, to accept one's self as human means to accept the compelling need for relationship and the dominant role which it plays in every life. The self needs the other in order to live, in order to grow, even in order to understand itself; for it is not, as we shall see when looking at it in more detail later, a matter of understanding the self in a logical, explanatory, theoretical way. The only way one truly knows the self is through interaction with another. Feeling changes and is known only in the very act of expression. The will is felt by putting it forth and by receiving in return the impact of another will, and we seek those who give us more accurately that response. Of all the parts of the self the hardest to admit is the part that needs. To acknowledge need is to realize the existence of the source of satisfaction outside of the self, and that is a fearful admission; for the need is comprised of impulse, and the impulse feels like life itself, and therefore at times it is as if the very source of life lodges outside the self—hence out of its control, leaving it vulnerable.

This leads us finally to the admission of human limitation, limitation overwhelmingly greater than we are ever willing to admit, even in the most ordinary aspects of living. In time, in duration, in energy, in vulnerability, in control over external circumstance, we are forced to see how little control we actually have. In the process of growth, that limit which every expression of the self must somewhere encounter moves from the outside gradually into the own self. For the child, this limit, as well as the ideal, is carried by the other, usually the parents, and every human being differs with respect to this internalization of limit. Without it, there is no true freedom. But it is safe to say that no individual ever reaches the goal of feeling the limit completely within, but always needs the outside as well, in some balance that constitutes the ever-changing but ultimate reality of human psychology.

Ultimately, then, we come to this conclusion: it is the own self that the helping person must first learn to accept, and through this process he becomes better able to permit the other to be himself. This comes about not because of any exaggerated detachment, but out of the thoroughly incomprehensible phenomenon of greater capacity to relate through greater separation. More self means more wholeness within, less necessitous need on the outside, but, miraculously, richer capacity for genuine relationship.

This chapter, despite its title, has concerned itself primarily with the psychology of the helping person, and now, in the chapter which follows, but with a new focus, namely, "understanding," we arrive at a consideration of the nature of a concept constantly utilized to describe a relationship. As introductory to this further detailed examination of the same situation to which we have been devoted in these pages, it is enough to say that, when the caseworker faces the client whom he has never seen before, he does not understand him in his individuality, but understands him only in such universal terms as that he, too, is capable of some fresh acceptance of himself. The caseworker knows, as well, the partial nature of this capacity in the client, as different from his own psychological comprehension as a helping person. On account of this very difference, the caseworker feels guilt which can mislead him, unless he is willing, too, to live out this difference from the client in every word and action, without apology and without denial and without disabling guilt. For the meaning of acceptance of the self, as applied to the helping person, is not complete without the honest and courageous acceptance of the difference inherent in the responsible and powerful role which the helper has dared to assume.

CHAPTER X

THE NATURE OF UNDERSTANDING IN CASEWORK HELP

THE WHOLE CHARACTER of the helping process changed and moved to new developmental levels when the concept of immediate response as the core of understanding came into full comprehension. From the moment of entering training in a functional setting, the student is in an experience to which this concept of the immediate response is central. It is again one of those arresting paradoxes which appear so often in psychological material that this concept, simple as it may seem, and desirable as it may appear, requires a long, slow developmental process to ensure acquiring the ability to respond that this concept holds out in promise. At the same time it can be said with equal assurance that, while this idea of fineness of response is a product and reward of deepening self-development, it is yet possible for the learner to make an immediate connection with it from the first. The beginning student experiences it in the kind of response he receives from teachers and supervisor, and, often to his surprise, he finds that in consequence he, too, is suddenly able to respond more freely and spontaneously to his clients.

There are many different kinds of understanding which the self believes it craves from the other, and all of these manifest themselves in one way or another in the helping situation. All are in a sense illusory and spurious, real as they may appear; while certainly not to be scorned, nevertheless they are only substitutes for the kind of understanding that eventually characterizes the genuine helping process.

First, there is the common understanding previously spoken of in the discussion of identification, which can only be characterized as sympathy, in which the self is met by another who seems to say to him, "How hard this has been; how much you have done; how I can feel for you!" In ordinary instances when two people begin to exchange experiences, the one telling and the other listening, it is likely to come about that the listener is suddenly reminded of a similar thing which happened to him, and as soon as he can politely do so he embarks upon a recollection of his own. It is interesting to consider what it is that passes between these two people that can be characterized as "understanding," and to realize how different it is from understanding in its functional, professional meaning. For here in the natural life situation it seems that the listener grieves with the griever, feels pain with the one who is in pain, lets fear grip him in reaction to the one possessed by fear, primarily because he himself has been through a like experience. Much of human response is of this kind, and in it experience becomes a give and take, back and forth, a discovery now of likeness, now of difference, a spinning out together of the commonplace detail of reminiscence. Here we have two people on an equal plane, relatively speaking, whose interest in each other grows out of self-centered interest in his own experience, however much this fact may be disguised. This is the exact opposite of the true helping situation, in which, as every responsible helping person soon discovers, the injection of personal stake to compare, match, or contrast the client's account with one's own experience immediately becomes an intrusion and a desertion of the client's center of interest. I recall having a supervisor tell me with that wonderful combination of delight because she now knew better, and despair that she should have made so grievous an error, that once, when her student poured out his fear of inheriting a tragic illness from a parent, she met it by admitting that she too had known a like fear. The mistake was instantly perceived through the student's instinctive rejection of this unhelpful kind of identification.

Again, there is the sense of understanding and unity between one's self and another that arises from a shared emotion, a common liking, a similar point of view, felt by both to be unique and different. Even to discover that another has felt the same way about a color or a taste or a special kind of weather adds richness and flavor to living. Yet, however beneficent and meaningful this kind of understanding, it too is not part of the structural base in a helping relationship, although it is inevitably present in one form or another. On occasion it forms the pathway by which an otherwise isolated, separated, and painfully different person begins to traverse the unknown and lets himself feel the earliest sign of uniting with an alien whole.

Yet another variety of understanding can only be described as "forgiveness," and often it seems to the helping person that it is this kind of understanding into which he falls unwittingly. The very position that he holds as helper, presupposing as it does that he possesses a key to the understanding of human dynamics, inevitably creates a pervading sense of forgiveness toward behavior which the individual himself may feel to be sinful, unworthy, and burdensome. By the act of unburdening, he rids himself of the weight and conflict momentarily, and discovers in the response of the helper that he is not as bad as he thought himself to be. To forgive is a benign and sometimes tender act, capable of a rich range, so that it is not a matter of whether it should or should not be; rather it is a matter of honesty and genuineness, in contrast to a false assumption of the right to forgive as if some Olympian source rested originally in the helper. Soon the quality of forgiveness, if it becomes a growing basis of unity between the self and the other, mounts to the point where it brings about increased denial of self-responsibility and renewed guilt feeling as a reaction to that same denial.

Very frequently the overburdened client comes with longing to be sided with against another, or against whatever the external threat or injustice is felt to be. He feels understanding in the person who agrees with him, who seems to accept exactly those arguments that he is constructing for his own justification. In this stage he depends to an agonizing degree upon external opinion, having to convince the other that he needs help and is worthy of it. Needless to say, all of this appearance of pressure in order to convince is a reflection of his mounting inner guilt, of effort to deny his own will, of unadmitted and unacknowledged fear of a new, unknown and possibly uncontrollable situation. How to contain all these strands of awareness at once: how to respond to the client's feeling that everything is against him, and yet refrain from identification with his false projection of blame upon the object—this is the great problem confronting the helping person which we are attempting to examine.

In every human self there is the universal longing at times to be understood intuitively, by a gesture, by silence, in short, by no effort of language, since language at best is always felt initially as separating rather than uniting. Indeed, this kind of momentary understanding is a blessed accompaniment of living and of relationship, provided it does not hold the self in necessitous need. For this, too, may become a negative will expression in its refusal to give any piece of the self, insisting upon being known the way one is without words. In the helping situation, but only as the fruit of developed relationship and as the product of true engagement, there are moments that are like this, informed with the sense of mystery, in the best meaning of that word. We can hold to this appreciation for the wordless connection, and yet acknowledge that only if the self can find ways to offer intrinsic pieces of its substance—only through the willing use of language, that universal means of conveying both thought and feeling—can any substantial relationship develop.

Finally, we must take cognizance of the kind of understanding which says, "You are like all others; this is natural, is to be expected, is universal." Much response in helping is like this and is indispensable and appropriate. Yet I have known a person, whom I was attempting to help, tighten up, withdraw, resist anew, in rejection of this emphasis upon likeness with all humanity, because at that very instant his own movement was already fixed upon the affirmation of uniqueness. The emphasis upon the universal, the common, the human, can at moments encourage the opposite of self-responsibility, thus increasing the need for rationalization and justification.

Now we are come at last to an effort to say more accurately and finely what is the true nature of understanding in casework help, for important as is each one of these facets of understanding which we have been examining, not any single one nor yet all together serves to answer this perplexing question satisfactorily. For now it becomes clear once more that the problem in our use of the word understanding arises because of the tendency to use this word always as if applied to understanding the client, the one seeking help, whereas its meaning can only be comprehended when permitted to assume its rightful and inevitable focus upon understanding the helping situation and the caseworker's own part in the process.

Actually, the arresting fact becomes plain that in any authentic helping process the client does not always feel understood: on the contrary, it is impossible that he should, since the very essence of movement originates in those moments when he is feeling difference and separation. To be sure, he does feel, as has already been pointed out in some of the earlier parts of this discussion, that he is understood in this helping situation in a way that he has never experienced before: this is different from anything he has ever known. But it is also true that when the whole of the situation is comprehended, that is, the completed process as it moves from the beginning phase into ending, he also at times feels painfully misunderstood, unaccepted the way he is, held to an external standard which is not yet his own, especially when the helper rejects the false self in a moment of crisis.

Therefore the key to the whole problem lodges in taking hold of both sides of this psychological concept at once: the heightened, intensified sense of a kind of understanding from the helping person different from that ever before known, and the penetrating experience of being misunderstood by the same person with whom he has had such an exceptional awareness of unity. Consequently it begins to appear that the word understanding does not serve our purpose for describing the attitude of the helping person, weighted as it always is with the one-sided implication of understanding the other; perhaps, therefore, we find the key to this problem only by searching for new ways to describe what it is that does actually take place.

Stated in general terms, the nature of understanding in functional helping is comprised of an immediate awareness of the dynamics of the present moment and of the immediate situation. This awareness on the part of the helper becomes manifest in responses which grow ever more accurate and reliable with the development of the helping self. The "immediate situation" to which we refer is obviously the helping situation; the place, the time, the persons, helper and the one who seeks help, the agency, intricate and multistructured, making itself felt in every step of the process. That to which the caseworker responds, then, is the will-impulse-feeling expression of the client as it is heightened, focused, and intensified by his effort to avoid the very help he sought.

In the light of this generalization, the crucial role played by the understanding of pure psychological dynamics involved in asking for or taking help becomes paramount, and momentarily it is almost as if to say, content does not matter. The life struggle for growth can be played out on any content, whatever the client chooses. In the last analysis, whatever the content, the client is acting, thinking, feeling, under the stimulus of the helping situation which is both pressure and freedom, in a special combination of the two. The first principle the beginning helper must always learn is that which establishes the primacy of the present relationship between the helper and the one who seeks help, a relationship that will become temporarily the center of the client's life if he can finally enter into this demanding process which identifies taking help with psychological growth.

In the chapters that follow, I shall attempt to examine more finely the vital movement into engagement between two human beings in the functional helping situation, and to bring back into its appropriate place the role played by content. Both of these aspects of the problem will serve to illuminate the concept of understanding. But, first, I should like to touch once more on the related question, out of what source this kind of understanding comes to the caseworker.

It is generally accepted that the caseworker understands how to help because he has himself taken help. He has been through the same situation, not in content, but in dynamics. He knows what it is to reveal his need and to take what it requires from a source that he does not control. The danger in this generalization lies in the temptation to oversimplify by concluding that by this is meant the learning of a technique, known because experienced for one's self, and therefore in turn applied to the client. But nothing could be farther from the truth, and nothing more destructive of the true meaning of this fundamental premise. It is exactly because no technique can be learned to be applied to another, and because there are no mechanical interpretations to fall back upon, that this kind of helping process is so difficult to learn.

The understanding of the student caseworker is imbued with the heightened awareness of process: what it means to be in a process and to feel its eventuation in a time rhythm. This understanding contains the awakening realization of the universal reactions of the human self to beginnings, to change, to the pull of involvement which cannot be controlled; to ending and separation experiences. The one who is learning to help in functional terms knows, through his own process, the pull of ambivalent forces, the striving of the will, the yielding, the release of new life which is the result. All of this is at the center of understanding, and is of a wholly different order from the kind of understanding which concentrates upon interpretation of the client's behavior.

The difference which distinguishes phases of maturity in development of a professional self is a difference observable and known in terms of authenticity of response. The natural self tends to project its own experience and assumes its truth for everyone. In this phase there is little separation between self and not-self, the latter being largely colored and shaped by internal need, so that the world becomes a part of the self as whole.

True, in a later phase of development—in any phase which is a product of inner growth—the self also must continue to project its own experience, but now this experience is more reliably universal, more aware, less the victim of illusion and denial. It is in order to live up to this demand of universality, to respond accurately, that the inner experience must be informed with precision, candor, and authenticity, which is the same as saying it must be lived truly and honestly. This is the core of the meaning of understanding.

CHAPTER XI

THE SIGNIFICANCE OF THE
IMMEDIATE PRESENT

AMONG ALL the concepts of which functional casework makes use, none is so difficult to understand, so hard to learn in actual doing, so elusive of precise definition, as the meaning of the immediate present in the helping situation. In fact, there is no other way about it than to admit at the ouset this limitation: that its meaning will defy those who search for it analytically. Only by a kind of yielding to the nature of the material with which we work: mobile, dynamic, fluid with the very stuff of life itself, understood momentarily and lost again, by its very motion incapable of being arrested long enough to become conceptual, can we hope to find whatever of understanding is possible. It is worth saying once again that the development of the professional self is marked by just this kind of willingness to understand in new ways—a willingness which asks as well the relinquishment of the search for unchanging assurance in a world comprised of change.

All that we have attempted to examine here as characteristic of the disciplined helper—identification, acceptance, engagement, understanding, and response—is so much preliminary exploration to bring us at last to this consideration of what actually occurs in the immediate present of the helping situation. For now we come face to face with the exacting demands upon the strength contained within the helper, and are ready to ask, to what purpose, to what use, to what end? To the purpose, we have said, that another human being may gain, through the use of the helper, more self, more life, and hence more capacity to cope with inner and outer reality.

This is a new kind of strength of which we strive to speak and to the learning of which we devote ourselves. I have spoken in a previous chapter of the striving toward fuller use of the capacity of the self as the only satisfying explanation to account for the motivation which brings any person into the helping role. Yet it is a very different kind of creativity from that to which we are accustomed, and in its very difference lies its unique character. Creativity, in its more natural expression, goes out to work change upon material, to effect through the material the image of the own idea, the own inner truth. The self pushes outward compellingly upon what is, with ongoing unity of will and impulse and emotion —whole, powerful, and expanded with spirit. It creates upon the material, to effect its change. It is the self projected, enlarged because it makes, shapes, and fashions, feels its strength, and is alive on account of it. For the helper, the situation seems just the reverse: what is required is the capacity to permit the other to create upon the self, and this is hardly a lesser thing but even an expansion of comprehending what creativity can be.

In this hour the helping person lives wholly on behalf of another's need, and that is indeed a very great deal to ask. It is perhaps one reason why this role comes more naturally to the woman than to the man, for characteristically the masculine will goes out upon the object with power, strength, intent, and direction. The woman by nature is more attuned to containment and lends herself more readily to the giving over of the whole self to the use of another. The biologically creative role is like this, for in the nine months of the uterine experience the whole focus of the organism changes to the nurture of the new being which takes from the fertile ground in which it is planted. It is this lending of the self to the use of another which must be comprehended: the organic sensitivity of a whole, big enough to contain, like the support of earth itself, capable of love and tenderness as well as unyielding difference.

It is this lending of the self to the use of another which is the first thing to be felt and known in learning to help. And, strangely enough, it is a very different thing from humility or depreciation of self, or overvaluation of the other. It comes about only through the full awareness and valuing of one's own self, through accepting the strength and becoming responsible for it. That this strength is needed to the utmost in any process of helping is what becomes gradually and then ever more compellingly realized as experience in helping matures.

There are many ways of describing for what purpose the helping person needs to be possessed of strength of unusual quality and depth. But each partial explanation or illustration serves only to becloud the one ultimate fact about the process of helping, and if this is first stated, looked upon with fresh eyes, examined, then every other facet of what transpires can be understood in relation to this central core.

The gist of the matter is that, in every helping process where something does indeed take place, there comes a time when all the strength of the client is gathered into one mighty effort to overcome the strength of the helping person; and if he succeeds, his movement is defeated, and if he does not succeed, he may have won new life. From that time on the process moves to new levels. This moment happens not rarely but abundantly. It is an inexplicable moment, and yet its outlines are sharp and vivid. It is the use of the self in this moment that the helping person strives to learn, and in comparison every other demand for response pales into relative unimportance. For now the demand upon the helping person is to hold steady and firm and unshakable against a powerful onslaught masked and disguised in content that can be very misleading.

It is not difficult to understand why the helping person

should find it so hard to meet this moment and to respond with discrimination and precision; the wonder is that it is learned at all, and that it can be borne, considering the combination of spontaneity and accuracy, feeling and strength, courage and doubt which so often resides in it. The doubt that besets the helping person and interferes with the full use of the self in this moment springs from the fact that this maintenance of the own strength, in the face of external effort to overcome it, is in itself a powerful will expression, and, as such, is imbued with guilt, as any expression of the human will inevitably is. Furthermore, one cannot maintain this kind of strength helpfully unless the feeling for the other person remains devoted to his life's movement, and includes and values the intrinsic genuine self. At bottom, the impact upon the client of this moment is the impact of knowing that even this expression of himself is valued, and to be valued really for what one is, is the most important thing, as he soon discovers.

To give an immediate response in a helping process puts upon the caseworker the responsibility for the awareness of that moment when the powerful will of the client is gathered into a focus to pit itself against the external strength, now felt to reside in the helper. Through some strange fact of being, yet not so strange, it is the essence of growth that the too-powerful, too-negative, too-resistive will, which craves to force the outer reality to yield to its need, must now instead yield itself to the greater strength outside its own singleness. At one and the same time, the person seeking help mobilizes every shred of available power to conquer the greater strength on the outside; but his greatest need is to meet, feel, and yield to a strength greater than his own. Every person can know this great need which lies at the bottom of all human experience, both in natural relationship and in functional relationship, and can realize as well, at least in some partial way, the burden and weight of carrying that strength internally; in a word, becoming responsible for it.

The Significance of the Present

We use the word yielding, with purpose to characterize this moment in time, and in its use know what depths of doubt and reservation can be stirred by this word which implies surrender, hence defeat. Yet when one comes to terms with its reality, the reward is a deepening comprehension of the dynamics of this change-imbued moment. The flood of emotion which frees the constricted will carries the movement into new and deeper levels.

What actually seems to occur is the making of that fundamental choice toward growth which is the crisis in the process. The negative organization of the will that has held the self in bondage breaks up, and emotion is fresh and real. Need—internal psychic need—heretofore feared and denied, is known, realized, possessed. The self rests, momentarily, in the support of a strength not its own. The emotion is peace after battle. The impulse which breaks through releasingly is suddenly the conveyor of energy and spontaneity. In this receptive, vulnerable, feeling phase, the new element which is other-than-self can be received instead of refused, and to that new element, in whatever content it takes form, the old self must find a new relation. This holds the key to all development of relationship to the outside world. It signalizes the capacity for and the realization of a constructive utilization of the inevitable. This is neither adjustment (which requires bending the self to conform to an outer mold) nor compromise (which suggests abandonment of a part of the true self). It is evidence of the creative power of the psychic energies in the self; hence, growth.

By the measure of his capacity to utilize this process the client also discovers new capacity to find relation to the others in his personal life experience. At bottom this has been his problem when he comes to the social agency, whatever form the outer reality may have assumed. The self is not whole without the capacity to relate to the other, and finding relation to the other means discovery that the other, too, has powerful will and impulse energies, which interact with his own, and which he cannot control. If he is to live at all, then he must find the way to accept this inevitable fact.

The immediate present is imbued with fear because it, more than the past or the future, contains the fear of living. It is this responsibility for living which the human self perversely tries to avoid at the same time that he craves it so compellingly. It is not a matter of getting rid of this fear, which in every instance is impossible, but wholly a matter of finding the way to live with the fear in such a way as to make life bearable; more than this, to turn the fear to creative use. In the unusual sense of unity which at times is felt in the helping situation, it is as if the fear diminishes or is at least momentarily supported in a whole larger than the own self. Having discovered that one can unite without being destroyed, one knows anew that the capacity to unite holds great promise for life. Within this unity, so dearly prized and newly won, comes the inevitable separation which this precipitating moment of difference has introduced. Now he is faced, not with the fear of unity, but more with the fear of separation: the isolated, single, separated sense of the own self, alone and unconnected with the supporting whole. To traverse this lack of connection, to recreate it, to find his way back toward the relationship with another is the crisis he cannot escape. His forward movement toward it is growth, no less. Upon the helping person rests the necessity to know and respond to that forward movement.

The desire of one who writes of this, as of the person who reads, must indeed be to find some way to convey in concrete, visual illustration the tangible evidence of how this pure psychological movement lives itself out in everyday experience. Somehow it seems impossible to convey at one and the same time the dynamics of the engagement between the helper and the one seeking help, and the specific content in which this engagement occurs. For that reason I have chosen to devote one chapter to a discussion of the meaning of content and its relation to psychological change.

The Significance of the Present

It now seems possible to lay the groundwork for a further generalization regarding content. We have stripped the meaning of immediate response of all but the clear, sharp focus of response to the expression of the will-impulse-feeling strivings of the client. We have attempted first to comprehend the dynamic of pure psychological movement which grows out of the awareness of the crisis and the movement that follows yielding. If the response of the helper is to content as a sheer matter of content, the helping potential is lost. Yet content holds an all-important place, for none of this is possible without the projection of the inner conflict upon outer, partialized bits of reality. And it is the character of this reality, the structural nature of the process, which now remains to be explored.

CHAPTER XII

THE RELATION OF CONTENT TO PSYCHOLOGICAL CHANGE

THERE COMES a moment in the training process when swift forward movement results from the sudden realization on the part of the student that it does not matter so much what one says, as that one becomes genuinely engaged with the client. To react spontaneously, to throw off the constricting intellectual bonds of necessity to find the right thing to say, is like discovering a whole new medium in which to work. The moment of this discovery is enlivening and usually comes about, if it happens at all, through some sudden illumination, never by a slow, laborious accretion of learning. It is the moment of recognition that the very helping situation itself is the crucial matter, and that whatever of therapeutic value is possible for the client resides in this new experience with a helping person who assists him toward self-understanding and a new capacity to will constructively. As one student put it in writing a final casework paper, "As we ponder we lose the moment and then it is too late; once we ponder, the emotion is gone and with it the feeling and the spontaneity."

Every helping person will bear testimony to this actual experience, that the best results are obtained and the most enlivening sense of engagement and movement is present "when there is no time to think." In these moments there is a realization of rhythm, of wholeness within the helping person, of willingness to risk, of freedom from caution—in a word, of courageous giving of the self to a process on behalf of another. From this exhilarating generalization it might be easy to jump to the conclusion that all that is required is absence of restraint, whereas the kind of spontaneity of which we speak is, as this whole discussion has tried to indicate, the product of a long, slow growth of internal discipline which produces just this freedom to use the self spontaneously in the functional situation as it unfolds.

We speak here of that same relation of form to creativity which is the essence of any discipline. Content in the helping process bears the same relation to psychological change as form to creativity: content is the form in which inner experience communicates itself. In ordinary experience we feel emotion about something; if we are afraid, we are afraid because of something; if we feel guilty, we locate the cause of the guilt upon a specific act or thought. Inner and outer, abstract and concrete, the psychic life and content are inseparable parts of a whole, two sides of the same phenomenon. It is only through the medium of content that there can be development in relationship, while at bottom the content corresponds exactly to pure psychological interaction between two human wills. I stress the area of ordinary experience because content plays precisely this crucial role in all human interaction, including the functional helping situation, yet at the same time it is essential to keep in mind that, as the discipline in the helping role grows and deepens, there comes about a corresponding enrichment of the helper's capacity to work with pure psychological movement and emotion almost without content. There comes as well a maturing realization that the fundamental emotions of fear and guilt are inherent in the life process itself, needing no justification or explanation in terms of external events. The possession of this knowledge constitutes one of the major differences between the helper and the one being helped, inasmuch as the latter seeks always to justify or explain in real terms.

It will readily be seen how this realization of the importance of pure psychological dynamics between two human beings in different roles, almost to the exclusion of content, is an indispensable phase in the process of learning to become a helper. In fact it can be said that, unless the student is capable of an exaggerated abandonment of content, he never wholly succeeds in throwing off the bondage to the reality content that is the natural characteristic of the beginner. He must learn to regard the will-impulse-feeling interaction between caseworker and client as the essence of the authentic helping situation. But in the process of establishing this concept the true significance and value of content may be overlooked, and, if this is so, then one important facet of the total situation is left obscure and inaccessible. It remains to ask, what is the significance of content; what relation does it bear to psychological change?

There are two key points in this problem of content which can guide the caseworker in dealing with its diverse detail. The first lies in the principle that the response of the caseworker must be not to content as such, but to the will-impulse-feeling expression of the self in relationship. In the functional helping situation, one side of the relationship is the client; the other side, the caseworker—agency-centered—who now constitutes for the client otherness, non-self, the external object upon which the client can project his conflict and his dynamic pattern of use of self in relationship. Accuracy of response in the caseworker lies in feeling sensitively what is projected upon and done to him as the helper, and this can be expressed in an infinite variety of content.

The second key point lies in the realization that the very uniqueness of casework arises from the discovery of the value for therapeutic results which comes about through devoted consideration for, and use of, content. The constant penetration of reality factors existing both in the client's situation and in the agency's function is the most meaningful factor for differentiating casework from therapy. The distinctive character of function in casework arises from this utilization of the potential for growth through the reworking of a concrete, partialized, limited, specific content within a process especially established in structure for this purpose. Parenthetically, it might be added that this same thing is true in the learning-teaching experience within the functional setting provided for casework training; namely, that, by a close adherence to all facets of the purpose that brings the student into training, therapeutic results are possible. As has been stated earlier, there is fear of this use of the word therapeutic, in part because the solid ground of function seems momentarily lost in confusion of casework with therapy. Yet one of the essential differences between the two, from the point of view of the process, lies in this important and significant area of the use of content.

For the caseworker, there are three identifiable phases of development in relation to this problem of the use of content. The first is characterized by an exaggerated attention to content. This is the natural attitude which the student first brings into training, and it is wholly logical, for, if one is to help with a reality problem, then what is more reasonable than that both the helper and the one being helped should focus wholly upon solving this problem. Let us say that in this phase content holds the center of the stage. Supervisors will recognize this phase as analogous to their own experience in learning to supervise, when their attention is concentrated upon the case, to the detriment of the worker's learning.

The second phase of learning is the one I speak of at the opening of this chapter, namely, the sudden awakening to the value of spontaneity in the helping situation. This is a moment of illumination, of newly acquired freedom, and often of some very much enlivened capacity to help. A quality comes into the interview which has been altogether lacking before.

In the third and final phase the helping person has taken full possession of the dynamics of psychological movement and the meaning of the current experience in the helping milieu, at the same time that he possesses a sensitive capacity to work in the medium of the content which is natural to the client.

Such schematization of phases is useful and meaningful only if viewed as a fluid and constantly shifting relation of parts to the whole. For this sequence of events could as well describe the continuous development of the experienced helper, reflecting as it does the constant swings and advances and retreats which make up the search for greater skill so long as this search is alive. There is no better way to highlight this very point than by reference again to that most meaningful statement of Rank's informed with new meaning for casework by Miss Robinson's quotation of it in *A Changing Psychology:* ". . . One must learn the speech of the other, and not force upon him the current idiom."[1] In this lies every facet of the meaning of content for which we search. In fuller context, Rank points out the relation of the universal and individual factors which correspond to the two sides of this phenomenon: ". . . The essential factor remains always the capacity to understand the individual from himself, in which process the common human element, certainly not to be denied, can constitute only the hypothesis, not the content of the understanding."[2]

This "capacity to understand the individual from himself" means a capacity to relate creatively to the content of the experience, as the individual himself fashions it, for this is the intrinsic essence of his uniqueness; it is the individual expression of the "I," and the generalization, so important to casework, of "respect for the individual" demands this utmost respect for the content, for the reality situation, the way the client sees it and works upon it. It is in this medium that he can create to the extent of which he is capable.

It is by no means an easy matter to differentiate between these two possible and contrasting attitudes toward content, the one attitude being a sensitive response to the client's individuality, the other attitude being the excessive and unsuitable concentration upon content which always interferes with effective helping. When the helping person becomes too centered in concern for the concrete reality problem which the client brings, a number of different results are bound to occur in one way or another in the course of events. When the helping person reaches out and touches the concrete reality problem, by suggestion, advice, excessive or inappropriate concern, then the immediate effect is likely to be that the client discovers the very channel for unburdening the weight of his problem: something he seeks but which will defeat him in the end if he is successful. Reference has already been made in this discussion to the universal tendency, on the part of the one who comes for help, to come with necessity to blame other persons, or to blame events over which he has no control, or circumstances which have victimized him, as the cause of his tribulations. He believes that change means change of the outside. He does not yet know, and cannot, that it is only through change within himself that he can achieve his desired goal; that he alone can do it. Readily the connection between the two attitudes is evident: the connection between the caseworker's overconcern for the reality problem and the client's desire to be rid of the burden. The problem becomes the caseworker's, and over and over again one sees a whole process continue indefinitely, with just this struggle unresolved.

The same struggle comes about when the helping person reaches out and takes hold of the concrete problem through some mistaken effort to share with the client the burden of solution of the reality problem. The reality situations of finding a job, or consulting a physician, or finding a place to live are particularly full of risk with respect to this undesirable result. One can hardly believe that the human self can for so long hold itself in bondage to the continuous need to force the other, the helping person, to carry this pack upon his back, when inherently he will fight every move which seems to indicate that his efforts have succeeded.

Here we have before us a valuable opportunity to see and

consider the relation between content and psychological change. We have spoken again and again, in different connections, of the one fundamental movement which takes place when the user of help takes over into himself both the problem and the responsibility for its solution. I use the figure of speech "pack on the back" advisedly, because it seems to me at times one can almost feel this in kinesthetic terms, and can know the moment this shift takes place from one's self, who holds the will-to-growth, to the one using help, who now takes it over. Unfortunately this does not stay put as simply as the carrying of a load, but moves again constantly back and forth. So that here the question, will he himself take this responsibility for this particular content, carries the full meaning of the imperative psychological change which must come about, if he is to use himself differently.

Likewise, the over-concentration of attention upon the content by the helping person soon shapes up to become the bone of contention over which the will-struggle eventuates. For now it becomes still more clear that if the helping situation ever runs into those rocky waters where but one goal is in sight, and this the goal of the helping person, then, indeed, the client, often to his own great disadvantage, will set his will against it. He opposes seldom, if ever, in the clear-cut discernible manner of open refusal of the plan of the caseworker, where it could certainly be got hold of, but more often in the subtler ways of resistance (characteristic of mankind, not evil in the client). He may appear to be in complete agreement with the caseworker, he may be making devoted efforts to achieve the goal, but with striking lack of success. "I will do what you want," he will say in complete submission and conformity. "If I can only find out exactly what you are asking of me, I assure you I will do it," he adds. Or, even more frustrating to the helper, the client acts precisely in accordance with what was agreed upon between them, and promptly the most undesirable consequences ensue from his praiseworthy efforts.

In other words, it is the content which eventually distills the situation into the pure form of the clash of two wills. It is for this reason that the use of a worker-conceived plan is imbued from the outset with the seeds of its own defeat.

So far it seems relatively simple to follow the course of this exploration, but now we come to more complex and more illusive phenomena. It would be an easy reaction to what has just been said to abandon altogether our interest in the reality problem which the client brings, lest any of these results be produced; lest, when the caseworker touches the problem, it cease to be the client's. Yet we have also said that it is of the essence of functional casework that there should be felt and expressed, throughout the process, utter regard and consideration for the content the client brings. "Getting at the feeling which lies back of his words"; "waiting for the relationship to develop in order that he may feel sufficiently at ease to reveal his true feelings"; "knowing that what he says when he first comes is not the true meaning, but eventually the true meaning will come forth"—all of these expressions which appear in casework literature are wholly alien to and destructive of the meaning we are attempting to examine. Actually every word the client speaks, from first to last, is important to him, of genuine meaning, hence to be valued and given consideration as a part of himself. If he has made a plan, as he so often has when he first comes to the agency, just because he must so desperately feel that he is not so badly off as he may appear to be, it is worthy of every attention from the caseworker. Out of their actual working together upon this problem and plan as he brings it will come the testing of what he has created; the caseworker need be in no haste to inject his own doubt.

I have spoken in the previous chapter of the crisis which originates, and which is present in every process, when the one being helped gathers all his strength into one focus and attempts to overcome the greater strength of the helping person. And I have said that if that outer strength holds he may possibly win new life, and if it succumbs the process fails. Now we are ready to develop in more detail what the nature of that engagement can be and often is, because the erroneous conclusion could be reached that this encounter of one strength with another is always a matter of two opposing judgments or opinions, of which that of the caseworker must prevail. Rarely is it this, although sometimes it may be; but if it is, then the clash of wills likely to occur is of that kind which, no matter what the outcome, results in the failure of the client to receive help. In fact, the very nature of the strength in the helping person may be evident not from his insistence upon a single outcome but rather in continuous capacity to make no issue of what the final outcome may be.

This is but a particular instance of the fundamental principle which can now be restated. In any process, the psychological dynamics are the same—they represent the universal, the common, the like, that which is always the same wherever authentic involvement in the giving and taking of help occurs. Content, on the other hand, represents that which is individual, unique, different. In consequence, the relation of content to psychological change becomes comprehensible only as the helper can leave behind the necessity to interpret content in mechanistic terms and respond to it instead as the conveyor of the real self, dynamically lived out in the present.

Any process will show universal points of crisis in psychological movement, but always through content which is unique. Perhaps we can understand the whole problem of the generic and specific in casework through this very point: what it takes, for instance, for a caseworker to move from one specific function to another. About this we believe two seemingly contradictory things: one, that there is a common base which is the same for every function; the other, that it is just the difference in the function itself which provides an indispensable ingredient in effective helping. The contradiction is resolved in the belief that the helping person must possess and carry from one function to another this deep level of understanding of psychological movement, which has the same essential outlines of movement in every process. At the same time it is the content, which is the form, the individualization of the function, which must be learned anew, and the learning of which requires a process of internalization in time.

There will be content in every process that reflects the tentativeness of the beginning movement, compounded as it is of wanting and not wanting at the same time. There will be the gathering toward the center of the first crisis, when the one seeking help tests his own strength against the helping person, feels the greater strength on the outside, halts ambivalently, struggles, then yields to it, and from it discovers he gains a new release toward forward movement. Then follows a new beginning, this time initiating the longer sweep of the continuing process, repeating again upon another level the ambivalence and tentativeness, the building toward a crisis, the crisis, the yielding, the new movement forward. Until at last comes ending, and at the crisis of ending, which represents more than any other point the imposition of an immovable limit, the whole activation of the will conflict poses once more the touch-and-go: will he, or will he not, take over his own growth movement?

For each of these points of crisis, and for each of the slower gradual sweeps of movement in the process, there is content suitable to the function and self-created by the client. It is with content that he creates. The fixed, unchangeable nature of his psychological make-up as a human being he cannot escape, and the agency structure in the helping situation precisely reflects this life reality; but in the medium of his own content he can create to the utmost of his capacity.

What the helping person feels, as he relates to the particular individual content of the one seeking help, is the effect of the will-impulse-feeling strivings as they become more intense, more sharply etched in outline, under the unusual circumstance of the functional helping situation. What he feels is movement toward the source of help, or movement away; effort to elicit emotion from the helper; effort to control his own; drive to exaggerate helplessness, or painful acknowledgment of need. He feels the will in all its force manifestations: to change the day, the time, the conditions; to change whatever it is the helping person has set up, no matter what its nature. He begins to feel the searching, the testing, the effort to discover: can the helping person really take me as I am? Will what I am shock, frighten, alienate this one who attempts to help? To understand this, one must recapitulate still another concept, namely, that the craving of the self to be understood is never satisfied by understanding of the good side alone. In some compelling manner, the striving of the self is toward a goal that the other regard him honestly, essentially in his essence. It does not matter, then, whether it is valued good or bad, generous or mean, big or petty, honest or calculating. The self wants to be known for itself, real, exact, accurate, genuine, honestly conceived. And when it happens between two people that some approximation of this utterly unachievable goal is reached, it is a moment of rare human experience indeed. Thus, when the one using help has first felt this sense of "he accepts me the way I am," he will keep on trying to discover whether this is indeed really the case—will it hold. He will go on producing more and more content by which to further this intention. For this purpose, content is truly inexhaustible. The will of the client is bent upon discovering where there is a weak spot, and if it can be found he will go through it—perversely, to be sure, for what he requires above all else (if the life impulse has any strength) is that he should not succeed in this endeavor. To this outer strength he craves to yield the too-tight organization of himself, but this does not happen until he has pitted his own will and yielded in the process.

With children, the use of content in this manner is much plainer than with adults, and to anyone attuned to these dynamics the fact is inescapable that the child seeks always to discover what will stop him, where that outer limit is, and whether the adult really means what he says. The content which children use, and especially that which adolescents use, is swift, directly inspired by the relation to the helper, much nearer the surface and uncomplicated by rationalization. It propels itself outward straight as an arrow upon the caseworker, with an arrow's intent to attack. This is one reason, if not the key reason, why it is so difficult to work with a child in the helping process, and why a child in the way he senses an adult's relation to him can be frightening in his immediate awareness. The caseworker can give sorely needed help to a foster parent on just this score, because a child will move from home to home, getting the better of every adult, until he encounters one strong enough to meet his strength with greater strength. One must distinguish, when speaking of this point of crisis, between the adult who opposes the will of the child out of fear that the child will get the better of him, and the adult whose action arises from a source essentially tender, and internally imbued with strength. At bottom, this is the core of the problem of the delinquent; and the source of help lies in his finding the combination of a strength which says, "this cannot be," at the same time that it is related to him compassionately.

Sometimes the use of content by the client is designed to enlist the caseworker as an ally against an unjust fate. He pictures himself as the helpless victim of circumstance—one who cannot be blamed, because what has happened has happened, and the odds against him have been too great. Any process which remains on this level becomes static. For as surely as content of this character appears, there is bound to be the equally compelling drive to be found responsible, reprehensible as the end result may be. At times the client will be insisting that he did this, caused this to happen, is responsible, when the caseworker is still sympathizing with him in his fate. Movement will come, life will be affirmed, help will be used, when the caseworker recognizes and responds to the self-responsibility which he affirms. For his need to establish this responsibility accurately can be understood only when placed side by side with the acknowledgment that, until he feels responsibility for what has been happening and is happening, he cannot mobilize his strength to encounter outer reality successfully.

The relation of past to present is of especial interest when examined from the particular focus of attempting to comprehend the relation of content to psychological change. Content from the past is unquestionably utilized repeatedly as a means by which to force the process out of the present into the past, where there is less fear. Content from the past can carry the full sweep of the overassertion of projected blame: what I am is because of what happened to me in the past; what my childhood lacked or had too much of; what others did or failed to do. Hence the past becomes a vital strand in disentangling self-responsibility, own will, admission of own will, from the projection upon others.

In the content of the past is located the stream of continuity of the self, both in individuality and in ancestry. The past gives expanse and enlargement to the self; one cannot be whole unless one possesses one's past, encompassing it lovingly whatever its content, for the very reason that it is a part of one's self. The process of growth seems to demand that in some manner the self rework a crisis in experience which lodges like an unassimilated weight on account of excessive guilt, or denied responsibility, or any other kind of denial which hides the real truth from the inner self. As I have witnessed again and again this process of growth which comes through the utilization of a piece of content from the past, it seems to be that what occurs is a sudden fresh sense of self and life arising as a result of the dropping away of the denial; a sudden realization of one's own expression of will. At the same time, the true emotion belonging to the past situation is felt genuinely, and this is possible exactly on account of the present experience in a growth process.

Content from the past tends always to be especially concerned with the relation of the self to the parents. Some schools of therapeutic psychology locate their search for cure upon the illumination of these early relations of child to parent, and formulate their solutions in causal explanation. This is vastly different from the concept here being developed. Here we are saying that, indeed, these early parental relations have been the milieu in which the child has grown. But it is because the parents represent the first objects of outer will—the crucial "otherness" of the child's life—that these relationships play so vital a role. Here the whole dynamic interplay of the pattern of self, consisting of psychological and physical need, of effort to satisfy that need, of willingness to admit the need, of will and the denial of will, of capacity to feel emotion, is played out in growth of the self. What the helper can know in the immediate moment of the helping situation is that this same dynamic pattern of the self, modified by the passage of time, by growth or lack of it, but especially by the impact of the current situation, will once more express itself authentically, and the outline of the pattern will be more precise, the more accurate the response of the helper and the richer the sense of life in the current process is.

Sometimes, in the process, the person using help comes to the threshold of comprehending this connection between past and present. He will say he knows that he must oppose the helper because he repeats the experience of the past when he opposed the imposition of his father's authority. But what he feels and actually responds to *is* the authority of the helper in the present moment—an authority which comes from the very fact of presuming to be one who can help; which comes from every reality factor in the helping situation, no matter how gentle the helper may be. It is only a question: will this be denied; will it be overasserted; or will it be acknowledged and utilized constructively?

Hence it is not that the one seeking help repeats an old experience out of need to return to the past. It is that the dynamic pattern of the self is actually and intensely alive at the moment, but in the content of the past it is more possible to communicate this fact with less fear, less guilt, less demand for being responsible in the present moment. This view of the relation of past content to the present places no requirement upon the one in the growth experience to use any particular piece of content, nor does a wealth of content have to be reworked in this manner. Any piece of content can convey the same dynamic movement, and the individuality of the self in the present is epitomized in this very selection of content and in the location of the vortex in which the life movement eventuates.

The more the content moves from past to present, the more likelihood there is of fear arising, and this is as true for the helper as for the one seeking help. It is that crisis which, of all points of crisis, asks the maximum in strength of the helper. A great variety of content presents itself in this especial moment, since it is the moment during which the one seeking help opens the innermost recesses of the self and puts into words the specific, the fact, upon which he locates his deepest fear. Since no human being, even the one who has disciplined himself to be a helper, is ever completely free of fear and guilt in the life process, this moment can become a true crisis, for the entanglement in another's fear is an eventuality to which live creatures are peculiarly susceptible. On exactly this point the disciplined helper differs from the one seeking help, for the essence of authentic growth is a constant change in which the self finds new relation to fear and increasing capacity to differentiate himself with respect to this emotion. This is a highly complex psychological phenomenon, and one which can scarcely be touched in so brief a manner, but neither would the subject of content be complete without inclusion of this point of major importance.

In bringing this chapter to a conclusion, there remains but one more point with respect to content which cannot be overlooked. I refer to the difference which exists between the caseworker's content and that of the client, a difference more often obliterated than acknowledged. The client is in every sense of the word a "lay" person, and thus much closer in ideology, values, prejudices, trusts, and distrusts to the general public than to the social worker. At times, social work tends to erase this fact by assuming likeness between itself and the client and difference between itself and the public. Actually, any semblance of likeness between social worker and client in content terms is projection. Likeness, which is essential in order to help, arises instead from the universals of human experience.

Agency content is created, by and large, by social workers, with respect to time, method, standards, money, and general outlook upon life. At the same time, the statement is validly made that the structure of a social agency must represent a segment of reality, a partial experience, in order to afford an effective setting for helping. A moment's thought will soon illuminate the startling and surprising character of the content a client meets when he comes to a social agency.

Content of infinite variety is implicit in what the agency stands for, in what the worker represents. The client will react to this content, if he is helped to reach these reactions. It is a content which, among other things, stands for change, growth, and life, and the potential for its realization. It is a content which, while seemingly unencumbered by a specific norm demanding a specific kind of life content, does nevertheless stand for a value whose attainment is cherished and whose realization is the hardest demand upon the human self. This is the demand—in the last analysis self-imposed— which asks that the self become responsible and carry its part in relationship with integrity and increasing willingness to trust itself to the life process.

If one accepts this conception of the relation of content to dynamics, then there is but one conclusion regarding reliance on the meaning of any particular piece of content: there can never be any one interpretation, and content out of process is practically meaningless. What may at one point of time, place, and process be a true indication of yielding, may at another be only another step into the dark helplessness of the client's fixed resistance. What may in one situation be evidence of increasing capacity for relationship, may in another be an equally powerful indication of absence of relationship. Knowing this, caseworkers can see how they could not, and should not, arrive at prior decisions before a process begins. What the caseworker can know reliably is what this human being does in the actuality of agency setting; whether he is capable of relating, is relatively responsible, reachable, accessible to communication. Even though this principle with respect to the necessity of process is acknowledged, efforts still persist in the direction of attempting to make a prior decision out of process, regarding the nature, extent, and degree of seriousness of the client's problem, in order to determine what kind of help he needs.

CHAPTER XIII

THE MOVEMENT OF THE SELF
IN CHOICE

I T BECOMES increasingly clear, as we follow step by step the exploration of these concepts in which functional helping is rooted, that we are dealing here with a process in which the client is helped to become free to choose, and that he does not bring this condition of freedom into the helping situation in any accessible or active form. Clear as this statement may seem, and however universal the agreement that helping aims toward precisely this end, of releasing capacity for choice, the reverse attitude prevails in both thought and action. At times caseworkers fall victim to an illusion to which mankind is peculiarly susceptible: that freedom is a natural state of being which will prevail so long as nothing interferes and provided the environment is favorably inclined toward its encouragement. We speak of leaving the client free to choose, of allowing him to discover his own way, of protecting his right to self-determination, without realizing the extent to which each of these descriptions of the condition of relationship between helper and helped is static and negative in the sense that each implies refraining from interference, rather than the active engagement which the helping process requires.

Accordingly, in order to comprehend the true nature of the movement of the self in choice, we must first open up and consider the more authentic realities of freedom, in terms of inner experience, psychologically explored. Interestingly enough, the words freedom and choice always go together in some intrinsic compatibility, since the state of inner being which we comprehend as freedom leads always to the en-larged capacity to choose; in a word, to affirm the will con-structively, to know what one wants, and to seek it effectively. The exploration of this problem has led us to the inescapable conclusion that inner psychic freedom is a state of being, achieved only through long and arduous and painful life experience. It is the product of growth and individuation and, even under the best of circumstances, is never wholly possessed. The most we can ever hope for is some partial realization of the answer to this longing to be free. In the helping process what takes place can never be more than the most limited, temporary, and unpretentious striving for new freedom; but this in no way demeans the goal, for the search gains new vitality out of the very admission of its partial nature, and sets in motion a growth process whose on-going impulse will continue to seek out new development.

This is the fundamental truth which every helping person must at bottom admit and accept, first for the own self, in order to hold it in constant relation to the helping process. It is precisely the fact that the client lacks freedom to choose and act which brings him to the source of help, and it is his location of the responsibility for this absence of free-dom upon the outside which keeps him from realizing the degree to which he can be an effective force to free himself.

But to a degree far greater than we are usually willing to admit, and to an extent that we are fearful to concede, the crisis in the helping process is more truthfully described as a process of helping the client achieve a new relation to the *inevitable,* instead of uncovering constantly new sources of choice. Through a state of affairs seen at times only as thoroughly contradictory and illogical, through this very acceptance of the inevitable, through admission of what can-not be different, of what will not succumb to the own will or force, the human self finds new life, new constructive use of himself. We speak in no sense of a fatalistic submission to what is, in hopelessness and despair, but we speak instead of the unquenchable life-force of the human spirit to grapple with outer circumstances anew.

From the moment of birth man experiences the first overpowering reality of the fixed nature of his environment. That he is born at all, in this moment of time rather than any other, of these parents; that he is endowed with a given physical constitution in sex, color, and appearance; that he is destined to play his part in an already existing environment—all these are reality factors which allow him little if any opportunity for his own choice. He shares in common with all humanity the attributes of being human, of a finite life, of the necessity to struggle in order to live at all, of a nature ambivalent with life and non-life, veined with fear and guilt, and impelled forward by a compelling search to complete himself. All his life, if he can but bear to admit it, he struggles with and against the unchangeable nature of the inner and outer reality, always with unpredictable but potentially creative results. In the span of a life's history he encounters and grapples with innumerable important occasions for choices. First these decisions are made for him by adults, such as where he shall live, what he shall wear and eat, to what school he shall go; later he takes these on himself as he moves into the crucial life decisions of an occupation, of relationship to the other, of movement from place to place, of creating a home, and somewhere, in some far less tangible way, the choice of the way and the depth of the fulfillment of the self. Indeed, the nature of the choice with which he is faced at these points of crisis is deep and complicated and sometimes overpowering in realization of the responsibility which the self cannot escape. In outer appearance, it is the multiplicity of choice and the burden of too much choice, rather than its limitation, which is more predominantly apparent. But beneath it all lies the first comprehensive life reality of the nature and extent of the limitation arising simultaneously from external environment and innate capacity of the self.

One can understand the meaning of this inevitability only by searching the everyday experience of one's own reality. On behalf of the client, we are likely to realize as well how much greater and more powerful are the odds against him, even if viewed in purely economic terms. This we need to realize and include within our thinking, but not to the exclusion of the fact which lies at a deeper level: that no matter how plentiful the reality choices appear to be in the helping situation, every client, and every person in the dynamics of the helping movement whatever the function, is finally and at last faced with the one, single, ultimate choice, will he choose growth or will he refuse it. In this moment of choice, its character is not imbued with variety—it is tight with singleness. He has sorted and sifted to this one point of impact, where the conditions of the helping situation and the character of the helper, upon whom he has located all manner of projections, constitute now the unchangeable, the inevitable; and the only question which remains becomes the same one of which we have already spoken—can he take in what is, permit the resultant disorganization of the status quo of the self, and through this means cross the threshold to the richer possibilities which await him. This is the precise moment of likeness between the helping situation and real life. He learns through new experience, through immediate experience, to will anew. He has met the outer reality, engaged with it, and moved into some fresh relation to it. And it is precisely because this same limitation is utterly natural to the helping situation, as it is to life itself, that the results can be what they are. Functional casework is sometimes accused of creating artificial limits or obstacles; sometimes students in the learning phase strive to create the limit in this same external or artificial way. But the progressive picture of the growth of skill has no such contrivance in it; if the helping process is real, the client searches for and finds the natural limits of the situation.

It is quite clear that this kind of choice does not take place in an intellectual process, or primarily through the exercise of reason which judiciously balances one alternative against another. The common view of the matter often maintains that emotion ought not to enter into the making of choices; that the choice is trustworthy only if it can be logically sustained by a literal weighing of values, by placing all the pros on one side of the scale and all the cons on the other, permitting whichever tilts heavier to determine the decision. Indeed, it is natural enough to draw this conclusion regarding the process of choice since, whenever the self is so engaged in choosing, it is true that its inner state seems to be describable as one in which the pros and cons thrash about, clash, separate, while one gains strength and another loses, until finally the moment can no longer be put off when the decision must be made and action taken.

The process of choice as we know it in helping bears no resemblance to a mechanical mental endeavor. The content of choosing carries and reflects the deeper psychological movement which is going on within the human self. In pure feeling, stripped of content, the experience of choice is an experience of the self in conflicted movement. The arresting fact is the seemingly nonintellectual nature of this movement at bottom, no matter what the justifications and rationalizations may be upon the surface. It is chaos, momentary or long lasting, consisting of clashes and divisions, unity and merging. It is fraught with discomfort, little discomforts in the form of irritation or big discomforts in the form of anguish and severing disunion. "At the instant of choice," says Kierkegaard, "he is in the most complete isolation, for he withdraws from his surroundings."[1]

It is the miraculous quality of living that some deep stream of the self flows along through time knowing its own direction for the sustenance of which it seems to select from its environment those bits of reality which carry this fundamental movement. At times the harmony of this inner direction is clear and unified. The self knows its way and chooses out of the common day rhythmically, with an organic sense of wholeness. At other times the disunity, the loss of relation, the loss of a focus for life itself seem to make of every tiniest commonplace decision an obstacle of wearying proportions. At times like these, even to decide what one wants to eat or what one should do next seems more than the available energy can cope with. It is then a blessed thing to have this question settled by another, without involvement of the self. In comparison, all love of freedom and all longing to "do it myself" fade into insignificance in the welcome relief of a situation or person which relieves the self of all responsibility.

Consequently, the helping person must also reckon with this powerful reverse of the desire to choose and to be independent. Even the best of helpers can be caught unwittingly in the temptation to project upon the other the pure, unadulterated supposition that the craving to be independent is the compelling factor. It is indeed a powerful craving, but it is just as true that there are times when the helping person knows, and is capable of utilizing fearlessly, the releasing, beneficent capacity of his own wholeness and strength to support momentarily the divided disunity of another.

It is the nature of this movement of the self in choice that it cannot happen at all except in time, and it is this which leads me to the conclusion, already put forth in the chapter on the client's initial movement toward the social agency, that the application process must contain at least three interviews, sufficiently spaced one from another so as to provide this essential time element in which reaction and development can take place. The three interviews constitute no arbitrary selection, since the accepted pattern of a completed process must allow for the beginning phase, the midpoint, and the ending phase. In the presence of the helper in the first interview, it is impossible for the applicant to discover, in all respects, what is himself and what is this powerful other with whom he has engaged. Neither can he discover this alone, but when he returns a second time he begins to work upon this question once more; he discovers that there are space and time in which to move around, and that allowance is made for the inevitable backward movement, which he must be able to admit and describe, if he is to be one who can utilize a continuing process.

Three interviews permit time, too, for the significant part played by the accidental intrusion of an external precipitant to take its course. The emphasis I have placed upon the deep stream of the self, which moves slowly and which carries the direction and purpose of the self, would not be complete without acknowledging at the same time the important and meaningful connection which exists between this fundamental self-direction and the accident of a chance happening or event. For example, when a student who has been in training for some time (and therefore has more capacity for accurate understanding of the experience) describes the series of events which brought him into training, he customarily describes a process long in the making, but very often a specific concrete event became the precipitant which moved him at last into action. We speak of this as the condition of "readiness" which develops in a long process of time, in which the external event finds fertile ground. This outer element is all-important in the process of choice, and the helping person, knowing this, can find ways to bring it into the process out of the natural happenings in the current situation.

The role of the helper in this process of enabling another to choose constructively might be said to consist of the capacity to relate simultaneously to this deepest level of the self, which carries the long slow direction, and to the surface level of the self, which carries the swift, more superficial levels of choice. Movement can perhaps be described as always having these two levels—at least two levels and seemingly at times many more. Knowing this, the helper accepts his unique role in this process in containing and holding the slower, more rhythmic movement while the client flounders around in indecision or premature decision, changes his mind a dozen times, tries out one thing, rejects another, and returns always to find the opportunity to reorganize his direction, until at last the precipitation of the ending creates the inescapable moment when he must take over into himself the responsibility for affirming, through word or action or both, that this is the way it will be.

This is the process of learning to choose, rich and comprised of plentiful activity. For choice cannot be made in a vacuum, nor can it be made in the head through thought alone. Choice becomes ever the more possible when there is content to be acted upon: things to do and problems to meet and solutions to try. Fear is easier to cope with when one can do something about the fear; sheer waiting and pondering are agony. Activity not only lends an outlet for the energy so stirred and aroused by the very helping situation itself, but it also plays that important role of facilitating discovery, through actual expression of the self, of what the self is like, and what it wants. It never ceases to fill me with wonder, each time I come upon the renewed recognition of how feeling changes through feeling: that is, through being expressed and lived out; how the will is better understood through willing and encountering the will of another; how every facet of experience, whether mistaken and painful or exhilarating and right, can be gathered into new comprehension by the self that is creatively focused, or, better said, in the moments when the self is creatively focused. When interviews are spaced at weekly intervals, as they very frequently are in the casework service, the hour of engagement between the helper and the one who seeks help can be intense, deeply disturbing, and penetrated by the new sense of life which every human being fears intensely yet craves so deeply. A week is none too long in which to thrash about in one's own aloneness—in confusion, in rebellion, in yielding, in conflict, all gathering toward the moment of return, in new organization, in new discovery of what the self is like by telling it to another whose responses are accurate. This is the part played by the focus: the penetration of the confusion, the break-up of the old constellation, as a result of which there ensues the giving way of the artificial defenses, and the mobilization of the self, made necessary by the very pressure of the next time now so imminent.

Sometimes it seems to happen that striking change in attitude and relationship comes about solely as the result of a client's yielding to emotion in relation to the helping person. Some casework material reflects this fact to a remarkable degree. What one sees in these circumstances is the initial tight organization of the client, coming forth in words and emotion that are hard, fixed, willful in the negative sense, destructive, and lacking in understanding of the part played by the own self. If and when a change of feeling does occur between the one seeking help and the helper when the emotion softens the will and true feeling bursts through, when the momentary relief from the tight organization is felt in this beneficent yielding to the emotion, then it is often highly possible that the fresh opening up of the capacity to feel love instead of hate makes itself manifest in every direction. Actually this has much that is characteristic of the growth process, and explains why so much helping appears to take place upon just this realization of unity with another. The helper who knows this organic wholeness can hold a total situation in momentary relief from disunity and separateness.

But no genuine growth will eventuate from this experience of unity alone. For now we come to the final piece which belongs in this consideration of the movement of the self in choice. If growth is in truth to be the outcome, then the final phase of the process requires of the one being helped that he take back into himself the will to do, and the belief that he has the strength to do; and, even more crucially, that he accept the final and ultimate outcome, that he must do it alone. This is the experience of separation, of utter aloneness, of final and inescapable responsibility. Throughout the helping process the helper has carried, in more or less degree, the will-to-growth, the identification with the potentiality of the client's self. At moments this is carried wholly by the helping person, but gradually, as the process develops, there are recurrent moments in which the client experiments with taking a piece of this other side back into some possessed and affirmed part of himself—all in gradual preparation for the terminating hour when the same thing must happen in final ending. He will try in every content that he knows to force the helping person to continue to carry this living side of himself, at the same time that the other movement in him is so powerful—the will to do it himself, to find the way himself, to possess and express his own, single, alone self. He will produce content to prove he has not been helped; he will reactivate all of his problem; he will seek to ensnare the helper in a new engagement of will. This is the reason why it is so valuable to set by agency structure the terminal point in the process, for it is only through long experience, and the finest of skill, that the helping person has what it takes to remain firm through all of this reactivation of problem, always produced no matter when the ending occurs. When time structure has been held to in this way, both helper and client know the inevitability of ending in this movement, with a deep feeling of satisfaction.

The one who has been helped has permitted himself to yield to another's whole; he has known vulnerability, incapable of defense when the core of the self is touched. He can leave the experience even though he desires to hold it, unique as it is in its quality of unity within a world where division is rampant. He will know the exhilarating, life-engendering sense of the strength now residing within his own self, where he finds the awareness of wholeness and unity heretofore sought for wholly outside. In this moment of time, where a true ending enables separation to be achieved and accepted, both helper and the one who has taken help know the truth which mankind denies—that freedom of choice can never be conferred as a gift from one to another, but must always be earned by the individual self.

NOTES

NOTE TO CHAPTER I

1. A recent publication undertakes to compare these differences, viz., *A Comparison of Diagnostic and Functional Casework Concepts*, Report of the Family Service Association of America Committee to Study Basic Concepts in Casework Practice, ed. Cora Kasius (New York: The Family Service Association of America, 1950).

NOTES TO CHAPTER II

1. The date 1880 is chosen because it appears to mark a significant turning point in the pre-casework period. Perhaps this is owing to the fact that the recorded history of social work year by year in the proceedings of national conferences begins at approximately this time.

2. The late Franklin K. Lane of California was Secretary of the Interior in the cabinet of President Wilson. He served from 1913 to 1920, retiring on March 1, 1920.

3. Mary E. Richmond, "Some Next Steps in Social Treatment," *Proceedings of the National Conference of Social Work*, 1920 (Chicago: University of Chicago Press, 1920), pp. 254-60.

4. *Ibid.*, p. 254.

5. *Ibid.*

6. Mary E. Richmond, *Friendly Visiting Among the Poor* (New York: The Macmillan Co., 1899).

7. The reader will note that the term "casework" is written in two different ways throughout these pages. This in itself is a change in custom reflected through language which, while apparently minor in importance, nevertheless reflects some change of a fundamental nature. Wherever quotations have been used from writing prior to 1930, the terms "social case work" or "case work" are consistently used. In my own writing I have maintained the accepted current use of the one word "casework."

8. George B. Buzelle, "Individuality in the Work of Charity," *Proceedings of the National Conference of Charities and Corrections*, 1886, ed. Isabel C. Barrows (Boston: Press of Geo. H. Ellis, 1886), pp. 185-88.

9. *Ibid.*, p. 187.

10. W. L. Bull, "Trampery: Its Causes, Present Aspects and Some Suggested Remedies," *Ibid.*, p. 188.

11. Alexander Johnson, "Preface," *Proceedings of the National Conference of Charities and Corrections*, at the Thirty-sixth Annual Ses-

sion held in the City of Buffalo, N. Y., June 9-16, 1909, ed. Alexander Johnson (Fort Wayne: Press of Fort Wayne Printing Co., 1909), pp. iii-iv.

12. Mary K. Simkovitch, "The Case Work Plane (or the Application of the C.O.S. Method to Families above the Poverty Line)," *Ibid.*, pp. 136-49.

13. *Ibid.*

14. Mary E. Richmond, *Social Diagnosis* (New York: Russell Sage Foundation, 1917).

15. See Virginia P. Robinson, *A Changing Psychology in Social Case Work* (Chapel Hill: The University of North Carolina Press, 1930), Part I. This book is only briefly referred to here, because in a later chapter its influence upon developments in social work is more fully examined.

NOTES TO CHAPTER III

1. Jessie Taft, "Progress in Social Case Work in Mental Hygiene," *Proceedings of the National Conference of Social Work,* 1923 (Chicago: University of Chicago Press, 1923), p. 338.

2 Grace F. Marcus, "How Case-Work Training May Be Adapted to Meet the Worker's Personal Problems," *Mental Hygiene,* XI (July, 1927), 455.

3. Jessie Taft, "The Function of a Mental Hygienist in a Children's Agency," *Proceedings of the National Conference of Social Work,* 1927 (Chicago: University of Chicago Press, 1927), p. 392.

4. Jessie Taft, "Time as the Medium of the Helping Process," *Jewish Social Service Quarterly,* XXVI (December, 1949), 189.

5. Jessie Taft, "The Function of a Mental Hygienist in a Children's Agency," p. 396.

6. *Ibid.*, pp. 396, 398.

7. See the most recent statement of these developments, Virginia P. Robinson, *The Dynamics of Supervision under Functional Controls* (Philadelphia: University of Pennsylvania Press, 1949), Chap. II, pp. 16-26; also, Jessie Taft, "The Function of the Personality Course in the Practice Unit," *Training for Skill in Social Case Work,* ed. Virginia P. Robinson (Philadelphia: University of Pennsylvania Press, 1942), p. 62.

8. Virginia P. Robinson, *A Changing Psychology in Social Case Work,* p. 127.

9. Jessie Taft, "Supervision of the Feeble-minded in the Community," *Proceedings of the National Conference of Social Work,* 1918 (Chicago: by the Conference, 1919), p. 548.

10. Jessie Taft, "Qualifications of the Psychiatric Social Worker," *Proceedings of the National Conference of Social Work,* 1919 (Chicago: by the Conference, 1920).

11. See Jessie Taft, "Conception of the Growth Process Underlying Social Casework Practice," *Social Casework,* XXXI (October, 1950), 311.

12. Virginia P. Robinson, "Organization of Field Work in a Professional School," *The Family*, I (October, 1920), 2.

13. *Ibid.*, p. 7.

14. Jessie Taft, "Problems of Social Case Work with Children," *Proceedings of the National Conference of Social Work*, 1920 (Chicago: University of Chicago Press, 1920), pp. 370-71.

15. *Ibid.*, p. 380.

16. Virginia P. Robinson, "Some Difficulties of Analyzing Social Interaction in the Interview," *Social Forces*, VI (June, 1928), 561.

17. Jessie Taft, "The Function of the Personality Course in the Practice Unit," *Training for Skill in Social Case Work*, p. 63.

NOTES TO CHAPTER IV

1. Virginia P. Robinson, *A Changing Psychology in Social Case Work*, p. xv.

2. Bertha Reynolds, "Review of A Changing Psychology in Social Case Work," *The Family*, XII (June, 1931), 111.

3. Virginia P. Robinson, "Psychoanalytic Contributions to Social Case-Work Treatment," *Mental Hygiene*, XV (July, 1931), 487-503.

4. Jessie Taft, "The Use of the Transfer within the Limits of the Office Interview," *The Family*, V (October, 1924), 143-46.

5. Virginia P. Robinson, *A Changing Psychology in Social Case Work*, p. 114.

6. Virginia P. Robinson, "Psychoanalytic Contributions to Social Case-Work Treatment," pp. 494-95.

7. Virginia P. Robinson, "A Discussion of Two Case Records Illustrating Personality Change," *Family Casework and Counseling, a Functional Approach*, ed. Jessie Taft (Philadelphia: University of Pennsylvania Press, 1948), p. 178.

8. The complete but concise statement of Dr. Taft's relation to psychotherapy, casework, and teaching, and its bearing upon the development of function, is to be found in a footnote in Chapter II, pp. 17-18, of Miss Robinson's most recent book, *The Dynamics of Supervision under Functional Controls*. The first part of this same chapter presents as well the most recent authoritative statement of Rank's relation to the development of the functional point of view.

9. Jessie Taft, *The Dynamics of Therapy in a Controlled Relationship* (New York: The Macmillan Co., 1937).

10. Jessie Taft (ed.), *The Relation of Function to Process in Social Case Work, Journal of Social Work Process*, Vol. I, No. 1, November, 1937 (Philadelphia: Pennsylvania School of Social Work, 1937).

11. Jessie Taft, "The Time Element in Therapy," *The American Journal of Orthopsychiatry* (January, 1933), pp. 65-79.

12. Otto Rank, *Will Therapy*, trans. Jessie Taft (New York: Alfred A. Knopf, 1936).

Notes

13. Otto Rank, *Truth and Reality*, trans. Jessie Taft (New York: Alfred A. Knopf, 1936).

14. Virginia P. Robinson, *Supervision in Social Case Work* (Chapel Hill: University of North Carolina Press, 1936).

NOTE TO CHAPTER VI

1. Rank, Otto, "Outline of a Genetic Psychology," p. 168. Unpublished material reproduced by the Pennsylvania School of Social Work from mimeographed notes of lectures which Dr. Rank released for use in the School.

NOTE TO CHAPTER VII

1. Virginia P. Robinson, "Some Difficulties of Analyzing Social Interaction in the Interview," p. 561.

NOTE TO CHAPTER VIII

1. Lawrence Pearsall Jacks, *Education Through Recreation* (New York: Harper & Bros., 1932), p. 41.

NOTES TO CHAPTER XII

1. Otto Rank, *Will Therapy*, trans. Jessie Taft (1 vol. ed.; New York: Alfred A. Knopf, 1945), p. 4.

2. *Ibid.*, p. 3.

NOTE TO CHAPTER XIII

1. Søren Kierkegaard, *Either/Or*, trans. Walter Lowrie (Princeton: Princeton University Press, 1944), II, 210.

THE NATURE OF POLICY
IN THE
ADMINISTRATION OF
PUBLIC ASSISTANCE

Anita J. Faatz

PENNSYLVANIA SCHOOL OF SOCIAL WORK
Affiliated with the
UNIVERSITY OF PENNSYLVANIA

[1943]

TABLE OF CONTENTS

FOREWORD

THE growing conviction that the structure and function of the social agency as a whole must play a decisive role in defining and sustaining the professional practice of social work in the service of the agency's clientele, has led the faculty of the Pennsylvania School of Social Work in recent years to give increasing attention to defining the elements of professional discipline which seem essential for the fulfillment of this role through the processes of over-all agency administration. Preparation for administration, as an area of professional social work practice, has become an integral part of the School's program.

Advanced students, who have brought into day-to-day discussion and into the preparation of theses, the outcomes of experience in responsible administrative posts, have stimulated these efforts and have contributed enormously to the clarification of social administration from this point of view.

The School is glad to make available herewith a significant contribution by Miss Anita J. Faatz, Assistant Director of the Maryland State Department of Public Welfare, concerning policy and policy-making, which is perhaps the most characteristic element of the administrative process in social work, as it relates to other areas of professional social work practice.

It is appropriate that this paper deals with the problem of policy in a public welfare agency, since it has been the rise of public welfare enterprise which has helped to focus attention upon the important role and the distinctive problems of administration in social work, and since, furthermore, there is every indication that public welfare service is destined to play a larger part in the total operations of social work in the future.

The School is indebted to the Department of Public Welfare of Maryland, and to its director, the Hon. J. Milton Patterson,

for cordial cooperation over a number of years in making available for educational use, as in this paper, the rich administrative experience of that department, and for encouragement of
educational preparation of personnel at all levels in the public
welfare service of the state.

KENNETH L. M. PRAY

Philadelphia

October 15, 1943

INTRODUCTION

OF ALL the significant changes which have taken place in the field of social work in the past decade, perhaps none has had so profound an effect upon practice as the increasing use of policy in the public assistance agency. If its full significance has not yet been realized, at least its reality cannot be gainsaid. The country over, public welfare departments have been engaged and are engaged in writing manuals defining policy and in this way they express the purpose, intention and conditions which determine the manner in which the agency offers and effectuates the service for which it was created.

This is not always looked upon as a forward-moving trend, at least not in all of its aspects. Some point to the amount and kind of written policy abroad in the country today and see in it much that is harsh and unworkable, what the average man calls "red tape," since its effect seems only to entangle and obstruct. Some see it as a movement away from concern for the individual, and, if that be true, a denial of the social case work nature of public assistance. Some say it is to be regretted that public agencies have to be so mechanical, so procedural. They accept this circumstance as inevitable and hope in some way it can be tolerated and softened and kept from growing too large in proportion, so that some of the quality of the service can be kept aloof from it, or be kept alive in spite of it. The agency is like that, they say, because something in the outside situation requires it to be.

Yet the vitality and vigor of the movement suggest that it must have grown in response to some immediate and primary need of the job itself, some recognition of the fact that public assistance cannot be offered without it. Time has served to accelerate its growth, rather than to diminish it, and this sturdy, persistent quality can be explained only by an assumption that it survives some test of use.

Formal policy making was not a characteristic activity of social work agencies prior to the 1930's. Consequently, its advent in the public agency cannot be traced to a traditional experience which came from the field of social work. Policy making was, and is, a common phenomenon in government agencies existing for other than social work purposes. However, there is no evidence that the newly formed public welfare department was so identified with government enterprise from the beginning that it took over this development as natural to itself.

At the same time one cannot overlook or minimize the influence of certain external factors which were present near the beginning and which undoubtedly propelled public welfare departments in this direction. There was the express provision, recurrent in state public welfare laws, that the power to make rules and regulations be lodged in the state department. Then there came the requirement of the Social Security Board that a state, in order to take advantage of federal financial participation, must submit a "Plan" of operation. These two factors alone would account in part for a state's activity in reducing plan to paper. They would not account, however, for a state's continued activity in defining, redefining, changing and extending its basic policy structure. No external requirement could sustain a process so full of vitality and movement. Its reason for being could be found only in terms of some internal necessity in the agency itself, in terms of the meaning of policy to the service which the agency offers.

Looking back at ten years of administration of public assistance in one agency, I am mindful of much that comes together today in new meaning, which deepens our understanding of the current situation and points the direction in which we seem to be moving.

From early 1933 until late 1935 the Maryland State Department of Public Welfare administered relief without a manual. What was more, it administered federal funds under federal direction with very little in-the way of standards or procedures. The only tangible policy then available which can be compared with the kind of operating manual which we use today was contained in two pamphlets issued by the Federal Emergency Relief Administration, which dealt with adequacy of relief, investigation and service and other similar matters.* Otherwise

---

* Federal Emergency Relief Administration. Rules and Regulations, Nos. 1, 2, 4 and 5; Rules and Regulations, No. 3. June and July, 1933. United States Government Printing Office.

the whole administration of the relief program—between federal and state, state and local agencies—was transacted on the basis of bulletins, circular letters, telegrams, directives. This was kaleidoscopic and swift in motion. Change, accelerated beyond all the usual tempo of living, was the order of the day. People had no time to learn to live with it. Either they found their own way of coming to terms with it swiftly, or they did not come to terms with it at all.

In a sense this might have been regarded as a real policy structure. It was different from that structure today in two main respects: It was constantly changing and it was organizational and program-making in nature, rather than standard-setting at the point where the service was offered.

If time permitted it would be interesting and profitable to examine what, even in this constant state of flux, was stable and usable. Some of the policy, brief and general as it was, had powerful identity, firm and supporting, which did much to shape the course of public assistance. Yet if we give full recognition to the possibility of finding more stable policy structure in those two years than we were aware of at the time, the fact remains that at that time in the public welfare department of Maryland there was very little to which one could point to show an articulated, formulated policy base.

An important series of events in the history of the nation, as well as in the experience of the public welfare department, operated to change this—a series beginning with the drafting and enactment of the Social Security Act, followed by the promulgation of state laws defining the basis of public assistance. The result was a rapid transition, which took place almost overnight, from general relief to differentiated categories of assistance.

It was at that point that we began to write manuals. In the State of Maryland, too, it was the first time that there was a law—anything, in fact, which specified conditions, which began to define the service we rendered. I recall, too, how much intention there was that the law be general, that it be flexible, that it leave to the department the determination of its concreteness.

We wanted, in those days, to work with malleable material because we did not know how to lay down a stable structure. In the fall of 1935 the first manual, the old age assistance manual, was written in our department. Later, but not until the fall of 1937, a general overall manual was written, covering all types of assistance. That still remains as the core of the policy structure of the agency. But since that time its content, in part, has been rewritten, added to, eliminated, in a hundred different ways, and what we issue today as manual, and how we issue it, bears little resemblance to our early efforts.

This historical material is important beyond its general interest, for the purpose of contrast. Against it, the essential outlines of the situation today begin to emerge in clear relief. For two years assistance was administered with practically no structural policy base. Then the first policy was written, precipitated somewhat by the Security Board requirements and the provisions of state law. With this beginning, the writing of policy seems to move far beyond the external requirements. It begins to yield up something of its own nature and meaning, its dynamic interplay in the agency at the point of service as well as in the administrative process, its implicit usefulness, which keeps it alive and vigorous. Remove the statutes from the law books, remove the requirements of the Security Board, and the chances are that any public welfare department which has learned to operate with a manual will find it can no longer get along without it. Responsible, accountable administration is not possible without it.

My purpose is to examine why that should be true. As one whose primary interest has been, and is, in the administrative process, I have come to believe that policy has a meaning in the agency and a vital quality which goes far beyond what we have yet comprehended. I see this as the beginning point, in fact the only workable beginning point, for an approach to the understanding of the administrative process. I believe if we could gain increased knowledge and understanding in this area, then some of the more perplexing and seemingly insoluble problems about administration would begin to solve themselves.

The reality with respect to the problem of administration is hard to admit. One looks at the field of social work as a whole, for signs of what it is thinking and expressing regarding this troublesome subject of administration, and one finds a multi-plicity of idea and feeling which is as varied as the universe, but which has one common denominator—an expression of how little we seem to know and how much we need to know.

For example, one of the observations not infrequently heard, both within and outside the field, is that social workers do not make good administrators. Many people in social work seem to share this uneasy feeling. Some react to it with an over-vigorous assertion that many social workers do make good administra-tors. Some react with reproach toward social work itself, for what they see as a too great preoccupation with the individual, to the exclusion of the social, economic and administrative set-ting. In particular, people have asked of schools of social work, and schools have asked of themselves, what can be done to pre-pare students more effectively for administration?

At one moment we are convinced that what is needed is for social workers to learn more about the methods of business. Social workers, we say, must gain more facility for working with money matters and columns of figures. They need to get over their dislike of, their boredom with, administration, and be willing to bear some of its less attractive responsibilities. Social workers are too professional, too technical; they do not understand the community point of view. If they could learn more about how to work with boards, how to work with lay persons, how to identify themselves with a legislative process, they could be better administrators.

Or on the other hand it will be said: Training and experience in case work should fit a person pre-eminently to carry out the duties of administration, rather than make him less fit. Only a person who knows and understands the service can administer the agency which renders that service. Moreover, case workers know something of human beings which should be useful in any area of work in administration. Not infrequently this affirma-tion of the possible use of some knowledge or skill from case work is accompanied by an uneasy feeling that the statement arises from a fragmentary, unresolved notion that case work can be turned by the user in any direction where he relates to another.

I do not mean to speak ironically or condemningly of this state of affairs. Anyone who reads this can add a thousandfold to the illustration of anxiety, contradiction, perplexity; can see in it the group expression, but also, to a large extent, can see himself mirrored in it, so that even within the same individual these swings from one extreme to another will manifest themselves.

With it all, it will be known that this is not mere theoretical speculation. There is the hard reality that social agencies do have painful, gruelling difficulties. Perhaps what we first need to realize is that some of this, perhaps a goodly portion of it, is part of growth in the organization. One would expect to find total peace only where there was no life. Knowing this, it is not necessary to deny the reality and validity of the struggle within an agency in order to wonder whether or not so much of it truly belongs there; whether some of it, at least, is not due to our lack of knowledge, or our failure to make use of what knowledge we have, and to the fact that at times we work in a clumsy, awkward manner, that we have not described the situation, defined it, analyzed it and seen it for what it is, and that the problem sometimes seems too broad in scope to lend itself to effective understanding.

My approach to this problem is by way of an observation which comes directly out of immediate, current, daily experience, an observation that much of the content of this striving to set up a responsible service is related to the matter of policy. I know this to be true to some extent in the agency with which I am identified; I find it reflected again and again in all my broader associations with social workers who are administrators and social workers who are not. The "for" and "against" is for more policy or against it, for answering more questions, or withholding those answers. What does this mean, what does that mean? There is too much structure, not enough structure. There is no agency to represent, or too much agency to represent. Too much is written, not enough is written. Everything takes too long, nothing takes long enough. Uniformity will destroy originality, lack of it is subjecting the client to individual judgment.

If this is so, then why should it be so? Is there something about policy itself which has the quality to call forth such response? Is it because other things, any other things, cause the distress, but policy is a convenient place to put it? Do we not know enough about what to put into the content of the policy, or how to write it?

There is only one way to get at this, and that is to examine policy itself—not static policy, because this would never begin to yield up its meaning—but policy in movement, policy as part of process in the agency. In describing what happens under these circumstances, in and by itself, even without analysis a simple, human language begins to emerge.

The main body of this discussion will be concerned with one specific piece of policy material as it begins, grows, becomes part of agency structure, and finally eventuates in active use. But first it seems necessary, for reasons which will appear in the material itself, to examine briefly the nature of the service to which this policy will be related.

THE NATURE OF THE SERVICE

IT IS customarily said of the Social Security Act that it creates public assistance as a right. A great deal of meaning, and properly so, is attached to this concept as a determinant of the way in which the service is offered. It has an important and significant bearing upon an understanding of the nature of policy.

The right which the law creates is a limited right; that is to say, it is not like the right to use the public parks, or the right to use the highway, or the right to protection from the fire department. These are rights enjoyed by all, practically without condition, and they may continue to be exercised so long as a person does not deprive himself of them by actions against the public good which result in taking away his freedom.

But the right to public assistance is available, as we well know, to only a very small portion of the population, not because others do not ask for it or wish to exercise the right, but because, even though they should attempt to do so, they would find, as many persons do, that they are not entitled to the right because they do not meet the conditions. In this sense the public assistance right is, in the dictionary meaning, "a claim recognized and delimited by law for the purpose of securing it." *

Language as formal as this has a forbidding sound, especially if one is mindful of the human quality of the service which we offer. Yet on longer acquaintance and with time for understanding, one recognizes in these words the first primary expression of the structure which makes it possible for the person to use the service. In a sense it creates the need for an agency. It sets up the structural base by which the agency defines the

---

* Webster's New International. Other definitions which follow are from the same source.

right, says what it has to offer and the conditions under which it offers it.

Viewed thus, it highlights the essential difference between the granting of assistance in accordance with the defined standards of a policy, and the granting of assistance in a manner which necessitates a high degree of individual discretion. The definition of the public assistance right creates the framework within which the applicant asks and the worker extends the service.

Since the law in most essential respects sets up only the outer boundaries of the right, the agency defines it further by the promulgation of policy. Policy is thus of crucial importance as a medium for defining the right: it is the substance of which the agency is made; the essence of what the worker represents; the form and structure within which the client attempts to clarify his eligibility.

Between the right and the applicant is the agency, the only means through which he can get to the substance of what he needs. By what the agency makes available to him for this purpose, by the help it gives him, and only in this way, can he get to it.

Policy thus becomes a primary source for understanding the concept of worker as representative of the agency, in contrast to worker as individual.

I know of no way to put meaning into this except in terms of the individual applicant who comes to the public assistance agency.

When a person decides to apply for assistance at a public welfare department he may or may not know what it will be like to find the office and come face to face with a person who, from that point on, will represent the public welfare department to him. If his dealings with the agency are brief, as they will be if he does not carry through his application, or as they will be if he is found ineligible in the early interview, then the person who first meets him and talks with him is, to a heightened degree, the personification of agency.

If he has continuing relationship with the agency, even over a long period of years, it is still true that he seems to see the agency in the terms and with the characteristics of the person who helps him avail himself of the service. Even when workers change he has the impression that the agency changes accordingly. This is the first and primary relationship in a public welfare department. It is the most customary and most taken for granted relationship in the department, at the same time it is the one most vested with meaning and significance.

Here, too, the concept of worker as representative of the agency comes to life. To the applicant the worker *is* the agency. One need only recall that the language of clients, when they talk with others in the agency, is almost invariably in terms of what the worker has or has not done; what the worker said or did not say; what he gave or did not give. Even when he sees the supervisor or executive; when he knows a board member; when he writes a letter to the President; or when he comes to the State Department for a "hearing" to review his application, it is usually the worker who is the focal person.

Recently a recipient came to the state department for a hearing when his assistance had been cancelled because he failed to report to the agency a change in circumstances which affected his need for assistance. I asked him whether he understood that it was an agency requirement that he report change of income of his son who lived in his home with him. He said, "I did and I didn't. For years Mrs. A. used to come to see me regularly. Whenever she came she would ask me what was different and I would tell her. Once John lost his job and we needed more money. She took care of that. When he went on W. P. A. she knew that and fixed it all up. But this last January Mrs. A. didn't come any more (reproach in his voice). A Mrs. B. came to see us and I told her that John was about to get a new job. I thought she knew. She never came back. What I want to know is, why is she now telling me I should have reported this? I thought the worker did that, I thought that was what a worker was for. That's what Mrs. A. used to do; I naturally thought Mrs. B. would do it, too."

Nothing could be more vivid than this in conveying the sense of worker. It is person related to person. If that suggests a contradiction of worker as representative of the agency, it is only because so far we have looked at only one aspect of this concept. Client does not see agency in the structural, im-personalized, organizational sense.

However, every client has some sense of agency when agency is truly there, and experience is bountiful with examples of how this makes itself felt. In a variety of ways he experiences an entity which is different from worker, but which worker carries to him. Here is an application which he is asked to sign; everyone signs it. This is his way of expressing his wish to consider his eligibility for assistance. Here are the condi-tions, not suddenly brought into being for him, but existing for everyone. These are the facts which the agency needs to know; this is how he may substantiate them. Here is the "budget"; now he receives a check signed with a name other than that of the worker. Sometimes he hears it said that first the "supervisor's" approval is needed. All this adds up to a sense of the outside, for both him and the worker, something definite, something tangible, something with which they begin to work.

Soon enough he will find that some of these requirements which are present in the situation are not all easy for him to accept; some of them are extremely difficult. Some, he will find, require great ingenuity on his part to find the source from which he can establish a fact to be as he has stated it. Some necessitate his going to other persons, for instance his children, to ask their participation. Some actually deny him what he has come for. Even though all this is true, the fact of the matter is that the structure which is the agency is his greatest protec-tion, and the concrete conditions presented to him make pos-sible a positive use of the agency.

The client who comes to the public assistance agency risks much, and the fear which he often brings is not out of pro-portion to the risk which is great, not only in his own feeling about it, but in reality. The reason that he risks so much is that the major condition of the right requires that a circum-stance of "need" must exist.

There is no word so relative, so individual, and yet so uni-versal as the word "need." Every human being has needs; the ingredient of all living is need. But what the client brings when he comes to the agency to apply for assistance is not, and can-not be, his total need. He comes today bringing one concrete specific need, namely, a need for money, because he, by his own valuation of it, does not have sufficient resource to provide shelter, food and other necessities for himself and his family. This is the only need, at the beginning, with which the agency can be, or has any right to be, concerned.

At the same time that this need which he brings is so imme-diate and current for himself and his family, it also has the highest potentiality for bringing together, in this one focal spot, past needs and deeper needs and complicated life situa-tions. There is hardly a public assistance application which does not illustrate the way in which the facts the agency re-quires touch off areas full of feeling and deep emotional con-tent for the applicant. It may be something as simple as his wish to hold on to his old homestead, which costs an exorbitant amount to maintain, whose upkeep, as a matter of fact, has hastened the need for assistance. It may be something as deep-seated as the question of support from a relative from whom he is long since estranged. It may be as full of conflict for him as a requirement that a medical statement is needed to clear up the question of whether he is or is not able to work. All the community standards to which the applicant may or may not have conformed may come to plague him at this point of application: whether he has been thrifty or spendthrift; whether he is energetic or lazy; whether he once misstated his age because he needed to be older or younger for the thing he wanted at the time.

Neither the client nor the worker can bear the responsibility, individually and in each situation anew, to find the boundaries which mark off the relevant from the irrelevant. The agency has an obligation to do that. It has an obligation to assure that the applicant who comes to the agency, actually with little choice because his need is great, is still left with freedom, with control of his situation in his own hands, and with his own self intact and unimpaired. In this respect both his concern and that of the agency are served by the same thing.

The objective of both applicant and the agency is to discover, together, whether or not his circumstances are within the conditions of assistance eligibility. He, and he alone, is in possession of the facts which can show what the result will be. This is his application for assistance. He can carry, and does if the agency permits him to, the kind of responsibility which means he can get to those facts if he knows what they are, why they are wanted, and what will be done with them. The agency's part is to explain the concrete conditions; his, to assemble and marshal his own energies and resources to work toward and with those conditions. Often he needs help to do this, help of the kind which means that his responsibility is not taken over by another, but is left with him, so that there is still something available to his use which supports and sustains as he carries it. He needs help when his feelings of fear, of anger, of protest, of dependency, or rebellion against dependency, so stand in his way that he cannot get to the facts which he needs, cannot use them when he does get to them, or cannot carry the responsibility which the agency asks of him. Throughout he remains always the central, active person.

If he receives a grant of assistance there are a number of things expected of him, on which, as a matter of fact, his continuing eligibility depends. He is expected to continue to be a responsible person, in that when there are changes in his circumstances he will be asked to take the initiative in bringing them to the agency. He will be expected, too, to make the maximum use of any resources which may be available to him, whether they be for seeking work, or for someone in his family to seek work, or for managing on his assistance grant. What is more, he will be expected to separate himself from the assistance grant if there is any remote possibility that his own resources can be assembled sufficiently to make that possible.

Herein lies the answer to skill in public assistance. This is not treatment, or therapy, or even a social service "over and above" the giving of assistance. But it is a process of helping that asks of the person who offers it, a disciplined use of the self in identification with agency. It is a process that shares much in common with family service, foster care and other case work services, at the same time that its own sharp and clear differences make it something else again. This is not to say that the public welfare department may not properly offer other services; it does and can, of great variety. But we have come increasingly to see the need that those services, if offered, shall be so clear and definite that the client knows what it is he comes for, so that he can be sure, beyond doubt, that his continued receipt of assistance is in no way dependent upon his acceptance of, or use of, those services. We would hope that in some way and under some circumstances he will find that in this process of applying for assistance, establishing eligibility, and continuing to maintain that eligibility, he has an experience in the use of himself which means for him a reorganization and strengthening of his own capacities.

To summarize: In order to understand the crucial role of policy it has been necessary to restate the entity of agency, to see this as upholding and effectuating the assistance right for which the applicant applies. This is especially important as far as the factor of "need" is concerned, since need is internal, individual, and cannot be determined for any person by agency. Only the applicant can know it for himself, and then only in part, as he tests it out against the objective external requirements of the agency. This, too, is a protection to the client and the worker, in that it sets the boundaries of the relevant and reduces the potentiality that the granting of assistance will carry with it control of the person by the agency and intrusion into areas of need which he would not voluntarily bring. In this setting the client will be the responsible, active person. He can clarify his need, select his use, take as much or as little help as he wishes. In order to do this, he makes use of the structure which the worker places at his disposal. By this means he holds the agency accountable.

Thus stated, the true reality of policy emerges. The full significance of its movement at any point where it changes or is extended is thrown into bold relief. When policy changes, agency changes; the structure which the worker uses changes; the structure which the client uses changes; the structure which supervision uses changes. What follows will be an attempt to illustrate, from agency experience, around one policy, what that can mean to agency and to the persons who are a part of it.

THE CIRCUMSTANCES WHICH INITIATE
A CHANGE OF POLICY

THE specific piece of material which I propose to use for this purpose is now known in the agency as "Rule and Regulation #19."* It defines the purpose and method of the initial investigation of an application for assistance, and of the periodic reconsideration of the grant. At various times, during its early stages, it was spoken of as a new policy to conserve travel, or as a clarification of policy regarding the necessity for visiting the home and use of the office interview, or as a policy defining the continuing relationship between the agency and the recipient of assistance.

The regulation was issued to the local departments to become effective on October 1, 1942. This date marks the ending of one phase of the process, which began at least a year earlier with the first faint and fragmentary recognition of the need for change. It marks also the beginning of a whole new phase, the beginning of the process of assimilation and use in the agency. I shall be dealing with both aspects of the process, that leading up to the date of release, and that following the date of release.

The change in structure which took place as a result of this regulation was both an extension and a replacement. It eliminated a paragraph from the current policy which read as follows:

"All three assistance laws also call for reconsideration of the grant (re-investigation) as frequently as the State Department shall require. Such investigation shall be made as least once every six months, and more frequently where indicated. An interview with the recipient designed to bring into the discussion any change in circumstance will satisfy the requirement for reinvestigation, unless there is some indication of change of circumstances, in which case this change should, of

---

* See Appendix.

[175]

course, be thoroughly explored as would have been done in the original investigation."

More significantly the new regulation extended policy into areas where nothing had been written previously.
If structure is what worker places at the disposal of client in order that he may be active in determining his eligibility, if it is the given, the stable, the point of reference in this relationship, then one might reason that the less it changed, the better. Looking at it in its most superficial aspects, it takes time for a local department to go through the steps of receiving a manual change, reading it, correcting the manuals, considering what it will mean in operation today and tomorrow and thereafter, acquainting the staff with it, weaving it into supervision, encompassing that constellation of activities which is lightly referred to by the single phrase "putting a manual change into effect." Change in manual is seldom welcome even when it has been wanted and even under the best of circumstances.

Yet everyone knows that a static situation does not prevail, nor would it be wanted if it could be had. The whole vitality of an organization is in its capacity for growth and that capacity is nurtured by the interplay of meaningful experience, forged into conscious direction. Thus change in structure, with full recognition of all that can mean for worker and for total agency, is desirable and natural to agency.

Knowing this, one begins to comprehend the close association between the administrative process, the movement of policy, and the reaction of the individual to change introduced from without. A public welfare department, like every other organization—governmental, industrial, commercial, civic—is a constellation of people brought together in a more or less consciously arranged pattern of interrelationship, whose common purpose is the purpose of the agency and each of whom carries some segment of the work of the agency. This makes of organization an essentially human enterprise. In its internal operation, it is people in action. In a public welfare department there is the additional reality which enhances its human quality: its service is to people, thousands of them, in a constant stream of movement through its doors.

It is hard to conceive of any person in the agency who is not affected to some extent by a policy change. Some policies are of such a nature that they are minor, affecting no one and nothing very deeply or significantly. Even with major policy changes some people in the organization will be lightly affected. The more really the policy touches or goes to the heart of the daily practice of the agency, the more profound and vigorous will be its effect upon those who make use of it.

Some aspect of the universal resistance to change is present in this situation. What it is, what its meaning is, in what respects it is like or different from other situations where change manifests itself, is the substance of a whole area of exploration to which the administrative process so far has given little attention. Here one can only take note of it and point to its potentiality for the understanding of administration and the skill of the administrator.

Policy, to be properly used, and to carry the quality of muscle, not steel, must have become a part of the person who uses it. Failure to make it one's own manifests itself a hundred different ways. Some persons will evade it, forget it, weaken its meaning; others will force it to be all that it is and five times more. They will drive with it, insist upon it, interpret it in its narrowest and most literal meanings, especially if these begin to negate its purpose. To some extent this always happens, in some ways, with some threads of activity, whenever a manual change is put into effect. I shall refer to this again and relate it to the discussion of the process whereby a policy is launched in the agency. Here it is important because of the way in which it illuminates what change in policy risks and what it sets in motion.

If an organization is aware of all this, it will be chary of every impulse which arises to modify policy. It will know that most changes in policy cannot take place lightly, or easily, or thoughtlessly, but only when some test of use indicates that it is essential. It may ask itself the questions: What would that test be? What are the circumstances which initiate a change in policy? How does the agency know when that moment has arrived? What does it weigh, first on one side, then on another?

Or does it weigh at all? Is its decision always, perhaps, precipitated by forces over which it has no control?

I have attempted to trace back to its source the first recognition of the need for change which culminated in a conscious decision to write Rule and Regulation #19. In doing this one is conscious of almost imperceptible beginnings, isolated, unrelated, and coming together here and there in a positive expression of need, until the whole channeled itself into an intention to write a new regulation.

Long before active work began on the new regulation, requests had been coming to the State Department for permission to depart from the so-called "six months" requirement. There were circumstances, said the local departments, where an interview every six months was not necessary. There was so little likelihood that the recipient's eligibility would change, so little reason for the agency to visit, that it seemed uneconomical to hold to this requirement. This was one way in which the need for change first began to express itself. Local departments asked that it be different.

Or, the State Department itself would become aware of some signs pointing to the desirability of reexamining this provision. The reading of records would illuminate the fact that visits were not being made every six months; that agencies, for whatever reason, were not observing this requirement. This would lead to a certain amount of discomfort both on the part of the State Department and the local departments: A requirement in the manual which is not held to, even though only a minute part of total structure, creates a feeble and uncertain spot in the whole relationship. The State Department knew something should be done about it.

Or, at group meetings when the need for more staff was emphasized, executives and supervisors would state that the agency was falling behind in reviews of eligibility. The staff was unable to keep current with its work. Could the requirement be lightened? Or could more staff be provided?

No single one of these things had the effect at that time of propelling the State Department into action to rewrite this requirement. Part of this was undoubtedly due to the fact that the whole agency was engaged in another major policy change* and there was not time to embark upon another. Part was undoubtedly due to the early recognition that this was not a simple matter of changing "six months" to some other arbitrarily chosen length of time. When the policy was first written, its content had been selected just as arbitrarily as that. In order to begin at all, manual had to be written almost overnight. Selection of content sprang out of immediate necessity to make decisions, right or wrong, trusting only to a reservoir of past experience, an intuitive sense of reasonableness, and a hope that the content would be sufficiently related to reality to be workable. Later, this method for determining standards could no longer suffice.

One other main current of inquiry and speculation can be identified as having had an important bearing upon the need to write this new regulation. At various times and in a variety of ways too numerous to mention, the question would be asked: What is "continuing eligibility"? What are we expected to do with it? What factors of eligibility do we review periodically? What is the basis for the continuing relationship between the agency and the client?

In the fall of 1941 came the first real impetus to do something about this part of the manual. This took place at a state-wide staff meeting, where a choice was made as to the next major piece of policy material to which the administration should turn its attention. Without much hesitation, three things were emphasized: the periodic reconsideration of the grant, the nature of the continuing relationship between the agency and the client, and the six months requirement for revisits.

Immediately following this meeting another event occurred, catastrophic in nature and one which can hardly be regarded as part of the normal forces at work in an agency. In December the United States went to war. Tires became practically unobtainable, gasoline was to be rationed, travel in the field, upon

---

* This was the section of the manual which defined requirements and resources, the so-called "needs" section of the manual, which had engaged the attention of the organization for about a year while it was in process of formulation.

which the agency was to a large extent dependent, had to be curtailed.

This need to consider how travel could be conserved was the precipitating agent which turned a fluid state into crystallized intention. This often seems to happen in the process of policy formulation. Obviously, the effect of a war is something which cannot be generalized in terms of usual operation of an agency. In this case it was the war which was the unique force, but in other situations it is often true that some specific event, some especially sharp need, some unforeseen happening, comes at a time when the agency is ready for it. By this means energy is harnessed to a specific purpose.

By January we knew, unmistakably, that all the little things which could be done and were already being done about conserving travel, such as increased planfulness, sharing rides, using public transportation, would not begin to suffice. The agency had come face to face with a need for extension of policy which, on first sight, might seem to require only a minor administrative routine, but which actually went to the heart of its practice. If travel was to be curtailed, this meant a reduction in the amount of the usual and traditional visiting to the homes of applicants and recipients. Careful economy was not enough —the agency had to insure that it did not travel one mile, nor use one bit of rubber, nor consume one gallon of gasoline, that was not essential to the service which it rendered.

Then, what was essential?

With the posing of this question the problem was formulated. It was now known that this further definition of structure, the need for which had for a long time and in many different ways been bubbling to the surface, would take place in an area where, up to now, we had practically no structure. We knew we would have to examine the purpose of the home visit. We were not unaware of the difficulties in approaching a problem as total as this, because it seemingly called into question the whole purpose and method of public assistance.

We had made a decision that more definition was needed, that change in policy was indicated. We knew in a general way the area in which this definition would take place. We had formulated the question. We moved now into a period of observation and study, when relevant experience began to be assembled and focused. We submitted it for group discussion. Gradually, through a process of discarding the irrelevant and unusable, selecting out the workable and usable, the material narrowed and sharpened, until the outline of its form and content as policy began to come into view. This was followed by the actual writing of the new policy, its preliminary release for criticism, testing and evaluation; its writing in final form; its adoption by the State Board.*

The dates here have some significance. The state-wide fall meeting to which I have already referred took place on the last three days of November, 1941. The regional group meetings took place in May and June, 1942.

On July 22 the first draft of Rule and Regulation #19 was ready; on July 25 it was discussed in staff meeting in the State Department. On September 4 it was adopted by the State Board of Welfare; on September 8 it was released to the local departments, and on October 1, 1942 it became effective.

This tempo is slow. At times it seems glacier-like. The realities of the situation are such that the pace is seldom, if ever, a true reflection of the tempo which the organization would take, if left entirely to the influence of the timing by which it can formulate and assimilate change. Such matters as amount of staff time available, time needed for arrangements of meetings, imperative interruptions of the kind which bear pre-cedence over any other activity, time needed for approvals, dates of board meetings and the like—all these things operate to slow down the process. This tends to obscure somewhat the true tempo of the organization, which, because it is an organi-zation moving, is seldom suited to the tempo of any given individual.

Furthermore, it is a tempo which not even the organization can afford very often or under most circumstances. It can hap-

---

* I am interested in looking at some notes which I kept as a reminder to myself of things which needed to be done. At the top of the sheet of paper on which there appears a list of dates with brief notations of steps taken, I had written, in December, "Tire situation." This is later crossed out and over it I have written "Home visits." Later this too, is deleted and in its place I have put "Rule and Regulation #19."

pen only, and is necessary only, around a major functional change. Many changes originate, are written, and go into effect in a relatively short span of time, with little discussion and sometimes none. Some parts of practice can be dealt with like that. Some ought not to be dealt with superficially, but are and have to be because of the realities of the situation. Sometimes change has to be made fast and sharp. It may even be, under some circumstances and taking all factors into account, that we would find change can best be related to in that way. There are times when the swift, fast clarity of a single administrative decision is the only thing which will serve the purpose.

No prescription, no predetermined pattern can settle this. There is something about the current situation itself, the immediate experience of the organization, in terms of the subject matter, the need, the relation to other activity, the status of experience regarding it, the readiness or lack of it on the part of staff, which must be utilized in finding the way. In this respect it is like other processes in which responsibility, control and skill are the essentials.

THE PROCESS OF DEFINITION

What do we define? How do we define?
How far do we define?

A KNOWLEDGE and conviction that structure needs to be defined in order to create entity of agency are not enough to accomplish the purpose. Structure has to be usable. And therein
lies another whole area of the problem.

Some policy consists of generalizations; some of specific
standards, or mandatory procedures. Total structure of an
agency usually makes use of all of these, ranging from the very
general to the very concrete.

Structure becomes unusable, or nearly so, for many reasons.
Some is unusable because it is unreasonable, harsh, or unrelated to the way in which people live and act. Some is complicated beyond understanding and seems nothing but obstacle
put in the way of client as he tries to get to his assistance, and
of worker, as he tries to help him in this. Some is inconsistent,
contradictory. Some is hard to use for the simple reason that
the manual is not arranged in a way that makes it easy to find
what one is looking for. All these things make for faulty, cumbersome structure.

Of all these, none seems to be so full of perplexity as is the
question of how far the agency defines, what it defines, in
order to create usable structure. How often it is said, "This is
something which can't be decided by regulation!" Or, in contrast, "This is something on which a policy has to be made!"
Both things are right, sometimes, in some ways. Not infrequently there is a great deal of fear attaching to the concern
that something will be defined too much; or that something
will be defined too little. In the first instance, the person seems

to be fearful of losing "individualization"; in the second, that there will be too much.

In the Maryland Department of Public Welfare there is a large, and in many respects, cumbersome manual. This is the policy structure of the agency. This is the agency—not the whole of it if one thinks, too, of the overall, unwritten, guiding intention—but a good substantial part of it. If one wishes to know what is this agency which the worker represents, then one points to the manual. It is a great assortment of much that is old and archaic, that creaks and lumbers as we try to use it; of standards, of procedures, of method, of a little philosophy, at points a little preaching and exhortation. Yet it is the agency. It has life and vitality, as well as parts that are vestigial.

It is also the definition of our function; not in the narrow sense that one would say, "It is not our function to administer the school attendance laws," but in the sense that function is "the natural and proper action of anything"; "the natural or characteristic action of any power or faculty . . ."; " a mode of conscious action." In a rare meaning, function means "doing." Perhaps it is as simple, and yet as profound, as saying: Definition of structure, function, policy, form, by whatever word one uses, is putting into words what the agency does and how it does it, and both must have direction and limitation.

Then along comes a new piece of manual material, Rule and Regulation #19, which, like any other piece of manual material, either replaces something in the manual or adds to what is already there. It is brief—relatively brief as manual material goes and considering the wide area it covers—; it is formalized, that is, it is written in the somewhat stilted language of regulation; it has form, like outline; it is sparse, limited and may not seem to have much warmth of human service on first reading. But in some respects it is like that in order to be architecturally "functional"; that is, designed for use, to serve a purpose.

It deals with a subject which, to my knowledge, is not often covered in policy—the purpose, extent and method of the initial investigation of eligibility, and of the periodic reconsideration of the grant. Likely it is one of those areas of which it would be commonly said, this cannot be covered by regulation. Yet, in my evaluation of it, and the use which has been made of it, it seems to illustrate some balance between defining too little and defining too much.

It also is an illustration of the way in which a policy sometimes grows out of experience, out of discussion; how the use of both of these, in process, mold policy, determine the area it will cover, forecast the form it will take, settle upon its intrinsic intention.

The substance of the problem with which this regulation deals was discussed in a series of regional group meetings which took place in May and June, 1942. There were three groups, each of which met three times, at intervals two weeks apart, with approximately two hours for each discussion. They were participated in by executives, district supervisors, supervisors of local welfare departments and state supervisory staff. There were about twelve persons in each group.

The subject matter to be discussed by each of these three groups had already been decided upon. I quote from the bulletin of assignment, made available to the groups by the State Department:

"Topic: Purpose of the Home Visit, With Special
Reference to Continuing Eligibility"

As will be observed, the groups were not discussing how to conserve travel, nor were they asked to write a policy or formulate a regulation.

The substance of the thinking as I have recorded it here grows chiefly out of the discussions of one of these groups, of which I was the discussion leader. Interwoven with it, however, is the thinking and discussion of the other two groups. The discussion leaders met during the course of the meetings and also afterward; minutes were recorded, and in the end all came together in a way that moved the material into a writing of the regulation.

We did not start with any written material, not even a statement of questions, and this is a difficult way to work. We were all aware of the common practice throughout the agency of making considerable use of the visit to the homes of applicants and recipients. We confronted ourselves with a stark, un-adorned question, which we asked almost as a challenge: "Why do we visit the home?"

At first this is like asking oneself the question, why does the sun rise? It is traditional, we have always done it, assistance has always been administered that way. We have made some use of the office interview, but never really established eligibility, or thought we could, without visiting the home. It is not easy to say why you do the habitual.

I speak with deep respect for the courage of these discussants, who stated so immediately and so searchingly any "why" which presented itself—just the way it was, just the way it seemed, with knowledge that later we would challenge all the reasons that had been given and subject them to some severe test of validity. We knew, too, that each, before we were through, would be challenging her own supporting structure, whatever that might be. We put everything into the picture we could. We visited because people couldn't come to the office, we visited in order to verify the address, or to verify resources, or to determine the suitability of the home. We visited because the worker had one call to make in the section and could save total travel for the community by visiting others at the same time. We visited because in that way we could interview more than one person, and sometimes we needed to interview other members of the household. We visited to see the relation of one member of the family to another.

The discussion moved fast and vigorously and much of its movement is lost in the telling. When we challenged, we asked, for instance, do we *really* verify anything by a visit? Many examples could be thought of to show how unreliable this was if its only purpose was to verify. In fact, as the concrete reasons began to grow feeble, we came closer and closer to something that went much deeper and that illustrated in a most vivid way the relation of policy making to practice—to the case work process itself. Part of the precipitation of this thinking came when we put the question: What would we answer a client who asked, "Why do you come to my home?"

Someone said, "I think clients prefer to come to the office.

It is more business-like." "But do they? I know clients who plead to have you come to their home to see for yourself how poor it is. They think you cannot understand their need unless you come and see." "But the opposite is the client who *doesn't* want you to see how poor he is; who can't bear to face it that way; who borrows better clothes to come to the office and who would take less and minimize his need rather than let it be what it is." Here is the gamut of individual difference. How can you write a policy to meet that!

Somehow it was said, probably not in one sentence but in fragments that began to fit themselves together into a whole, for most clients this coming to the home may have more and a different meaning than we realize. When he comes to the office, the situation is limited to what he brings. In some respects, not all, it is much less total than going to his home. When we go to the home, how can we avoid confusing him as to our intention? Is the agency concerned with his total living? Do we care if his house is untidy? Are we going to be impressed if we see "good wholesome food" cooking on the stove, or the reverse? Will the grant be influenced if we, the visitor, are put in a bad humor by the interruptions of four children who come in and out, in shouting efforts to divert attention? All this, and much more, must be there.

It would have been easy, in the first freshness of re-examination of old practice, to throw the whole aside and say, "It never had any use anyway!" In some way, at some time, it seemed as if each of us almost said that and then moved away from it again. Because now the reaction set in, something that felt like, "But wait a minute. This is all very well. Yet there must have been some reason for, some use in, a way of doing which has lasted long and been used unquestioningly by many people."

We said, for instance, visual learning seems to be extremely important for the beginning worker. Some workers will never have a feeling of what sheer, harsh deprivation is like until they see it. They will know it only intellectually and one would wonder whether they could then truly know it. We would hesitate to remove this until we were sure that a suitable substitute could be put to the worker's use.

We said, some people really are more comfortable in their own homes. Some persons, especially in the country, have had a degree of isolation that is not often realized. They never go more than a few miles away. They would be at a disadvantage in strange surroundings. We did not deny the reality of this. We recognized, too, that there were times when we always visited, such as for instance when a person due to illness or physical disability could not come to the office.

At this point one might say that we had made little progress since what it all comes to is this: Sometimes a visit is desirable and sometimes it is not, and this depends on many variables and intangibles that cannot be defined. Still we moved, and that a long way, because we had examined consciously what some of those variables and intangibles might be which go into a choice of method. I am sure it was out of this discussion that there began to evolve in my own thinking the crucial significance of *purpose,* which later holds such a predominant part in the regulation.

There is one more trend which I wish to pick up, one which seems in a way the richest strand of all. It had to do with a consideration of how often we would need to have an interview, or to visit, after the grant was made. Here again we were confronted with *purpose.* There had been considerable emphasis upon the need for clarity in the intake interview, as a way in which to reduce the number of subsequent visits which would be required. We illustrated this fruitfully. We believed in it so hard, momentarily, that we spoke as if much would be solved if we could make the explanation at intake so clear and so simple and so full that henceforth client would understand in every way, his continuing relationship to the agency.

But human beings are not like that, we reflected. They do not learn through words alone. No matter how clear the explanation, the client does not learn his relationship to the agency or the conditions under which he receives his grant, through a single interview. Clear words help; of that there is no doubt. But here is an applicant who has always thought of his old age benefit as a "pension." He has read about it in the paper, he has heard it discussed over the radio, he wrote to his congressman about it. A pension means to him just what the word commonly implies,—a set sum for the rest of his life as a kind of reward for hard and useful living. Then he comes to the agency and it is called "assistance." His ear will hear the difference in words. It may irritate him a little that the familiar is called something strange. He may be one of those who senses and resents its cousinship to "relief," and he has not come for relief. In fact, when he accepts it and receives a grant, he may be able to do that only because he still must believe it is a "pension" and takes it on his own terms, because that is the only basis on which he can accept it.

In this setting and with the reality of his own conviction, we ask him to understand that he must report "change in circumstance" to the agency. What do we mean by a change? We illustrate: If he should earn any money, if his son should get an increase in wages resulting in more income, if he changes his address. He will react to this in any one of a thousand ways, especially if he has a need to deny it, even to the point of forgetting entirely that he was ever expected to report change.

This situation is rich with meaning from the standpoint of understanding the skill required of the worker, the content of policy, the importance of understanding of human beings in order to administer assistance. I have seen just this situation, where a grant was cancelled because the recipient, while he had heard, physically, really had not heard, in fact, because he could not; where the agency knew, and honestly, that it had explained "change" and that he had not met the condition.

No; words will not serve as the only means by which the client finds out what the agency is like and what it means. Someone suggested that before a recipient can understand what a change in calculation of his grant means, he has to work through that kind of change with the agency. You might explain to him, with all the clarity of which you are capable, that the amount of his assistance can change up or down, if his requirements change or if his resources alter. However, until the agency has actually worked through a new calculation of grant, until it has shown him how change in circumstances alters his grant, he will not know, fully enough to use it, what that means.

Some will, more than others. Some will need a continuous relationship to the agency, at least in the early days of the grant, in order to develop their own responsibility for that relationship. One cannot take responsibility for what one can-not understand, and the ability to understand will vary widely. Here again we were faced with individualization in the midst of formulating a policy.

At this point we were forging ahead in our understanding of the stuff of which the continuing relationship between agency and recipient is made, a relationship with a specific purpose, with specific limitations; perhaps only a part of the whole pur-pose, perhaps so far stated in only a fragmentary way, but still with some essence of the reality of the situation implicit in it. We were molding the form and structure of the agency.

I have referred several times throughout this discussion to the influence upon this policy of the consideration given to the way in which people react to situation. I have illustrated from client experience; I have mentioned our concern with the worker's visual knowing of human deprivation through the seeing of what deprivation is like in its outer form. We did not close this discussion without a look at the reaction of the board member and of the total agency.

The board member, we said, is used to having us visit the home. He will not feel safe if we do not visit. Workers will not feel safe in giving up something they have so long relied upon. Supervisors will not feel safe when the records give so little feel of the situation. This will all be new and strange. Hastily we said, *we* would not feel safe. And with this recognition we knew what new stresses would be felt by supervision in order to use the new policy effectively.

In concluding this part of the discussion, which began with the question, how we define, what we define, how far we define, I would like to point, in summary, to some of the characteristics of this regulation as it took final form.

It relies upon a concept of *purpose* to hold it together and to afford the basis of operation. It does not give a specific answer to questions of how, when and what. It states:

"The purpose of the investigation shall be:

1. To permit the applicant to state his need in his own terms; why he is applying for assistance, and to explore with him in a preliminary way, what use he has made or might make of his own resources in lieu of application for assistance.

2. If he decides to make application for assistance, to acquaint him with the provisions of the laws, regulations and other requirements relevant to his application.

3. To inform him of the nature of the proofs required to establish eligibility and to help him in securing those proofs insofar as he needs and wishes such help.

4. To examine the proofs as to their validity for the purpose of establishing eligibility.

5. To arrive at a decision with respect to eligibility.

6. To discuss with the applicant the manner of calculating the amount of the grant and to arrive at a decision regarding the amount of the grant.

7. To inform the applicant of the decision.

8. To discuss with him the conditions applicable to his acceptance of a grant; the nature of his responsibility to report relevant changes; the periodic reconsideration of the grant; and any other conditions or arrangements which, in the opinion of the local department, require consideration."

The policy then goes on to leave to the local department the choice of method by which it will carry out the purpose, "whether by interview in the office or in the home, telephone, correspondence, search of records, etc.," provided, however, that the local department in the selection of the method assures that certain conditions are met; namely, that all factors of eligibility be covered; that all parts of the purpose as expressed in the regulation be carried out; that every investigation include at least one interview with the applicant himself; that the timing of the interview and the manner of the interview be designed "for understanding by the recipient and for facilitation of the continuing relationship"; and lastly, provided that

> " . . . no application shall be left pending beyond a reasonable period of time, or rejected, for reasons solely related to travel."

There is the additional safeguard that the case record be required to reflect accurately the manner in which the purpose of the investigation was covered.

The second part of the regulation makes use of a similar device for defining the *purpose* of the periodic reconsideration of the grant and leaving the selection of *method* to the local department. There is no specification of how often or at what intervals visits should be made. The discussion which I have just described eleminated any belief which may have remained in the validity of routine, periodic visits which would fall always at certain specified times for all recipients, an implication which was present in the old policy. The new regulation makes use only of outer limits:

> "Every grant shall be reconsidered: whenever . . . "

certain circumstances arise which are generally described,

> "provided, that every grant shall be reconsidered once in every six months."

and provided also:

> "That an interview with the recipient shall be required not less than once a year."

These two time limits are sheer, arbitrary outer limit, based on a taking-for-granted that agency and recipient cannot keep up even the most superficial acquaintance if they communicate with each other less often than that.

At the same time it is to be noted that the regulation will not be satisfied with reconsideration once every six months, interviews once a year. There is no intention that this pattern fall in that way. There is likelihood that it may; in some situations this will be all that is required. There is likelihood, too, in setting an outer limit, that it will tend to create a pattern in that direction. But the regulation requires a great deal more of a local department than this. It requires that the *purpose* be understood and that it allow its method to be determined by the *purpose*. It holds the agency to limit itself only to facts "relevant to assistance or other service."

It has one other extremely characteristic factor to be noted: It presupposes that the applicant or recipient shall be the active person, carrying responsibility, making decisions, selecting his way and finding his proof, using the agency to help him as he needs help.

This is, at one and the same time, the hardest kind of structure to use and yet the only kind which can be truly useful.

THE PROCESS OF ASSIMILATION OF POLICY IN THE AGENCY

ON THE day when a policy goes into effect something happens to it which changes its whole character. Prior to that, actually, it is not a policy, only a collection of ideas moving into form and shape, subject to any amount or kind of revision, not bar- ring complete rewriting. In this "prior" period it already may be having a powerful influence in the agency because the idea itself has struck a spark and its vitality has made itself felt.

But on the effective date the ideas become policy and agency begins the process of assimilation. This is more than just adding something additional to an already existing structure. A new focal point has been introduced. It is as if the agency reorgan- izes itself around a new center. The marshalling of energy, the organization of work, the preoccupation with subject matter, seem to be drawn toward the center of this vortex set up by the new policy.

To attempt to describe what takes place in the movement of a total organization under these circumstances is like trying to put on paper the essence of living itself. Yet somehow, if we are ever to understand anything of administration, an effort has to be made to try to describe it, and to describe it in such a way that its essential dynamic quality is not lost. Only in this way can we begin to achieve some control of the process. Now it must seem at times to persons in a large organization as if they and it are swept around by forces which are bewildering, because so little understood, and frightening, because so seem- ingly out of control.

The first thing which needs to be comprehended in all its fullest meaning is the significance of size and distance. One reason why the problems of administration begin to show up in public agencies is a sheer matter of numbers and widely separated areas.

Take for instance this organization about which I am writing. At the time this policy went into effect there were approximately seven hundred people employed, serving a total caseload of twenty-three thousand, with a monthly new application count of twelve hundred. As public welfare agencies go, this is small, very small, but when viewed from the standpoint of human communication, it is colossal.

Nor is it just a matter of numbers. It is distance, too. An organization of seven hundred people, all working under one roof, is different from an organization divided into twenty-four separate agencies each with its own individuality and separateness. Each person in each of these offices is expected to have a sense of belonging not only to the one local department in which he works, but also to a state-wide organization, and even to a nation-wide wholeness which is the Security program.

When a new policy is issued this size and distance exaggerates itself tenfold. Here is the Director of the Department, the source, the fountainhead of the authority with which the new regulation is vested. He is also the person ultimately accountable for the effective carrying out of the service. By himself, however, he cannot carry out this responsibility, excepting only if the amount of work is so small that it can be carried by a one-person agency, and then administrative process is entirely merged in the service. As soon as the task to be done is more than one person can fulfill, then there begins a division of work into more and more segments and the arena spreads and the number of persons increases until the distance between Director who releases, and worker who uses, is great. The simplest, the most natural method of communicating ideas, intention, purpose, the use of language in a person to person relationship, is gone, and in its place there are just two channels open to the executive: the written word, and the transmission of the oral word from person to person, through a channel of supervision which ultimately reaches the worker.

If the instruction which he attempts to communicate is definite, limited in subject matter to something which does not affect the agency very deeply, dealing with a kind of concrete-ness which does not lend itself to much interpretative variation, then the process of assimilation is relatively simple. It is hard to think of much in a social agency, however, which is like that. Even an announcement of new office hours, specific and definite as that is, puts into the supervisory process, as everyone well knows, a whole new set of feelings to be dealt with before the job can get done.

When on the other hand the subject matter and the nature of the material to be communicated is substantive, as is that contained in Rule and Regulation #19, then the process of assimilation becomes much more complex.

The reason is that there is no way that agency can assimilate a new policy as an agency, mechanically. Agency is wholly dependent for its expression upon the persons who represent it. Remove the individual expression of it and all that is left is office, desks, telephones, files and a manual of policy which is academic and theoretical. It is inanimate matter, no matter how carefully designed.

This does not imply that a policy is no more than a piece of paper with words written upon it. Through all its comings and goings when it is being prepared for release—its last writing, its editing, the cutting of stencils, running through the mimeo-graph machine, sorting, stapling, counting, putting into the envelopes for mailing—it is at the same time being vested with an authority which is given it by the Director and the State Board. This is nothing flimsy or tentative. It comes out of the most fundamental source of power which society possesses—the voting legislative body which purportedly translates and effec-tuates the wishes of the majority of the people into conscious intention to turn back to themselves a governmental service. This is always characteristic of structure in a public agency.

This is its nature when it leaves the State office. It is received, read, given its place in the manual, perhaps left resting on desks, discussed a little at first. In a sense it has become structure, but only in the most partial way. It is not structure with any reality until the individuals who will use it have come to terms with it. What they can do with it in this process is as varied as the

potentialities of human behavior.

Immediately after the release of a new policy an agency goes through a period during which everyone in the agency has to learn to use it. That seems like a very obvious statement. Perhaps it has suffered on that account. We have overlooked what it means to the agency, to the service to the client, when several hundred of individuals are learning, all at once, how to use a new piece of structure; assimilating the new piece of structure; actually making structure of it, by a process of learning to use it.

It does not seem to me that agencies have ever known that this was so, much less understood that it had to be that way, and prepared to give the agency the resilience and the sturdiness which it would need in order to withstand that. Nor have we ever to my knowledge tried to adapt the making of policy, the release of policy, the assimilation of policy, to that universal and inevitable response.

Just here an agency which is in possession of knowledge and skill regarding the human ways of learning and how resistance to change and learning may manifest itself, has resources at its command the potentialities for which seem almost unlimited. In attempting to describe what some of these reactions are like and what the effect on the service may be, I do so knowing full well how fragmentary this must be and how much more of experience must go into it before it can be meaningful.

First one has to know and understand the negative nature of the responses which are universal, however individually they may be expressed. A policy, despite all the positive quality with which it is endowed and despite all the positive expression of wish for it, is always, in the last analysis, a limitation. It excludes far more than it includes. It limits the free and unrestricted activity of every individual in the organization.

Moreover it is an external limitation. This is true no matter to what extent it has been worked upon, taken to pieces, put back together again, by participating discussion on the part of staff. Perhaps, just on account of this participation it may seem the more alien when finally received, because in its final form it will never be what any given individual wished it to be. It is a composite of what many individuals contributed to it. When it leaves the director's office, having ceased to be something that can be modified and molded, something that responds and yields to thinking and the wish to make it different, it has taken on, instead, the role of authority which I have already described. This gives it both the strength and rigidity of a restriction. It is something new and different, something which is at once wanted and unwanted by the people who must now learn to use it.

These two qualities, limitation and outsideness—to say noth-ing of a certain necessity that the agency must inevitably put into it, to see that the service reaches the client, which must feel like compulsion to learn,—complicates the process, which is at one and the same time the process of assimilation in the agency and the process of learning by individuals.

For one thing, it seems to happen in this period following the release of a new policy that the balance which the organization is always striving for, as between too much form on the one hand and not enough on the other, is temporarily disturbed. During ordinary times, day in and day out, it is as if the organi-zation in its total movement is always striving to achieve this balance, actually never does, but is constantly changing around it. It is a kind of ambivalence within an organization between two opposite poles of the same thing. Without form, no crea-tivity is possible; with too much, creativity dies. The search is for structure that is usable and sustaining, the pitfall is a literal prescription of method. This duality is always present.

Then a new policy is released which has the effect of intro-ducing new definition. This gives new impetus to the need for concreteness, spurs it on wherever the agency is susceptible to it. We are most familiar with this struggle as it manifests itself in every beginning worker who comes to the agency. We know that we have to reckon with the desire to be told how, to have answers to questions, to find rules to be guided by. This is part of learning. We know that. We recognize, too, the signs of growth when a worker moves into a new use of her-self around this point and is able therefore to carry a job more responsibly.

What we are seemingly less familiar with is the way in which this same phenomenon can express itself throughout an agency, must express itself at some times and in some ways in all of us. It is as if every individual, too, must always be achiev-ing this balance, for himself, internally. Most of the time the agency sustains this, supports the individual in that movement. The individual learns to find a wholeness in that source from which he can make fullest use of his own strength. The new policy disrupts that, too.

This is hard under any circumstances, hard on the individual and hard on the organization. There is an interplay of forces, some of which are positive and some of which are negative.

For example, one knows to begin with that asking questions about the policy is one way by which people learn what it is like, one way by which they make it part of themselves. Here is a word—what does it mean? Here is a phrase—what does it mean? Here is one sentence—it contradicts another. Here is a case situation—these are the facts—how would you apply this policy to it? What would be the result? What would be the answer? What would I do in applying this policy if this were the case, if that were the case?

Just here lies also the source of stress and strain for the or-ganization. By this much of a delicate tipping of the balance it begins to move from this essential use into the mechanization of the policy itself. Definition begins to beget definition. It now takes on the aspect of question-asking and answer-seeking for the answer's sake, and it is not long before there can be abroad in the organization a drive for concreteness, with such gather-ing momentum that it begins to kill life. It can spread like a prairie fire throughout the agency.

All the while the agency will know, too, that it is almost impossible to conceive of a policy which, after release, will not require some clarification, some further definition. I have never known one which did not need some of this, and the only way to get to it is to have it criticized and questioned by the users. But neither do I know any more difficult spot in administration than holding this balance while the policy is being struggled with by a total organization—questioned as part of learning to work with it, questioned in order to improve its content, questioned as an expression of the move into mechanization, at times questioned as an unmixed expression of negative reaction to it.

This explains, I believe, why a faulty policy can do so much damage, of a kind and to a degree that is far beyond a mere matter of clear or unclear writing. If the policy requires a great deal of interpretation after its release to make it usable it becomes feeble and unreliable. It serves to spread and intensify the need for more concreteness. It bcomes impossible to separate and know the difference between the situation where answer is truly needed, and the situation where learning is expressing itself and what is really sought is not answer, but help in using policy. The policy will not under those circumstances hold firm as structure.

Nor is exaggerated insistence upon more concreteness the only kind of negative reaction against the policy in these early days after its release. Sometimes, for instance, there is no use of it at all. It makes no effective impression upon the agency or the individuals in it. This, it will be said, is nothing new; it is like what we are now doing; it changes nothing. The policy could stay like this indefinitely in any given local department, on the belief that it was already being used; and therefore it is never assimilated, except only on a most superficial level, unless activated again by some outside influence.

Or sometimes there is too much dependence on, or wrong use of, the new policy, with the possibility of considerable hardship upon the applicant and recipient. One effective way to resist a policy is to misuse it; not deliberately, to be sure, on the basis of a conscious choice to defeat the policy by misuse, but with much the same effect, perhaps even exaggerated because so unconscious. Every time a new policy is released the agency takes, more or less, this risk. By the very extent to which the policy is written to avoid too great concreteness, it almost certainly leaves the way open to misinterpretation of meaning. This is especially true where individuals bring to it some conviction of their own for which they seek support in the regulation itself. They will find it there, if there is any way to do so, by putting own meaning into the language.

One last example: there is a way to deny a policy by placing responsibility for it wholly outside the local department, or outside the individual who uses it. This, it will be said of policy, is because the State, not we, has willed it so. To the client it will be put in varying terms: "Because we are required to do so by the State, it is necessary for us to . . . ." This immediately implies rejection of the policy by the person who offers the service. The client cannot mistake it in feeling. His own need to struggle against it is completely fortified by the worker's need to do likewise. By this much, he has more difficulty in making use of it to meet his own necessity, if he can do so at all. The unavoidable result of this must be that any effective use of the agency by the client is interrupted for as long as the tendency to place the policy entirely outside persists.

Thus the usual non-giving, denying, negative aspects of the job, which the worker has to learn to carry along with the positive, are accentuated and intensified by the release of a new policy.

Thus far I have stressed only the negative aspects of the process of assimilation, and it remains only to point out that a supervisory process must be strong enough to carry this. The supervisor, at whatever level in the organization, must recognize that these reactions are present, must bring them into the open, must facilitate the release of feeling emanating from them, must give the kind of help which another needs in working through to a more positive use of the policy.

There is still another facet to this supervisory responsibility during the period of assimilation, which is, in fact, the objective above all others, and that is, to carry from Director to worker the positive concept, the intention, the principle—in feeling tone as well as in theory—which has given rise to the regulation and out of which whatever concreteness it has gets its sustenance. It is for this purpose that supervision releases the negative, to make it possible for individuals to relate positively and creatively to the material. This regulation is an idea which has to be carried. It cannot be transmitted, readymade, from person to person. There is no way that it can happen at all, excepting that one person helps the other to learn it, and that is of an-other quality entirely.

One is likely to think of structure much more readily in the relationship between worker and client than elsewhere in the agency. This is because the subject matter is related chiefly to the client, it is also because we know more about it there. We move beyond this, however, to understand the essential im-portance of structure in the relationship between supervisor and worker, between executive and supervisor, between state department and local department.

It is in a sense stating the obvious to say that here is no dif-ferent, special structure set up for the supervisory or the ad-ministrative process. There is something additional, perhaps, in terms of responsibility, which affects the relationship. But the core of what one supervises by, or what one makes use of in supervision, is again the manual, the same function of the agency. Rule and Regulation #19 becomes a new focal point in supervision. When structure changes, therefore, it changes not only where the service is offered. It changes in every rela-tionship throughout the agency, including supervision.

At the time when the worker first begins to work with a new policy, to express the reactions, or some of them, to which reference has been made in the previous pages, the supervisor in every level in the organization is likewise beginning to work with it. Seldom, if ever, is there opportunity in advance for the person who has to give help to seek the help which he him-self may need in order to learn the use of the policy. Everyone is learning at once.

This places upon the supervisor an additional burden. Ex-perienced as she may be in the capacity to keep herself from intruding where the worker makes use of help, this is the more difficult when she, too, is coming to terms with the new policy, is, herself, in process of making it her own. If a supervisor, as sometimes happens, fails to recognize her own negative re-actions to the policy, the worker's use of it is seriously inter-fered with.

This is like saying that all we know of supervision, all that supervision has to give, is needed at this point. It is my intention to leave it there, to do no more than point to the essential role of the supervisory process in this process of assimilating new policy; but also to conclude this discussion by pointing to one particular aspect of supervision which has strategic importance here but which may easily be overlooked.

When Rule and Regulation #19 was released to the local departments it was mailed with the following covering letter:

"The effective date for this regulation is October 1, 1942.

"Please begin consideration immediately of the introduction of this regulation into the regular work of the agency; so that it will be possible for you to plan in advance for conference with the Field Supervisor at time of next visit.

"It is contemplated that early in our experience with this regulation, the State Department will initiate a review of practice of local departments in order to determine (1) whether the minimum requirements of the regulation are being carried out; (2) how the local department is exercising its discretionary powers; and (3) what evidence is available to indicate whether the regulation is accomplishing its objective in a workable manner.

"This review of practice will be explained in greater detail and discussed with you by the Field Supervisor. The review will begin in each local department not later than January 1, 1943.

"The State Board of Welfare will reconsider the provisions of the regulation after the results of six months' experience are available."

This was an effort on the part of the State Department to put more structure into the relationship between state and local departments around this one specific piece of material. That was not accidental, but the result of long working toward an experimental use of new clarity in this not-too-well understood relationship between the agency which supervises and the agency which is supervised.

It will be noted how specific this is in forecast of what is to be expected and how the State Department also puts into the picture what it anticipates as essential responsibility on the part of the local department. It contemplates, for instance, that the regulation cannot be introduced into the regular work of the agency without prior consideration. It lets the local department know that on this the help of the field supervisor will be needed, and sets the structure for that by reference to planning for the conference.

It also looks far enough into the future to see one of the many things which is likely to happen around a regulation of this kind, in order to put into the situation, early, enough that is known and definite to release some of the anxiety which may accompany it. Whenever discretionary responsibility is given over to another there may go with it the implication that no accountability is to be expected. If I am given freedom to act, to make decisions, by my own judgment, then how can you, who frees me thus, hold me to a known standard of perform-ance?

This regulation is particularly fraught with possibility for this assumption. The instruction which the local department is to follow is general:

"The method to be used for any part or all of the investigation in order to secure the necessary proofs . . . shall be left to the discretion of the local department, provided . . . ."

that six conditions are met. For the State Department to go back at some later point of time and begin to raise question with the local department as to the validity of the judgments which it has made seems to go contrary to the implied freedom stated in the regulation.

This is difficult under any circumstances, but in any event it cannot be done at all without letting the local department know well in advance that this is part of the plan. It is not unbounded freedom in exercise of judgment which is intended; it is ex-pectation of judgment to be responsibly carried and for which the local department will be held to accountability.

It is obvious immediately how important it becomes to know the basis upon which this will take place. It could so easily appear to be the pitting of one individual judgment against another. Wherever this would be present as a possibility, the local department could not be free to use its own capacity in working with the material. Its responsibility, its own identity, would become hopelessly confused with the responsibility of the State Department. In protest and in effort to avoid, it would seem to have no way out excepting to refuse to make any judg-ments at all, or to make them so rebelliously and defiantly as to make all accountability impossible.

The structure which the State Department attempts to introduce makes it possible for the two agencies to remain separate, at the same time that they are part of a whole. An executive of a local department is the representative of agency in relationships which turn in many directions—to staff, to board, to community and to State Department. An executive occupies a position which calls for a high degree of initiative and which expects of the person an ability to carry a job responsibly and to operate with freedom and independence. In a sense, supervision by another part of the agency, by the state department, can seem to be full of contradiction of this freedom, and even intrusion. It is only as this supervision is carried by a person who, also, has a unique sense of representing agency, of carrying structure and using structure, and only as the agency learns to know how to put in this support, that the relationship can have anything usable and durable in it.

We are just beginning to learn, I believe, how essential it is that these conditions be stated at the time the new policy is released.

THE PARTICIPATION OF STAFF IN POLICY FORMULATION

I WOULD need to rely upon the foregoing section to support the conclusion that policy is constructed, not written. It is a process of assembling a carefully wrought design from meticulously fashioned pieces.

No policy has easy sailing when it is first launched, or any time thereafter, as a matter of fact. It has to have a sturdy resilience to serve the purpose I have so partially described. It has to have strength of a sort that has not often been recognized, because the difficulties and confusion which result when it is feeble have seldom been traced back to their right source.

Persons who construct policy soon learn how demanding this task is. The more they learn, the harder it becomes. People who do not customarily construct policy but who attempt to do it occasionally are likely to react to its difficulties by flight to the conclusion that there is some special, technical knowledge and skill in policy writing which can belong only to those who write.

People who say it is hard to construct policy are right, eminently so. But the reason to which they attribute this is not usually the correct one. There is no magic by which policy comes into being. Neither is there a technique or a prescription as to how it should be done. The reason that policy is hard to construct is that it grows by process. It is fashioned from the raw materials of current experience. It takes its form and content from use and purpose. When do we need a policy? When structure needs it to enhance its usefulness. What do we define and how far? When the intuitive balance between that which is structural, in the true sense, and that which is mechanical, is given free play and trusted because it grows out of identification with the service.

Viewed in this way, the whole question of staff participation, which plays such an important part in all considerations of the administrative process, falls into a new perspective. What consideration is given it here is not by way of opening up the large and challenging question of staff participation as a whole, but only to relate it to this description of the movement of agency around and in reaction to policy.

Any approach to the subject, no matter what the focus, requires some examination of the true role and responsibility of the administrator, because only then can we ask the true role and responsibility of the staff group. The administrator has a responsibility which (excepting for certain aspects of Board, or review by outside body, etc., which are not particularly pertinent to this point) is single, ultimate and unshareable. It is compounded of authority, the source of which has already been referred to, and accountability, which he alone can assume. He can delegate through every step but the final one; he can use resources, knowledge, skill, of individuals or of groups, but when the final point has been reached where it must be said, "It is to be this way," then only the administrator can say that. The agency needs it that way in order to operate.

This alone would not necessarily lead to the conclusion that policy making cannot be assigned to a group, for the administrator could still assume ultimate responsibility for establishing as policy whatever finally emerged from the group. But there seem to be other reasons for wondering, and questioning, whether the practice of actually assigning to a group the writing of policy can ever be effective or satisfactory, either to the group or the agency.

This is not to suggest that the staff does not have a true and real part in the period of formulation of a policy. I would like to try to get to the problem by looking, briefly, at what the role of the staff may be.

The truest base which a staff can bring to policy is a richness and wealth of experience which can be found nowhere else in the organization. The immediacy of it, the spontaneity of it, its essence as living experience—what is more, the way in which staff subjects it to use and responsibility—these are qualities which only staff can bring and they know it and know it truly. There is nothing artificial in this. They know without it the lifestream of the organization would dry up. Thus they could have no resistance toward having the agency use it and use it to the full.

The description of the discussions which took place prior to the formulation of Rule and Regulation #19 illustrate to some extent, I believe, what the substantive part of group discussion can be, without assuming actual responsibility for the writing of policy.

However, there is another equally important reason for staff's active participation during the period of formulation of policy, of one of which we have been all too little aware. It is a reason which grows out of conscious recognition of what the period of assimilation of policy is like.

If all the getting acquainted with a new policy, all the reaction to its newness, all the learning of its meaning, have to take place after it goes into effect, then the client is bound to feel the full effect of it. The whole agency will have intensified, concentrated reaction, exaggerated beyond any necessity for it. The first time the individual sees the policy is in its finished form. At that time it will yield in no way to a wish to mold it, or to make it different.

As I think about the need—the real need and not an artificial one—for discussion of a policy in its formative stage, there is present all the genuineness of giving to every individual the utmost opportunity to begin to relate positively and responsibly to it. Staff sees it for the first time when it is only proposed, when it might or might not be put into effect at all. It can be criticized without limit. Suggestions can be made which might, or might not, affect its final form. Whatever negative reactions the individual may have toward it begin to work through in this process. Experience and the idea interact, and movement, not blocking, can take place.

Group discussion or committee work is not the only way. The more varied the adventures of the piece of material can be at this point, the better. The harder it is hauled around, the tougher the use, the better. This can be in every spot in the agency. Unfortunately, it is not often enough that the worker gets an opportunity to do this, too, to State policy.

If these two reasons are felt to be substantial, are used and accepted as the basis for staff's relation to it, then the period of formulation of the policy will have unity with the later period of release. It will mean that in the process of taking it to pieces and putting it back together again only those things which have a right relation to the service can withstand the test and it will be, as nearly as it can be, related to the service.

There is a certain amount of discomfort and uneasiness which arises out of the part which staff plays in the formulation of policy and there is not a little futility and dissatisfaction which grows out of much well-intentioned staff participation. To some extent this may be due to superficial and unsuitable reasons or to lack of clarification of the basis on which the participants are asked to share this experience. For example, the idea that this is a democratic, as opposed to an autocratic, mode of operation is not too well formulated. Does that imply the rule of the majority? If so, then is the staff the majority which should have that rule?

Or sometimes it seems to me that those who plan for so-called "participation" do so with an intention to win consent. The policy will be more readily accepted if people feel they have some part in it. This attitude, whether open or veiled, has in it a suggestion of manipulation which could never form the base for any workable engagement with the material. Here there is a preconceived pattern into which the group must be fitted. This kind of feeling will be openly present if a finished product is turned over to a group which has been called together and asked to discuss it. Then the individuals will know that they have not had a part that is real. To avoid this an agency may swing to the opposite extreme; in order to give the sense of realness, of true participation, the whole task is turned over to the group and this is equally untrue and unreal.

Or the group may have a sense that the reason they are being asked to participate is to dissipate, spread and make less poignant the ultimate responsibility of the administrator. If the writer of the policy has to face what it will be like in use, then it may be easier to bear if there is a way to say, if the policy does not work, "You, too, shared in the making. You had an opportunity to foresee this and make it different." This implication can be very subtly undermining in an agency. It removes the right of the individual to oppose the policy as much as he wishes and needs to oppose it after it has been released. It removes the focus and keeps an issue from becoming clear.

An administrator, or the person who constructs the final policy, can never fail to take complete responsibility for what finally emerges and this requires both a denial, in a sense, of what others have contributed and an ability to depersonalize it and make it agency. There has to be a great deal of sureness and security in the amount that has been contributed by others to be able to let it be like this. Then there need be no shouting to acclaim how much the staff has had opportunity to participate.

CONCLUSION

THE literature of administration, whether by power of the words themselves or by some element of usefulness inherent in them, has organized its content around a few constantly recurring words: planning, organizing, staffing, directing, coordinating, reporting and budgeting, and these, it is pointed out, are of the essence of the administrator's job.* These are words which describe action on the part of the administrator, and it is interesting that they have so much movement in them.

There is an essential rightness about the special emphasis which has been placed upon the word coordination, as being at the heart of the administrator's function. This recognition of the need to divide work, the separateness of the parts, and the resulting necessity to draw them together again into a whole, has become something of a commonplace. Yet always when we talk about coordination, when we read about coordination, we seem to take flight into generalities which have a certain power to stimulate thought but an equal power to perpetuate the generality. It does not seem to me that we have made even a beginning in knowing what this word means.

One has to return again to the fact that this specific service which we offer, public assistance, can be rendered only in agency setting by agency representatives. All of the administrative process is focused toward making this possible. In the last analysis, it is always the worker and the worker alone who can either express or defeat the intent of the agency.

An agency without unity is one in which the individuals operate as individuals, and then administration carries very little indeed. There will still be the necessity to secure funds, to make a budget and establish a bank account, to set up a method for paying expenses and accounting for them, to have comfortable housing, fairly efficient telephone and mail service and files in which materials can be found when needed, but this is not the administrative process. It is only as an agency begins to introduce conscious intention to relate these services

---

* See, for example, Gulick, Luther, Notes on the Theory of Organization; and Urwick, L., Scientific Principles and Organization.

to each other and to the primary service for which it exists, and as it moves on from this to creating and recreating its own unity and purpose, in a movement that is never completed but always in process, that the entity of the agency begins to have form and outline—that there is any agency to represent.

What seems to be asked of the administrator is that he possess an unusual capacity for carrying, at one and the same time, both the whole which is the agency, and the parts, which are the individuals; that he sustains, with resilience and life, but still with firmness, the total movement of the agency, at the same time that the myriad individual movements are given freedom but not allowed to engulf the whole. One has only to look at what an administrator's office is like to sense some of the full impact of this reality. At this terminal point, in this one concentrated spot, comes together at one time or another all that is the agency. Channels and cross channels of infinite variety lead in and out in many directions, to and from the outer world which is the agency's environment, to and from the internal organization which is the staff.

This requires an ability to carry structure in a new way, a way that is different from and yet essentially like what is asked of every other person in the agency. Whatever the difference, it arises in a measure from the fact that the movement is likely to be deeper and swifter, it encompasses more area, the forces which impinge upon the structure, either with or against it, have more strength. It takes firmness of a unique kind to hold to structure under those circumstances.

Yet there is no place in an organization where structure is more essential than just here, in its leadership, and no place in the organization where what is asked of it is as full of seeming contradiction and paradox. We say that this sense of the individual must be acute—the individual client, the individual worker, the individual supervisor, the individual local department—but not for one moment may the administrator relinquish the sense of the whole. We ask for movement and change, responsiveness to change, but at the same time for stability and consistency. We ask for freedom for each individual within the organization to utilize capacity and own strength, separately and creatively, but we ask simultaneously for a sturdy, structural limitation which is the agency. We uphold the value of staff experience and its vitality to shape agency policy and direction, but we are quick to respond apprehensively to any inference of abdication on the part of the administration from responsibility which it should rightly bear. We try at times to persuade the administration to relax from that to which it holds, at the same time that we expect it to know that our freedom to do just that depends upon our underlying assurance that it *will* hold firm to its essential structure.

This totality is what seems to me to make the administrative skill such a difficult one to achieve. The imperative necessity to "coordinate" is present in every organization; there is no other way about it. To this necessity, however, there are many ways to react. One is toward ever greater mechanization, in a constant effort to achieve a sufficiently static condition to lend itself to single control. Another is toward ever greater relinquishing of the administrative responsibility, leaving the individuals to operate without agency support. Both of these tendencies within an organization would make it spiritless or would generate fruitless conflict.

Neither of these can make possible the kind of agency in which a case work service can be responsibly given. It does not seem to me that there is any way for us excepting the hard way, in this striving to set up a fluid, facilitating, supporting agency. In order to accept this, agencies would need to be satisfied for a long time to come—could be satisfied, I think—with very imperfect agency operation, provided it could be known that the essential elements were present: that is, understanding of the individual, however he is related to the organization; conviction with respect to the value of structure; a feeling for movement and growth; a sense of process and time; and a respect for the ordinary, daily experience of the agency as the medium in which we work.

APPENDIX

STATE DEPARTMENT OF PUBLIC WELFARE

120 W. Redwood Street

Baltimore, Md.

RULE AND REGULATION #19 (GENERAL)

Investigation of Application and Periodic Reconsideration
of the Grant

I—The purpose of this Regulation is:

A—To effectuate the following provisions of the public assistance laws.
Old Age Assistance and Public Assistance to the Needy Blind

"Whenever a County Department receives an application for assistance under this article, an investigation and record shall promptly be made . . . ." (Sec. 8, O.A.A. and Sec. 18, P.A.N.B.)

All assistance grants made under this article shall be reconsidered by the County Department as frequently as may be required by the rules of the State Department." (Sec. 15, O.A.A. and Sec. 24, P.A.N.B.)

Aid to Dependent Children

"Whenever a local unit receives a notification of the dependency of a child or an application for assistance, an investigation and record shall promptly be made . . . . The investigation shall include a visit to the home of the child and of the person who will have the custody of the child . . . ." (Sec. 43, A.D.C.)
"All assistance granted under this sub-title shall be reconsidered as frequently as may be required." (Sec. 46, A.D.C.)

B—To prescribe a method of investigation and periodic reconsideration and standards and frequency of interview and field visit applicable to Aid to Dependent Children, Old Age Assistance, Public Assistance to the Needy Blind, General Public Assistance, foster care and other services provided by the local public welfare departments.

C—To prescribe regulations within which a local department may plan to conserve travel consistent with the war effort.

D—It is not the intention of this regulation to eliminate the home visit as an essential part of the administration of public assistance and other social services; it is the intention of the regulation to relate the use of the home visit to the purpose to be accomplished, as set forth in this regulation.

[214]

'II—Investigation of Application for Public Assistance

A—Purpose. The purpose of the investigation shall be:

1. To permit the applicant to state his need in his own terms; why he is applying for assistance, and to explore with him in a preliminary way, what use he has made or might make of own resources in lieu of application for assistance.

2. If he decides to make application for assistance, to acquaint him with the provisions of the laws, regulations and other requirements relevant to his application.

3. To inform him of the nature of the proofs required to establish eligibility and to help him in securing those proofs insofar as he needs and wishes such help.

4. To examine the proofs as to their validity for the purpose of establishing eligibility.

5. To arrive at a decision with respect to eligibility.

6. To discuss with the applicant the manner of calculating the amount of the grant and to arrive at a decision regarding the amount of the grant.

7. To inform the applicant of the decision.

8. To discuss with him the conditions applicable to his acceptance of a grant; the nature of his responsibility to report relevant changes; the periodic reconsideration of the grant; and any other conditions or arrangements which, in the opinion of the local department, require consideration.

B—Extent and Method of Investigation

1. The investigation shall cover all factors of eligibility enumerated in the State plan for each type of assistance; but shall cover only those facts relevant to the application for assistance or other services.

2. The method to be used for any part or all of the investigation in order to secure the necessary proofs, whether interview in the office or in the home, telephone, correspondence, search of records, etc., shall be left to the discretion of the local department provided the following conditions are met:

   a. That the investigation shall cover all of the 8 enumerated parts of the purpose in Section II-A above.

   b. That the investigation shall conform with existing requirements located elsewhere in the State Plan relevant to method of investigation.

c. That every investigation shall include at least one interview with the applicant himself and more if indicated.

d. That the interview or interviews take place at such time and in such manner that Item 8 in the Section II-A above, be covered adequately for understanding by the recipient and for facilitation of the continuing relationship.

e. That ADC must include a visit to the home of the child and of the person who will have the custody of the child before the grant is made.

f. That no application shall be left pending beyond a reasonable period of time, or rejected, for reasons solely related to travel, when in accordance with usual practice the agency would have made a visit under similar circumstances.

C—Recording

1. The case record shall record accurately the manner in which the purpose of the investigation was covered and must show that the investigation met the conditions set by this regulation in every respect.

2. The case record must reflect accurately the proof of eligibility as required elsewhere in the State Plan.

III—Periodic Reconsideration of Public Assistance Grant

A—Every grant shall be reconsidered:

1. Whenever facts of relevant change are reported to the local department by the recipient or by someone on his behalf.

2. Whenever such facts of relevant change come to the attention of the agency from other responsible sources.

3. Whenever agency policy changes with respect to a particular factor.

4. Provided, that every grant shall be reconsidered once in every six months.

B—The purpose of the reconsideration shall be:

1. To review those factors in eligibility which the State Plan sets by policy for periodic reconsideration; and those factors in eligibility which the agency has reason to believe may change.

2. To review the amount of the grant.

3. To review with the recipient the nature of his responsibility in reporting relevant changes; to discuss with him the manner of reconsidering the amount of the grant; the conditions applicable to his receipt of a grant; the periodic reconsideration of the grant;

and any other conditions or arrangements which in the opinion of the local department, require consideration.

C—The method of reconsideration may be by interview in the office or in the home, by mail, by telephone, etc.; or it may be by review of the case record by the agency, with a decision that no action is necessary; or it may be by development of a concrete plan by the agency for application of new policy to continuing grants; provided:

1. That if a decision is made that no action is necessary at the end of six months, the record shall clearly show on what that decision is based; and

2. That an interview with the recipient shall be required not less than once a year.

D—The case record shall show accurately and completely that the requirements of this regulation with respect to periodic reconsideration have been met.

IV—Foster Care and Other Services

A—The purpose of the investigation for foster care (of the child, his family and foster home) shall be that outlined in Section 0 of the State Manual.

B—Direct inspection of the foster home and regular visits to the child in foster care are essential to the discharge of the agency's responsibility toward the child and therefore may not be curtailed beyond the point consistent with good practice in normal times.

C—Interviews and field visits for carrying out other defined services encompassed by the State Plan shall be within the discretion of the local department; provided that the local department exercises due care in the expenditure of time and funds for travel.

V—General Conditions

A—No proof of eligibility or coverage of investigation required by the State Plan may be omitted or curtailed on account of necessity to conserve travel or for any other reason.

B—No assistance may be paid until eligibility has been established in full, excepting that emergency assistance from general public assistance may be granted by the local department when the agency has reasonable evidence that emergent need exists.

Passed by the State Board of Public Welfare on September 4, 1942

Effective October 1, 1942

Other Selected Writings

NOTE TO THE READER

Following are the original publication locations of the articles reprinted in this volume.

INDIVIDUALS IN ASSOCIATION

An account of how the Otto Rank Association
came to be formed

The paper delivered by Rank at Yale University in 1929, published here for the first time, contains the essence of what he calls the "purely individual." He writes, "My aim is to enable the individual first to find himself and then to develop himself." Of all the Rankian conceptions, this is the one which, in the fine shadings of meaning, most distinguishes his thought. The individual is the creator, the artist, of his own personality.

It is often pointed out that Rank abhorred system, pattern, even theory although he created theory himself. Whatever was static, intellectually parched, or wherever life was constricted by force from without, all this he felt to be opposed to the upsurge of impulsion from the life source in the self. It was growth that interested him, not cure. And growth for the moment at least is a lonely business. Rank created alone, almost in total separation from his former professional associates.

People say, organization is the last thing Rank would have wanted for himself. Perhaps this is so; there is no way to find the certain answer. To those of us who formed this association the argument was not real enough to stand in our way. For there is work to be done and work needs structure.

But beyond this—beyond the structure needed for the accomplishment of work—lies the need of the individual for association with others. In theory alone, if we were to place it there, Rank's conception of the "birth of individuality" is only half of the experience which involves the role played by "otherness"—by everything that is not self: things, people, circumstance. The theory of the will is rooted deepest where two wills meet, where the self discovers more of its own identity through the awareness of likeness and difference. These concepts of Rank's along with his many others may remain as verities, but the creation of particulars, of new lucid experience must go on continuously otherwise the static takes over. It used to be said among those of us on the faculty of the Pennsylvania School of Social Work (who were undertaking the almost impossible task of sustaining the student through a growth experience while he was learning to help others): each day we have to create ourselves anew in order to give what it takes.

Operating in association, "joining," must derive the odious connotations which sometimes surround it when the act of joining stems from inner emptiness which the person trys to fill by more external activity, thereby keeping himself in motion and occupied with outer demands. But an association which is formed by individuals who, having much within themselves, want more becomes a valuable experience.

We hope we can be forgiven for the presumption that conceives its goal to be the latter kind of association. Those of us who are dedicated to Rankian ideals—or functional psychological conceptions—have been increasingly separate, alone in a sense. For the purpose of going further, only a new coming together in new ways will suffice.

★ ★ ★ ★

Where the idea for The Otto Rank Association first began is hard to find. In retrospect it seems not to have had any one single beginning but many, growing into a river of idea and feeling with direction and course noticeable only after the fact rather than before. Certainly there was no prior design or projected plan fully conceived. It is indeed true that the association has developed in process. Looking backward one can see some of the steps by which it all came about.

When Dr. Jessie Taft died on June 6, 1960, the one person to whom everyone had turned for answers to questions about Rank, was gone. The questions which came to her over the years were sometimes concrete (in what field of knowledge did Rank receive his doctor's degree at the University of Vienna?) sometimes far-reaching: where can I learn more about the Rankian method of helping? To every letter that came she gave an answer that involved herself, taking pains with detail and reflecting the precision that characterized every word she ever wrote. Over the years she had received royalties paid to her as the translator of *Will Therapy* and *Truth and Reality* and this money she had put aside in a special account to be used, as she put it, to "further the interests of the Rank publications."

Even during Dr. Taft's lifetime complicated questions had begun to arise regarding such matters as granting permission to quote or publish Rank's work. Moreover, the Rank Collection although safely deposited in Special Collections of Columbia University Libraries, could easily be lost, at least for many years. The Library, as is wholly proper, does not assume the responsibility for stimulating interest in the use of its collections beyond making known their availability to any one interested in serious scholarship. The last projects on which Dr. Taft was at work after she finished her biographical study of Rank were a translation of Rank's earliest book *Der Künstler* (of which she completed one chapter) and the pursuit of a publisher for *The Genetic Psychology*.

It is a story previously told but one that nevertheless belongs in this account of how The Otto Rank Association came into being, that there were in the basement of the Pennsylvania School of Social Work several trunks-full of Rank's papers sent to Dr. Taft after his death in October 1939. During the years when I was on the faculty of the School a serious effort was begun to take on these materials but our intentions came to nothing. It is easy for me to understand now in retrospect why this was so, for the task was enormous. Only later when in retirement Dr. Taft herself took possession of these materials did it come clear how much work was involved in their disposition. Not only concrete work but deep involvement in the awakening of past experience.

Nevertheless the work was undertaken, she and Miss Robinson together on the third floor of their Flourtown home, sorting, arranging, at last packaging twelve boxes for shipment to New York. One cannot go over materials so alive although dormant without the chaos of feeling churned in so doing. At last, the feeling must be put back out, given form and meaning, and the outcome in this case was Dr. Taft's book, *Otto Rank, A Biographical study based on notebooks, letters, collected writings, therapeutic achievements and personal associations.*

From the beginning in 1954 I was deeply involved in all that was going on. While the work on the third floor of the Flourtown house proceeded, I began the search for a place to which the collection could be given. We knew nothing of the library world that concerns itself with the preservation of papers; we came upon it with surprise, and increasing interest, and relief, finding that every last detail of just such a situation as ours had been thought through and provided for. I followed the trail of helpful information: first from the library that I knew well, namely, the Enoch Pratt Library of Baltimore, then to the Library of Congress, then to university libraries, the last of which was Columbia where the gift finally went.

With some reluctance I must speak briefly in deeply personal terms for I find no other way to convey a true account. It was perhaps a natural outcome of my work with Dr. Taft over the years that she should have put into my hands the continuing responsibility for using this sum of money "in the interest of the Rank publications." She told me this while we were all still at work, but I scarcely heard her say it, excepting on a level buried in some dark recess of myself. It was of course because I would not give the thought of death any reality. Even when her book was finished, in print, there to be opened and read, and even though I knew the intensity of the ending reaction that followed, I still had my eyes upon the more that was to come.

It was natural, I said, that she felt in me the continuity that might be carried forward. I was younger by twenty years and I was passionately interested in this psychology. So I took the responsibility with what now seems to me surprisingly little question. I was about to write that I was at once excited and staggered by the responsibility but this was not true at the time. I simply took it and did what I had to do, mainly legal things dictated by the lawyer. It is only later that the realization, at first held in check by will and external reality, breaks out of the compartment in which it is contained and makes itself known. Then one must face it and engage with it and find the new relation out of which the next steps emerge.

I well remember the day when a trusted professional friend said to me as we walked down the street together after an earnest talk about just these matters of which I am now writing, "Did you choose this or was it a responsibility put upon you?" I knew the answer at once, pure and clear; I had indeed chosen it, chosen it in the way that all crucial choices are made, by little daily acts that soon shape a direction made up of that very thing we mean when we speak of choosing one's own identity. The commitment had been there as long as I could remember, and the only false move would have been to refuse it.

＊　　＊　　＊　　＊

From the name of this association one might naturally draw the conclusion that our objective is to see that Rank's work is accorded the recognition it deserves. There would be plenty of reason for this, considering the blanket of silence that has dropped down upon both his name and his work.

But for many reasons this would be a shabby objective. Rank needs no special pleaders—in the long run his work will be rediscovered even without any effort on our part. Moreover, an association dedicated only to an *external* purpose, that is, doing something for the sake of another, is bound to be shallow and short-lived. To associate with others can have only one true purpose, namely, to find not alone but with others, heightened interest, a quickened sense of one's own search for meaning, and an experience that is exhilarating. The need for a structure by which the practical matters could be carried was perhaps the incentive that pushed us on. But the answer to the question, what is the central purpose of the association, is immediately found. It is to bring into communication persons interested in these conceptions. *Interested*, that is, in keeping alive what has in the past had an extraordinary vitality, where many have found an experience of growth that held excitement, expansion, and illumination.

*   *   *   *

I am tempted to leave what I have just said standing as it is upon a positive assertion, but to do so would leave unnoticed the specific objections that have been raised to the formation of an association of this kind. It would be easy if these objections were thoughtless hit-or-miss opposition bound to arise in any event. But this is not the case. It is because the doubts spoken and written to us prevail also within each of us and on this account need to be explored.

I have already spoken of the resistance felt to any move that tends to become systematized. But there are other facets to this objection, not the least of which being the fear that the sharp difference once existing in social work now happily quiescent will once again set points of view in opposition. Those who have as their first concern the development of the profession of social work along lines that seem to them authentic and reliable, need have no concern over the effect of this association. It is indeed part of our intention to disentangle the Rankian conceptions from the social work milieu where they became imbedded and to trace them as well through the contents of art, mythology, drama, and literature where his ideas have had enormous impact.

Within recent months, in correspondence with Miss Robinson, a psychiatrist of noteworthy position expressed his opposition to "orthodoxy" which designated itself Freudian or Jungian or Rankian. In reply Miss Robinson wrote:

"It [your letter] poses for me again the question I often ask myself: Why do we set up a new organization in this field. In giving a name one is setting up a difference, attracting members who are willing to identify with that difference, to explore it in contrast to what is already existent under other names. This asks for scholarship but it also demands conviction and whether they can move hand in hand or whether conviction by its very psychological nature becomes orthodoxy, I do not know. But I shall be working on this question for myself and am grateful to you for taking the time and pains to put this question to me out of your experience and conviction."

It is in order to free the opportunity to "work on this question" whatever the question may be provided it is worthy of serious thought, that an association such as this finds it reason for being. To examine this question as a seriously searching person would, whether to identify one's self with a difference, or whether to search for likeness in whatever impinges, this is indeed at the heart of the matter.

But if one identifies with a difference, feels that difference in encounter and impact, there arises a simultaneous need for some unity, some identification with a whole beyond the lone self. It is perhaps safe to say that every one of us within reach of these pages wishes unremittingly for more expansion, more understanding, more skill, more life. There are two ways in which this can be found, and generally speaking they must go on simultaneously. One way is alone, through ever deeper concentration and absorption with the kaleidoscopic human experience with which every helping person and every artist is concerned. The other way is through relationship. We wish for and crave good talk, searching talk, and harbor the illusion that good talk just happens between two or more people, usually late at night, over a cup of coffee and a sandwich. But this experience is rare, so rare that we remember the occasions vividly and wish for their recurrence.

I have known the experience of what can only be called the creation of insights and illuminated thought, but for me it occurs when there is focus, and leadership, and process that is at first patient with mundane beginnings but finds through the content of most ordinary experience the form of a clear psychological truth. I know it in the classroom where I have been a part of its occurrence many times. And I know it in the one to one helping relation where two people develop extraordinary communication and understanding. Here the key word is "develop"—time, and process of which time is the essence, and freedom from the imposition of one will upon the other.

The greatest problem that exists for this association is to temper the visionary idea that animates us to the realities of what can actually be accomplished. To the members it must be said: we can promise very little at the beginning. It can scarcely seem worthwhile if measured by production. But if the scope of ten years or more during which this association will develop is not too uncongenial to one's wish for action, then we can say with confidence that something will come of it. We are not free from the common complaint of not enough time to work and not enough money to print, but neither are we despairing.

There are now 213 members of the association who have by their membership indicated their willingness to work as individuals in a new association and to find there whatever may come of a process which like all process is unpredictable in advance.

[228]

THE SEARCH AND THE GOAL*

The train of thought which I hope to develop this afternoon in itself has a goal. It is an ambitious goal, perhaps too ambitious, and experimental in every sense of the word. For what we should like to do—what my assignment is—is to present to you a theme on which the association will be at work during the year that lies ahead, a theme with a focus and a form, with an idea that we hope will enlist your interest in such a way that those of you who are here today, and the members who are not, will be aware of this theme and even working on it in your own way in your daily practice.

What is ambitious about it (I have had to struggle with the sense of its being almost pretentious) is the notion that an idea can animate and give continuity to an association. Stated in the purpose of this association is the proposition that we develop interest in and explore the Rankian conceptions. Not to find answers or to force ideas upon anyone, but to explore, to bring to life, to animate certain conceptions which are already familiar to us but also inexhaustible. Rank's thought, his life-work, is so rich and varied, it is imperative to limit ourselves: to choose a subject and to design the method by which we will examine that subject. It is this first sketching of the subject that I hope to accomplish today.

Even though I am aware of our professional make-up—that we are social workers, therapists, teachers, administrators in education or other fields, or retired from these demanding professions,—nevertheless I am speaking as it were to ourselves as

* Paper delivered at the meeting of The Otto Rank Association held in Doylestown, Pa. on May 13, 1967.

human beings. Because all that I have to say is in my feeling about it applicable first and foremost to ourselves, to our own lives and strivings, and to the extent that we feel and live these strands accurately, to that extent are we able to respond more accurately to others. Our over-all topic is the search for form and this search prevails for each of us. As some of you know one of the most absorbing topics for me in recent years has been the way in which *work* satisfies that search for form, what Rollo May calls the *passion* for form, an experience for which the word *passion* is eminently suited.

When I say that we are selecting a theme and letting that theme animate a process of thinking, writing, and planning, for the twelve months ahead, I mean to suggest something as concrete as planning for our next meeting; as concrete as urging you to feel and explore this same theme in your own practice; an inducement perhaps to you to venture some writing on your own. Of these practical aspects I will say more at the conclusion of my paper, but at first what I have to say is abstract and theoretical, as it cannot escape being, but I hope your train of thought will follow along with mine and that as I go you may have some reflections and thoughts that you too may wish to express later this afternoon. So with this introduction may I now plunge into the heart of what I have to say.

*   *   *   *

The subject that is of compelling interest today is the subject of *identity*. Dr. Erik Erikson of Boston is perhaps more responsible than anyone for recognizing the crisis of identity. It has become the key to understanding much about human development as reflected for instance in a biography of Keats in which the author, Aileen Ward, discovers a world opening to her when she realizes Keats' affirmation of identity; or one finds it in as poignant a work as Jung's Autobiography, *Memories, Dreams,*

Reflections, where he describes his search late in life for "who I am."

But now one begins to find the same subject in all kinds of popular guise: *Life Magazine* which is now running a series of articles on the pursuit of individuality; an editorial in the *New York Times* bearing on the anti-poverty program to which was given the title "A chance to find himself"—in other words acclaiming the purpose of a whole nation now to give to every individual the chance to find himself.

Our interest in this subject, too, has been concentrated and at times absorbing, and once you begin to follow a single idea the idea can at last take possession of you to such an extent that everywhere in the written word whether in profound writing or in fugitive daily writing, you can begin to find illustration and experience that illuminates the subject being pursued.

But along with my interest I began to feel a certain disquietude and at times almost impatience with the word "identity" and the discussion of it that I found. I knew that part of my discomfort was due to distress at popularizing so complicated and difficult a concept. This was the most superficial layer of my protest: one hates to see a serious and rich area of life drained of meaning. But I knew too that part of my discomfort arose from the sudden realization that the attainment of identity was being spoken of as if it were within reach of everyone: as if all we needed to do was put out a hand and take it in order to be ourselves. As you well know, nothing could be further from the truth. All the axioms that have to do with understanding one's self, such as Pindar's command which Rank quotes: "Be what you are!" or Shakespeare's "This above all: to thine own self be true." Or Aristotle's "Know thyself."—all these distill into one outcry, a goal of majestic proportion: to be what I am. But every writer of any profundity or sensibility knows what we all know in our experience: how it must be earned rather than grasped, what a lifetime it takes, and how the sense of "I" comes and goes in a process that continues as long as there is life.

All of this leads to an observation that many of you have already made on your own, but let me put it into words for us, namely, that Rank's conceptions, the so-called Rankian psychology, have a priceless contribution to make to the contemporary interest in the search for identity—not the answer, not the final word certainly, and never the finished logical answer which Rank abhorred—but the way to explore, the way to search, the way to seek, realizing this extraordinary thing about life that once a goal is seemingly reached it is already gone on behalf of the next one that is forming.

It is therefore my intention this afternoon to enumerate— actually enumerate and state with the utmost brevity—the primary tenets on which one might say we are agreed, the base on which we stand, the solid ground from which we can venture into territory that is less well known. I would propose that those ideas on which we might all agree even though it may be necessary for each one of us to find his own words for expressing them, are five in number:

(1) We accept for ourselves, and then for others, this primary fact: the two-sided nature of all living. It is not ambivalence that characterizes the neurotic (observes Rank) but one-sidedness. The two sides of experience, outer and inner, first to be found in nature in the regular recurrences in the environment, then to be found in the psychic life, of ebb and flow, waxing and waning—all the illustration of contrast that we can find, is utterly necessary to living. It is a source not only of inner conflict, but also the source of inner balance and brief attainment of harmony. There would be no life without contrast. When we are truly helping we confirm in the individual

with whom we are engaged the life and richness in his volatile feelings.

(2) The belief in the possibility of inner freedom, responsibility, and choice for every adult—in the potentiality for, not the existence of any of these states—is central to our theme. The prevalence of the two sides manifests itself here as elsewhere: i.e. the possibility, the promise, but the high risk that the possibility may be thwarted, constrained, only partially realized or not realized at all.

(3) Rank's contrast between knowing and experiencing comes ever home to our awareness. Experiencing in the present with fresh feeling and emotional understanding is the therapeutic factor that can change the pattern of the self, not in the sense that the pattern is made over, but in the sense that the interplay of will, impulse, and emotion find a new relation to living. To want to know too much is to constrict experience; to experience only without the pleasurable experience of understanding is equally a loss. The neurotic is one who tries by excessive pursuit of knowledge, certainty, and causation to control life, thereby to atrophy life, to lock it in stalemate.

(4) We come now to the proposition, that the individual must do it himself. It is his own utterance about himself, not the interpretation of the therapist, that is the key; without question every one of us, every individual, craves to shape, describe, project his own ideal of himself or his guilt for himself. "I willed it so." But at the same time the compelling opposite intrudes itself to recognition, must be recognized, heralded in the familiar quoted words of Rank, "the ego needs the thou." It takes an other, to find one's self. Speaking in very practical concrete terms, there can be no question but that in the process of growth one chooses the other as ideal, for aspiration, to be like, to make one's own self like, or one chooses for difference.

And this is as important for the growing child as is the matter of physical nourishment.

(5) Fifth and last, all of these psychological movements, the inner experience of finding the self, can take place only in a form, a gestalt, a process. Rank created this form out of himself as an individual therapist. But for many of us the form is the given, the reality of the setting in which we work, the deeply psychological, not superficial meaning of function. Movement is rhythmic, process that is truly process is rhythmic thereby sustaining and releasing the chance to rework experience, to search for understanding, to enunciate goals.

In summary I would thus say that these constitute the base on which we stand, (1) the two-sided nature of all living; (2) the acclaim of the creative will, that is, the emphasis upon capacity, responsibility and freedom in contrast to the sometimes prevalent view of man as the victim of early causation; (3) experiencing as the opposite of the effort to control life through knowledge, (4) the need to shape one's self from one's own ideal formation, even though the need for the other is inescapable, and (5) none of these movements of the self can occur except in form, in process.

★   ★   ★   ★

This brings me to the next point of departure, the matter of goals, and it is around and about the word "goal" that my thoughts now shape themselves. What can we say of goal, what reflections are stirred by putting the question to myself, do I have a goal or goals? Have I had them in the past and if so what can I say of their nature? And how can I feel the shaping of goal in the process of giving help to others? Goal is an important aspect of identity—of what Rank calls the self-ideal formation—of this there can be no doubt.

As I have thought about these questions I have been aware first of all of two kinds of goal: the first, a specific, concrete, actual, practical goal, accurately characterized as external, projected, usually realizable and providing accomplishment, the completed act of beginning and ending (of which I will have more to say when I come to speak of the search for form). This kind of goal may be trivial or serious, short time or long time, the outcome affecting life very little or very much, depending on the content. Some people wish for a certain kind of automobile, or a certain kind of house, or furnishings for the house and by a sequence of disciplined steps and acts of will they achieve what they are after. Or a young man for whom the opportunity is almost absent determines to have a college education whereupon he sets about to design a program and takes the disciplined steps to achieve his goal. Sometimes, but usually only for genius, the setting of a goal for a life's career is firmly fixed even in childhood. Agnes deMille declared at an early age, "I will be a dancer." Keats pronounced himself to be a poet. For most of us our deepest goal and purpose in life grows however in a very different way.

It seems to be true that there is an inner, organic, intuitive, non-verbal search for a goal. In some inner center of the self, without consciousness except at times, there is an impulsion that carries us in a certain direction. Certainly it must be true that man shares with all living matter, plant and animal, the impulse to survive, to follow its destiny, such as one sees in plant life where the plant puts out every effort to reinstate its living pattern. But for man who in contrast has intellect and knowledge, the obediance to the purely biological goal lessens, and the formation of goal becomes a matter of shaping an organization through the creative strivings of the will that bring impulse and emotion into harmony with these strivings. It is as if we move in accord with what we are, as if we feel our way along, as if we obey an inner destiny to which we yield willingly and at times with elation and delight.

Sometimes the goal may emerge solely from the unrest and dissatisfaction which characterizes the need for change: something must be different, we say. When this occurs, and a new goal shapes from it, every reason may be found to justify and confirm the goal, but at bottom it arose from the vapors of need to move, to change.

Once we have acknowledged this deep stream of a life that carries us in a direction, whose nature we cannot wholly grasp, we can leave it on behalf of affirming the essential part played by the external, short-time, specific goals in a life's course. This is the way by which it seems possible to pursue and reach long-time goals, by steps of little short-time goals when from one accomplishment the direction and content of the next step is revealed.

What I have said about goals thus far does not, as you well know, begin to touch the mysterious question, how the individual does in fact shape his own ideals, how he chooses growth if he does at all, what part the "other" plays in this process. This is the less well-known territory which we hope to explore.

* * * *

Now, in nearing the conclusion of what I have to say, I want to turn my attention and yours to the matter of *form,* of form in *motion,* which is process. And in order to limit myself in this vast subject, also giving rich inducement to thought and work, I have selected the time-phase of "ending" on which to comment briefly. The word "ending" has had a special meaning for those of us who have worked with, been helped by Rankian conceptions. Rank saw in ending the precipitant of the whole pattern of the self in its way of separating, giving or demanding, feeling or denial of feeling. We are accustomed to think mainly about the ending in a therapeutic process, or a helping process, or a learning process. I want to suggest to you another facet of ending.

It is this: the experience of ending, completion, finishing, occurs abundantly in many aspects of our ordinary living. The experience of completion is another aspect of living of which we can suitably say, it is vital. Any work that is creative, and any work that is simply ordinary, passes through a period of confusion, on the higher levels even of chaos, of unbounded, soaring, imaginative thought. The satisfaction that resides in the completion of a piece of work arises from the deepest psychological level, in that material has been shaped, given form, carried through a process, and finished. Whatever goes on continuously gets nowhere. It goes on and on without rising and falling, or ever coming to a head.

It seems to me that this has a vital connection with goal, but it would be beyond my reach at the moment to be able to make that connection. I can see that it lies in that interesting observation that the conclusion of one goal leads to another, and perhaps the most simple and meaningful part of goal-forming lies not in being able to say, "This is what I want of life" but instead, to be able to go on from one completed experience to another until goal shapes and direction forms in a way that could never be created by the intellect alone.

As I was in the very midst of working upon this topic, the search and the goal, there came in the mail the *Journal of Individual Psychology* in which the lead article is entitled "The Drive in Living Matter to Perfect Itself" by a biologist, Dr. Albert Szent-Gyoergyi, who works at the Marine Biological Laboratory, at Woods Hole. It is a superb article for our purpose and I hope if you are anywhere within reach of this periodical you will read it. I want to quote a few sentences from what he writes. He supposes "an innate 'drive' in living matter to perfect itself." "By drive I denote here simply the ability of life to maintain and improve itself. You know this from your daily life. You know well that if you use your car too much and your legs too little, your car gets worn out while your legs atrophy, just fade away. This is one of the most characteristic differences between the living and the non-living. The non-living is worn out by use, while the living is improved, developed by it. Life keeps life going, building up and improving itself, while inactivity makes it go to pieces." And further: "Things can be put together at random or in a meaningful way. In the latter case new qualities are developed. This is 'organization.' There are many levels of organization. Organization in living systems goes much farther than in non-living ones; hence the specific qualities of the former which are not found in the inanimate world. To understand life all levels of organization have to be studied. In the non-living rest preserves and function destroys. In the biosphere function builds and maintains, while the non-living systems degenerate in activity."

★ ★ ★ ★

Now I shall pause, to ask where does all of this leave us, to what does it point?

A few things that are more concrete I can say: that we hope to make this theme the direction for planning for the next meeting whenever that may be. We will be working unceasingly on these ideas. We think of you as teaching, counseling, giving casework service, helping in a therapeutic process; and we are enlivened by the thought of the meaning that could be found in this concrete and particular experience when illuminated by a focused topic.

Most important of all, we want to open the way for more individuals in our membership to take part in the program, to present their experience and to share in substantive discussions of content, of theory, of method.

Thus far the *Journal* is committed to enlarging its scope, that is, to go beyond Rank's interest in the philosophy of helping to his prevailing lifetime interest as expressed in the last paragraph of *Beyond Psychology:*

" This book is an attempt to picture human life, not only as I have studied it in many forms for more than a generation, but as I have achieved it for myself, in experience, beyond the compulsion to change it in accordance with any man-made ideology. Man is born beyond psychology and he dies beyond it but he can *live* beyond it only through vital experience of his own—in religious terms, through revelation, conversion, or re-birth. My own life work is completed, the subjects of my former interest, the hero, the artist, the neurotic appear once more upon the stage, not only as participants in the eternal drama of life but after the curtain has gone down, unmasked, undressed, unpretentious, not as punctured illusions, but as human beings who require no interpreter."

"As human beings who require no interpreter. . . ."

Thus in the very way I have traced the formation of small goals from which others grow, our way might be said to be wholly experimental, feeling our way along, not knowing any specific objective or having any prescribed way. What I have hoped to do was to awaken your interest in a topic, in a focus, and with this as a guide, we can move toward ever-increasing growth of the association and of your part in it.

RELATIONSHIP IN THE
HELPING PROCESS:
Listening and Response

After I had worded this title, "Relationship in the Helping Process: Listening and Response," I had many reactions to, and afterthoughts about, my own choice of a topic. I sat at my typewriter and wrote it down on a piece of paper and observed it as if the words were not my own and as if I were seeing them for the first time. And this happened because I had just come from reading the daily *New York Times,* and it could have been any day: What I was thinking was, what use, what place does a topic like this have in the world today, and who cares, or who will listen? The one-to-one relationship, and what goes on inside the one lone human being as he struggles just to keep alive, much less to grow, to endure the pain that development and self-responsibility entail—this I asked: How can it be heard?

But when Mr. Auman invited me to come to speak to you, an invitation which I accepted at once with pleasure—I had no trouble voicing the topic on which I would like to speak, because always what is most alive for anyone is what interests him most at the moment, what it is his mind and reverie and feeling are at work on. Always at the center of one's self, if one listens quietly, there is that center that holds the delicate quiet power of a magnet, to keep the self and the movements of the self located in a center that is reliable.

What I am interested in is "listening" and "response." To place these unlimited topics in a context of meaning I choose of course to locate them in the context of the helping process, because otherwise I could be talking about listening to the clerk at the supermarket, or to my neighbor tell about her roses, or to my accountant on the subject of a trial balance which I do not understand. All of these are interesting of course, because listening is the commonest of activities, hearing that one of our senses always in use. I listen to noise, to tenderly spoken words in a movie I have just seen, to ordinary speech, to rhythm, to sound imposed upon me against my will or to sound of my own choice.

But "listening" in the helping process, this is another matter again. And listening when helping involves two people, in a one-to-one relationship. It is a very special kind of relationship of which I will have more to say later.

But let me first return to Mr. Auman and his invitation to me to speak to you. When I asked him if there was any particular thing about which you wanted me to speak (I would try, whatever it was) he said, graciously accepting first my own interest, "they would like you to comment on the work of Jessie Taft as you knew her, what kind of person she was, what influence she had on Rank, etc." and later he added "about the ORA" (Otto Rank Association)—I said to him of course I would, and I added with a sweeping statement which even now on reflection is still true: within any topic that we would choose I can speak of Dr. Taft. And what I meant by this was: there are sentences uttered sometimes by someone somewhere that are like flashes of light in darkness, momentarily lighting up everything within range, and if human experience per se is within that range, it is lighted up. Dr. Taft was one who not infrequently uttered such sentences, and I do not intend to concede in any way that this is an overstatement.

So now as I begin to speak about, reflect upon, voice out loud my reverie about *listening,* I start with a memory that is brief, swift, exact. I can see the setting in Dr. Taft's office, I can feel my own strained fear. She was helping me as I was learning to help in individual conference. I must have said to her, often I did not know what to say in answer! I can recall the exact words she said to me, "You don't have to hear everything they say, nor respond to it. Just sit back in your chair and listen when you feel like it."

Now I am not quite sure that the last words are exact. The effect upon me was one of shock—her attitude was so casual, so uncommitted, so effortless. It was as if she was encouraging me to do something irresponsible, or at worst sloppy and lazy. Further, here was I in her office, sitting opposite her at her desk, there to be helped and to be listened to, yet she was handing out this advice. I have never forgotten, and the longer I live, the more I can embroider the truth of this with detail.

On the faculty of the University of Pennsylvania School of Social Work we *learned* to teach, and we were helped in a process, and our practice was the teaching of a class of demanding students. There never was a class that I approached as the time drew near, without fear, and never for a moment can I forget, either, Miss Robinson's sober observation, in order to do what we do we must remake ourselves afresh every day. When you teach what we were teaching you teach out of the stuff of yourself, and more and more this demands being able to use every shred of one's self, freely.

My experience of taking help in a process that demanded growth was in a function where the goal was specific: to become a teacher. And as you can see, this differs drastically from a process of therapy where there is no specific goal. And on this too I will have more to say.

I have known three people thus far in my lifetime of whom it seems to me it can be said, they are free to use the whole of themselves: Miss Robinson, Dr. Taft, and more recently in my acquaintance, Anais Nin who came to speak at the afternoon session of the ORA. "Free to use the Whole of One's Self" can scarcely be made more explicit—it is felt and sensed rather than defined. It is perhaps what we all wish for ourselves. It is not an outpouring—it is a use within a form in which the personal has acquired general meaning.

On the seventh of June it will be eight years since Dr. Taft's death. She was a teacher and therapist who, once encountered, was never forgotten. Everyone who knew her professionally says this of her; she was what she wrote, that is, there was an unmistakable wholeness and consistency between her work and her self. The most loved of her articles was perhaps "Living and Feeling," in which she acclaims the emotions and speaks that truth which many remember, namely, that the price of suppressing negative feeling is not to be able to feel at all. And contrary to all popular belief— or perhaps now becoming more and more popular—she urges parents to be *parents* not therapists. She was as good a therapist as she was because her feelings were as swift as lightning. But she carried a great responsibility on account of it, and I can remember with a twinge of poignant reminiscence, when I was admitting how angry I had become, she said, "the trouble is when you get angry you make yourself vulnerable."

Now, in these introductory remarks which still belong to my beginning, before I take the plunge and lure you or lead you into a forest of ideas, I must utter certain principles, or propositions, or truths taken-for-granted by me out of which I construct a kind of foundation or roadbed solid enough and reliable enough to let us take off into the "unknowns".

The first is that the word "will" is central to our thought. It is central in the psychology of Rank. It is central for me. It is central to relationship, whether is be the one-to-one relationship, or the relationship of teacher to class, or of people to their president, or of children to their neighbors. Recently I have read with great care and written a review of a book by Dr. Leslie Farber the title of which is *Ways of the Will,* and in it, in the opening pages, he is discussing therapy with the late renowned Dr. Martin Buber and he asks Dr. Buber what does therapy most need? And the answer Dr. Buber gave was, "a psychology of will" which is the first time I have every seen any written statement by a therapist or psychoanalyst, or psychiatrist, or psychologist, that an understanding of "will" is imperative.

Rank makes this fundamental statement about will: "What is naturally and spontaneously effective . . . therapeutically, is the same thing that is patent in every relationship between two human beings, namely the will."

In 1930 Miss Robinson called relationship "the most incomprehensible phenomenon in human development . . . of this tendency" she continued, "to seek relationship, of the characteristic pattern with which each chooses a one-person or a group relationship, of the uses which each makes of it, of its meaning to an individual, little has been said. Relationship has been taken for granted as the fundamental background and reality of human development."

Is this still true almost forty years later? Do we understand very much more now about relationship than was understood at the time Miss Robinson was writing? It does not seem to me that we do, in theoretical terms, and perhaps this is just as well, perhaps its very essence would be lost if we were able at last to understand what can very well be the secret of life itself. So I am not going about this with any intention to be logical or systematic or definitive: rather to be content with catching any wisp of truth that illuminates like a flash and is gone again. I have more opportunity now (than you may have in a busy demanding day) to scan the literature.

The only place I find flashes of truth about relationship is in novels or biography or autobiography. Here the human self is often revealed in its need for relationship and the way it goes about satisfying that need, and one can respond to and accept and say to it a "yes," I too know that it is this way.

Relationship in the helping process is a relationship both like and different from private personal relationship. At its best and when it really works, it is life intensified, more life rather than less, meanings that are more lucid, emotions that are richer and more powerful, and out of it all an exhilaration in an expanded sense of self that ordinary life seldom affords. But I think this can happen only if one really finds deep satisfaction and glow in the process of helping.

The *difference* between personal relationship and the helping relationship is crucial. Its essential nature is that it takes place within form, within boundaries. You may not agree with me when I stress the fact that relationship in the helping process is a controlled relationship, thus unlike private or personal relationships which in a way may be describable as having some limits, but actually not in the sense in which the word applied to the relationship in helping. In that book of Dr. Taft's which so many of us know and have used (it appeared in paperback a few years ago) the title of which is usually shortened to "The Dynamics of Therapy" the full title is "The Dynamics of Therapy in a *Controlled* Relationship"—and so indeed it is as one reads the two full records of process with children. But the word control in this sense is a very special sense, meaning form, limit, focus, development, growth. If one puts one's whole attention upon the word "growth" then one could scarcely need any proof or any argument to establish the fact that psychological growth, like biological growth, can occur only within a form. What is controlled in this relationship, however, is not the client or patient, who is left even more free because of the form within which he is working; nor is it control of the self in the sense of caution and restraint. The control lies in the depth of knowledge of process and its phases and the experiences that are common but also always fresh in its unfolding. Nothing is more restrictive of freedom than no boundary, no limit anywhere. We would each have to search within our own experience to find any evidence of truth in what I have just said.

Lastly I want to say a word about the applicability of my remarks to those who are recognized to be mentally ill, because I shall be speaking throughout without any dividing line between those who are more or less "normal" and those who may be suffering from some pathology. And this is because I believe that at bottom the same insights, the same sense of process, the same considerations about growth, and certainly the expressions of the will, bear a likeness whether we are speaking about the average or the extremes. In this same book to which I have already referred Dr. Farber draws most of his illustrations regarding the ways of the will from his experience with schizophrenic patients but even as he does so he continues always to draw general observations that, as he says, apply to all of us.

I take it for granted then that you will know that I am speaking about growth, psychological growth, assuming it to be at the heart of our goal. For in the average span of life the demand is always on us to grow or stagnate; and for the individual who is sick, his turn away from illness toward more life is an event of growth.

Now I turn my attention to the word and the act of listening. And find as I might have known that the only way I can approach it is to ask myself, how does it feel to me when I am listening when I am working in process with someone? I grasp at the first idea that occurs to me and it is: that when I am genuinely listening I am listening with my whole self. Not the ears alone or the intellect alone, but with attention that seems almost impenetrable. Now as you will readily see, by this remark I am jumping to the end of our reflections, because it is the point I might make in forming a conclusion at the end. And in a way it is a strange thing to say; it is as if attention becomes and is the whole. Heightened attention, yet in a way inattentive. My version of what Dr. Taft meant by her comforting remark was just this tantalizing combination of attention and inattention that can be the most genuine kind of relationship.

No doubt you know the book called "Listening with the Third Ear" of which I have never read a line, but the title plagues me because I dislike it so. Its implications are that one detects, uses a device unknown to and unseen by the other, as if you must secretly discover what it is the person means, not what he is actually saying. Moreover, it gives first place to observation, by eye and whatever the third ear is, in order to do what? To study and know the other in his essence because *you* find it and discover it, not that he willingly reveals it to you. It seems to me the title of this book stands for the very opposite of what true listening can be.

In the early phase of working on this paper (in what is normally referred to as the "pencil sharpening" stage) I took a look at Webster's Unabridged and there I found a phrase much more to my liking. The Anglo-Saxon root of to listen, is "to wait in suspense." I entertain this notion happily: "to wait in suspense."

One must remember that in genuine listening the start is always "cold" in any single interview, more so of course at the start of the process. One of the features of process is that listening becomes ever more possible because relationship is developing and recurrences appear in utterances in which one begins to feel changes, contradictions, advances and back slidings. The coldness in the start of any process, whether in a single interview or a series of interviews, is what one learns to live with and constitutes perhaps one of the factors in the "control" of the process. That is, one is responsible (not the client) for keeping matters moving even though for some dark moments it seems neither of you is getting anywhere.

As best I can get to it, interest is the key word and not a very original word at that! It seems to me that at the peak of listening there is fervent interest of the kind that very little on the outside can disturb. But what this interest is, is again a matter of tantalizing concern. I must first say what it is not: It is not a sentimental optimistic remark about "people"— how interesting they are, how I like "to work with them" and how in the long run they all mean well. At times everyone is a bore starting first of all with myself being a bore to myself. And many people are so a good part of the time. Mark too, that boredom is the death of the helping process, and, if you will not take me too seriously or too totally, I can try hearing myself say: in fact the growth process is one by which one dispels boredom.

Neither do I think that what is at the heart of interest is a collector's instinct in learning and proving certain facts about human nature—a study, for instance, to which these painful struggling facts of human existence which he is bringing to you are fitted into a psychological theory. I think I believe that if this interest in theory is the central interest, then there can be no true interest in the sense in which I mean it.

Now let me see if I can convey to you what I do feel lies at the heart of listening: it is the being part of a search—he is searching for some key that will unlock some unused portion of his life and he is more able to do it in your presence, because of what you are and how you are and the fact that he wants to make it plain to you. Do not minimize the importance of wanting to make something plain to another: not that he does not at the same time and at bottom want to make it plain to himself. But the chances are he would not or could not do it alone.

This brings me to the threshold of consideration: what is he searching for and why is he there? The most usual answer might be, to define his problem and find a better solution to his problem. Well yes, that is part of the story, but to me an increasingly small part. What he is trying to get to is the definition of himself, or, better said he is painting a portrait of himself, in words, and in this way is hopefully finding a sense of self more than he has had.

As best I can get to it, there is a magnetic quality about an individual who starts on a new attempt (to discover) who he is, to shape himself as he wills it to be. I say a "new attempt" because from birth he has been trying to do this and succeeding or not succeeding in a variety of ways. But when he comes in this very special way that is in process, with a caseworker or therapist, and within a form set up wholly for him, then something can indeed happen, and it is like standing on the threshold of an event or a series of events. And what one does one's self can effect the outcome. In this configuration there is life, excitement in the best sense of the word, suspense, risk, unknowns, everything that is the opposite of being cut and dried. It is boredom, emptiness, the static, the fixed, that is the worst of all, and anything that breaks this open is welcomed with open arms.

So I would say that when I listen it is with interest and interest gives birth to attention, and attention can narrow and become single in its purpose.

Simply stated, I think it is my interest that awakens his energy to do more with it.

Sometimes I have put to the person with whom I am working the question: do you know or do you remember what it was like for you when you were very young—as an infant or a very young child? Do you have the sense of having been loved and cared for, or is it the opposite? In my experience, almost at once the response is animated and the reflective answer comes easily or at least not willfully withheld. My purpose is not to interpret or diagnose overdependence, desertion, that characterized the mother child relationship, but how it felt to him: for the past lives on in this sense of union and separation, and the pattern of how one moves through these experiences is a mobile pattern throughout life: not a determinative controlling factor, but a dynamic changing pattern.

But how it felt to me *then* is precious—it is part of what we mean when we say that in order to have identity today one must possess, contain, carry forward the parts of identity that existed way back then. The satisfying quality is not that the experience was good or bad, but in getting the image clear.

Which brings me to one last point in this part of my remarks: there seems always to be at least one spot in one's past experience that one works and reworks in order to get the image clear. Not only is it unnecessary but hampering to anticipate that *all* parts of one's past have to be made conscious if one is to be "cured." Surely everyone must see by now that this is interminable—that it truly is infinite in the human imagination even though repetitious.

If the individual remembers and reconsiders and sees new light on what up to now has been hidden in denial, he will have a sense of new release. And the reason he is able to do it is that now, something in his willing, his emotion, his relationship to you the helping person, perhaps at the bottom of it all the continuity of the process, has enabled him to do now what he was not able to do before.

I see a new emphasis in the goal of helping—to enable this individual to paint the portrait of himself, and of course this will include if he really gets to it, both the bad and the good. I have thought so much and spoken so much about the two-sided nature of all living that I tire of my own words. But the other day as I was working on this I opened my favorite paperback edition of William James and I happened to turn to a page where he was writing on this very subject, and there I stumbled on his use of Goethe to make his point (this from *Faust*) "two souls dwell within his breast." I refer again to Dr. Farber's book *Ways of the Will* where, also, I recently found a passage of illumination on this point. He says in essence that the therapist is likely to suffer from standards of "perfectibility" that creep into his intentions. If we believe man to be perfectible then he is forever striving toward a goal not only impossible but clearly undesirable. Writes Farber:

> When man believes in his perfectibility, he experiences his own real being almost as a disease, a fatal sickness whose cure—perfection—seems unattainable for himself....
>
> Man knew himself to be an imperfect creature, and his own imperfectibility was as esstential to his definition of himself as were the sins that he committed, the temptations that raged in his heart, the virtues that he honored, the faith or hope that he cherished.
>
> History, literature, philosophy—all of which have not only always recognized human imperfectibility but have constantly warned man against the grave dangers of believing himself perfectible.

I want above everything when I am helping to enable the individual to discover in a moment of time, what he wants to be and to do. The pitfall lies in the two extremes: reaching too high, or not reaching high enough. Both are ways to avoid the reality of discipline and responsibility. The one lets the imagination and the illusion be the satisfaction, the latter fears the work, the dedication, the fear that is involved.

Out of all of this I have shaped an idea that animates my own thought; it is this: that to work toward the verbal expression of the creative strands of the self must take precedence over the continuous work on "problem." Those who come to us for help may indeed be entangled in problem. But they may also be there because they are experiencing the first stirrings of the need to grow, the phase of distress and echo of the desperate words "something has to change; something must be different." And you cannot tell in advance which it is, nor do you need to know, for the actuality will emerge, and will reveal itself. But I become more and more convinced that the problem area is only the portal, the entry to the first phase of a road that is cleared week in and week out culminating at last in the affirmation of a new sense of self.

Process has above all else rhythm, and rhythm spells continuity and development. It works because it is a segment of life heightened and intensified where emotion is real, not spurious, and because it is at the same time a segment of life designed especially for this purpose. During the time when we are working in interview with someone who has come for help, we are listening in a way that is exclusively for him, and for the first time perhaps he knows that he is *heard*.

TWO REALMS OF THE WILL: SEPARATE OR PHASES IN A PROCESS?

A Review of *The Ways of the Will* by Leslie H. Farber. Basic Books, 1966.

The first important book in recent times to grapple with the problem of will begins with this sentence, "Often a man can become absorbed by a radical issue long before he knows its name." The issue that compelled the author's attention was "the problem of will in human affairs." Only years later when reading an essay by Allen Tate, and still later in talk with Dr. Martin Buber, did he see and name the central core of his interest. Putting to Dr. Buber the question, what does the future hold for psychotherapy (what does it most need?), Dr. Buber answered "a psychology of will."

When first reading these opening pages of the preface my reaction was a mixture of surprise, shock, and delight. The delight arose like a silent burst of applause. The surprise and disbelief were occasioned by the almost incredible revelation that neither Dr. Buber nor Dr. Farber seemed to know that a psychology of will already existed—whether or not they agreed with its basic conceptions was beside the point.

Some five or six pages later the partial answer to this puzzling question appears. Having stated his observation that will is ignored in psychology and psychotherapy Dr. Farber pauses to say "Because he would seem to be the exception, some mention must be made here of Otto Rank." Whereupon he disposes of Rank in two pages of misconception so gross as to be shocking.[1]   One sentence alone reveals the distortion: "Rank regarded will as a life force, muffled and dampened by the moralities of religion that reduced man to guilt and impotence."

Yet, despite this perfunctory treatment of Rank, this is an extraordinarily valuable and absorbing book. I have read every word of it with care, have found in it that rare and happy encounter that starts thought racing. To understand will as I claim to know it from long years of study and teaching (to say nothing of experience with my own will and the will of others) demands content strong and authentic to stand up to the searching examination that the theory of the will can give it. This Dr. Farber's book does—it sustains itself throughout with the ring of truth and he can be forgiven because of what he *has* done without reproaching him for what he has not done. For anyone interested in the will psychology this book allures with enrichment. The style has genuine literary quality—brilliant, moving, witty to the point of cutting satire.

Note must be taken at once that Dr. Farber makes no claim to having constructed a psychology of will. He speaks of these chapters as "Essays toward a Psychology and Psychopathology of the Will"; *toward,* not yet arrived. Not that any sensible psychology ever would claim to have arrived, but in a special sense these are essays "toward." The very word he selects for his title, "ways" of the will, is suggestive, accurate, discriminating, also indicative of a frame of mind, as if to say, let us see where this takes us.

[1] It seems to be a valid observation that when writing psychologically, from the interior of the author's own experience, he must inevitably start *de novo,* pushing everything else aside lest it get in the way of his own as yet elusive thoughts. Such thoughts must be coaxed and welcomed without outer noise or interference. Farber himself says something like this later on in another connection: "This is why we counsel the young writer to have his own full say before he resorts to bibliography"; and, it is: "Only after a prolonged acquaintance with an author that the man himself will begin to emerge somewhat from his work."

Accepting as the reader must this condition of exploration and going as a willing participant into the searching, pursuing, tentative nature of this course, he may have no ground to expect or ask for a sudden clear assertion. Yet a recurrent exasperation occurs because Dr. Farber, seeing so much, suddenly fails to see (or at least to express) what he himself has conjured up, what is crystal clear before his very eyes.

What I miss is the strong sweep of a declaration that accepts the will, that accords to it its vital role in every human life. It is as if Farber walks up to the very edge, then backs away—and cannot quite say it. One finishes the book with the hovering impression that the will is a disorder, that its expressions are pathological, its strength destructive (as indeed it can be). Echoes of words ring in one's ears: the isolated will, the distention of the will, the will pursuing its tyrannical course. How, one might ask, could it be otherwise since Dr. Farber is after all a psychotherapist, his content (whatever else it may also be) is richly and abundantly the content of the schizophrenic and hysteric. So this is naturally the world in which he finds his illustration, always dramatic, always true to life, always stimulating. But the will in his pages remains tainted with the implication that something is other than it ought to be.

Yet if the question were put, does Dr. Farber in fact realize the will as belonging to the human condition, the answer (from the evidence in this book) must certainly be "yes." He is writing about all of us including himself. He does not hesitate to say this "is the lot of each of us. The temptations of the will beset us all." One of the charms of the book (and it is like a charm) is the magnetic power of his descriptions of the human condition, finely traced, emotionally precise: of pity, of envy, of despair, of the willful conversationalist. In his devastating, satiric portrayal of the research which attempts to bring sex into the laboratory, he achieves his purpose by wit and brilliant intensification of incongruities, bordering on the sensational. His account of the "candidate" undergoing analysis in the discipline of becoming an analyst is not only candid and genuine (also tinged with his own style of humor) but revelatory to any one who has been through the experience of learning to help while giving help to others.

It is this quality of candor that is so winning and disarming. He never engages in that dissection of the other, the patient, ad nauseum, to which so much psychoanalytic and psychological literature is devoted. He is writing, there can be no doubt, from the center of himself; about the therapist and the therapeutic encounter, from the side of the therapist which is after all "his" side. By this one factor alone, and others too, he shows beyond doubt that he is animated by the principle that to know the other, to respond accurately to the other, one must know one's self.

Nevertheless, despite all that has been said arguing for the fact that Farber *does* give welcome to the will as part of the human condition, it seems to carry always the taint of what is reprehensible. This may be altogether a result of comparison with Rank who heralds the will, the "conscious creative activity of will" and who strides ahead with declaration: "What is naturally and spontaneously effective . . . therapeutically, is the same thing that is patent in every relationship between two human beings, namely the will." Then Rank looks squarely at the fact of the universal resistance to "the acceptance of will as a psychological factor of the first rank" and asks,

> "Why must will be denied if it actually plays so great a role in reality . . . Why is the will valued as bad, evil, reprehensible, unwelcome, when it is the power which consciously and positively, yet even creatively, forms both the self and the environment?"

If you know Rank's work you know that he asked "why" not to find a cause to be eradicated for purposes of cure, but in order to understand the dynamics of the experience.

In a number of important respects, Rank and Farber work from the same base, although in very different ways. At the heart of Farber's thought is the proposition that "will is the mover of life in a given direction"; so too for Rank man's creative strivings lie in his "inexhaustible willing." "If the will is affirmed and not negated or denied, there results the life instinct, and happiness, like salvation, is found in life and experience, in the creation and acceptance of both without having to ask how, whither, what and why." Both men feel the two-sided character of will: Farber who works with what he calls the two realms of the will, Rank for whom the duality appears as will and counter will. Rank's theory is developed far beyond the points at which Farber's book stops: for example his conceptions of fear, of guilt, of the totality for which man strives, of the excessive effort to control life by knowledge, of the process by which the negative will is transformed to positive expression.

Yet the very difference in Dr. Farber's book is what makes it rich and stimulating, namely, the actuality of experience. His pages overflow with particulars of life and drama, and his portrayal of the two realms of the will, the contrast that sharpens the differences, is brilliantly drawn:

> "I can will knowledge but not wisdom; going to bed, but not sleeping, eating but not hunger; meekness but not humility; scrupulosity but not virtue; self-assertion or bravado, but not courage; lust, but not love; commiseration, but not sympathy; congratulations but not admiration; religiosity, but not faith; reading but not understanding."

He makes this observation: "The problem of will lies in our recurring temptation to apply the will of the second realm to those portions of life that not only will not comply, but that will become distorted under such coercion." It is clear that for Farber the first realm carries the highest good; life in the first realm is organic, silently strong, in motion, unwillful, unselfconscious, the "mover of life." Will in the second realm "a necessary nuisance" is conscious of itself, felt as a thrust, felt as isolated will, pushing, commanding, demanding, assertive, controlling. He quotes Yeats: "the will trying to do the work of the imagination."[2]

Let us return to the passage just quoted and lift from this the word "coercion" for the purpose of examining further the meaning of the two realms of the will. There are certain portions of life, says Farber, that can be experienced only within the will of the first realm (some examples have already been quoted); but coerced by the will of the second realm these coveted experiences vanish, and the more they elude our grasp, the more willful becomes the effort to force them to do our bidding. We try to "will what cannot be willed" and there lies the core of the problem.

The image that shapes itself in visual abstraction is an image of two realms prevailing side by side, one of which is over-used, spawning willfulness and force. But another kind of image suggests itself; would it not be more accurate to conceive of the realms as following each other as phase follows phase, as passages in a process, movement from one to the other by which higher levels are reached?

In my experience it is impossible to reach the realm of the will where the self is whole and productive without passing

---

[2] The difficulty in using a word such as "will" in so many different ways is illustrated here. Undoubtedly Yeats in this observation was thinking of will as force—what we sometimes must express by "pure will" or "willful." Yet truly creative will—the self when in possession of all its faculties, as illustrated for example by the superb figure-skating of Miss Fleming at the Winter Olympics,—*is* imagination as it is also impulse, emotion, form, discipline, "wedded" as Farber later uses the term, into creation.

through earlier more willful steps.[3] Let me try to make my meaning clear by use of one of Farber's illustrations, reading (which can be willed), understanding (which cannot). The start of difficult reading always demands the application of some will at the beginning—willful if you please. A discipline is imposed upon the self because a more or less distant goal—to understand—is strong enough for whatever reason to yield one's self to the discipline. I cannot reach the first realm where I find luminosity, movement, exhilaration, understanding—in short a kind of wholeness of self—unless I go through the essential steps that belong to the more willful realm. Feeling the experience thus one would speak not of the "problem" of the will, but of the "dynamics" of the will or by whatever other motion-word one prefers.

Dr. Farber's deepest concern, there can be no doubt, is with that stage of being which can only be described as "wholeness," vague and unsatisfactory as that term may be. We all know what it is when we feel it. Valery, the French poet, has a happy phrase that describes the condition as one of "humming at the center." We all know too what Farber means when he voices "the urgency we all feel to experience wholeness . . . so vital to our lives." But his attention is so powerfully drawn to the description of the ways by which will tries to force the feeling of wholeness that he leaves incomplete any consideration of the varied ways in which the creative will does succeed in finding wholeness. His interest is caught in what he calls "the feverish exertion of will" as it seeks to create "the illusion of wholeness forcibly grasped rather than gained or granted."

The detail by which he traces the efforts of the will to achieve spurious wholeness is finely drawn and comes from the depth of a rich sensibility. If pressed to characterize the age in which we

[3] One of the most interesting treatments of the passage through phases is that of William James in an essay entitled "The Energies of Men" now available in a Cardinal paperback (*Great Essays,* #C-113). "The normal opener of deeper and deeper levels of energy is the will. The difficulty is to use it, to make the effort which the word volition implies."

live he would (although disliking labels) call it "the age of the disordered will." The disability of the will is the rift within the self of man—the rift between the will and its object, as a result of which he tries to heal the split by an act of will—an attempt doomed to failure. In his effort to win unity, man tries many ways, among them the use of drugs which "offer the illusion of healing the split between the will and its refractory object. The resulting feeling of wholeness may not be a responsible one, but at least within that wholeness . . . there seems to be, briefly and subjectively, a responsible and vigorous will."

It seems to me that the only passage in this book (aside from the introductory pages dealing with the first realm of the will) where Farber's attention is irresistibly drawn toward description of the state of being that is the genuine feeling of wholeness occurs in the chapter "Will and Anxiety." But even here as we shall see, he writes in the subjunctive mood: it might be or it could be or it would be, not, *is*:

> "At the same time that our lives are occupied by deliberate efforts of the will, toward both appropriate and inappropriate ends, with or without drugs we suffer a mounting hunger for a sovereign and irreducible will, so wedded to our reason, our emotions, our imagination, our intentions, and our bodies that, only after a given enterprise has come to an end, can we retrospectively infer that will was present at all. In other words, within such totality, will, being unconscious, would not be a matter of experience, even though we might later try to portray the essence of the enterprise as one in which we wished with our whole heart or willed with all our being. The predominant experience within this realm would be one of freedom, as opposed to the bondage of the isolated will. The goal of will within this realm would be one of direction rather than of specific object or achievement, although naturally the

course of this will would be dotted inconspicuously by such concrete items. Never a permanent state and always limited in duration, it would give way over and over again to the more self-conscious will with which we are necessarily more familiar."

What is this mounting hunger of which he speaks? Hunger for "a sovereign and irreducible will" through which if I read Farber correctly, the longing for totality is satisfied. Indeed, there can be no doubt of the truth of this observation: the experience of willing is pleasurable, satisfying, exhilarating. At the moment when the will is victorious, "sovereign" given full rein, it satisfies a special hunger even if the result is a Pyrrhic victory, or even if destruction is its goal.

My quarrel with Farber is, that he seems to see the healing of "the split" "the rift" (within the self) in only one way,[4] whereas in truth the ways in which the will satisfies the hunger for the feeling of wholeness are many and extraordinarily rich. The very opposite of the "sovereign" will is the will in surrender —not captured, but willingly yielding itself whether to an other, or to the human condition, or to the nature of the materials or circumstances with which it works. The result is a comforting wholeness. There is wholeness that forms slowly within the interior of the self alone, as for instance in the process of effective work, physical or mental. There is wholeness in unity between one's self and the environment; (spring is in the air and spring is in myself.) There is (to touch all too briefly on a very complex subject) unity in relationship where neither will is "sovereign."

In dwelling thus upon a need and its satisfaction, the implica-

[4] Consider, too, in this connection the following sentence: "The more dependent a person becomes in this illusion of wholeness the less he is able to experience true wholeness in dialogue, and at the point where he is no longer capable of dialogue, he can be said to be *addicted* to his will," which would seem to imply that "true wholeness" is to be found in dialogue, when the will presumably would be harmoniously united with "emotion, reason, imagination, intention, body."

tion is unavoidable that what we have been speaking of as "the feeling of wholeness" satisfies a vital hunger. Even the brief but deeply satisfying experience of elation comes not from division but unity. How one-sided, if we permit it to remain so! The feeling of oneness, of totality cannot last very long, nor can any act of will sustain it beyond a brief period.

For the direction of all growth, painful as the thought may be, is toward individuation and individuation produces separation. Farber quotes Buber: "Mankind's great chance lies precisely in the unlikeness of men, in the unlikeness of their qualities and inclinations."—a psychology of difference. Yet the attribute hardest to bear in the human condition is difference.

It does not seem to me that Farber introduces soon enough nor thoroughly enough, that special quality of the will which is its capacity for change: both changeableness which is transitory and swift or slow, not really producing change; and development which is in a direction and irreversible. The will craves unity and finds it; the will craves separation and produces it, thus finding its own painful way to fulfill the essence of its being.

* * *

The question finally frames itself: what is Dr. Farber at last saying in this book—is there a clear thrust of focus, problem, proposition, that emerges at the end? The answer lies again in his title: he seems content to have portrayed with luminosity some ways of the will and in so doing to have thrown momentary light on certain obscure areas of the human condition. Take for instance his last chapter "Perfectibility and the Psychoanalytic Candidate." What is he saying about "perfectibility"? The illusion of perfectibility of man is not only false but corrosive and creeps slyly but unacknowledged into the goal of therapy.

What he has to say about this subject, as of others, is fresh and original, not a repetition of a rather tiresome plaint, "Being human I admit I cannot be perfect." Instead, he welcomes the imperfectibility of man as a condition of his humanity. "When man believes in his perfectibility, he experiences his own real being almost as a disease, a fatal sickness whose cure—perfection —seems unobtainable." Then Farber turns for confirmation to other sources (art, literature, philosophy, etc.): "all of which have not only always recognized human imperfectibility, but have constantly warned man against the grave dangers of believing himself perfectible."

Grave danger, indeed, for "man knew himself to be an imperfect creature and his own imperfectibility was as essential to his definition of himself as were the sins that he committed, the temptations that raged in his heart, the virtues that he honored, the faith or hope that he cherished."

Farber returns in his final words to the recurrent theme "we must remind ourselves that, though imperfect, we may still become whole." The "heresy of perfectibility" he says, destroys "our potentiality for wholeness."

The whole of this book can be read as a discussion of the practical problems faced by the therapist, and if read in this way, many useful thoughts are imbedded in his pages: on the fallacy of man's "immodest effort 'to know' rather than to 'imagine' what the patient in his essence is"; of the distortions of science when applied to man, of the value of facing one's own despair, of the need in every helping person for confirmation. For seeing the collision of wills in therapy there could be no better illustrations, starting even with Freud's famous case of "Dora."

But if one reads this book on this level its essential quality will be missed. Once its content penetrates to the inner experience of the reader, the impression is inescapable that this book is, in Farber's own words, "enacted somewhat larger than life," expanding the ordinary insights of daily living into new perspectives.

AN ILLUSTRATION OF THE
EXPERIENCE OF CHANGE AS SEEN
IN CONRAD'S *SECRET SHARER**

The novel which I have chosen to discuss to illustrate the experience of change is Conrad's *Secret Sharer*, a short novel less than fifty pages, a taut, exciting tale of adventure. It can be read as I imagine it often is and as I read it first myself, for the suspense, the danger, as the reader is swept forward in mounting emotion and tension. It can also be read for the spell it casts, of pure enchantment, as one is carried away by Conrad's exquisite word pictures.

My interest in this novel however is in the portrayal of the inner experience, the sense of movement, of relationship, and the authentic portrayal of growth in the course of which a young man who is, when the story opens, "a stranger to himself" takes at the end, in five short days, full command and possession of himself, his ship, and his crew; but not until he has risked his ship, his life and the life of others.

I recall Professor Guerard's words in the passage quoted in our program: if we are moved by a novel, our emotions stirred, if we have given way to its enchantment, we are not the same again. I have no difficulty believing this although I do not altogether understand it. I know that one common interest which holds us together in this room is our shared interest in understanding what we call "human nature"—understanding in the partial way open to us the movements and process of living. And

* Paper delivered at the meeting of The Otto Rank Association, held on October 25, 1969, in Doylestown, Pennsylvania.

[261]

this is singularly true of those who are engaged in the helping professions.

Theory formation, important as it is, is bound to be static, cerebral, devoid of emotion. We try through theory to study emotion unemotionally only to find as we soon do that this is doomed to destroy the very quality we are attempting to understand. Thus it is not surprising that we have turned to literature —the novel, the short story, and autobiography—for examining the meaning of will, impulse, change; in the work of art the experience can live and grants us lucid insights that would escape us if we pursued them through definition.

In Rank's conception the artist, by which as you know he meant not exclusively the painter but every personality of creative tendencies, is an individual of richer emotion, more intense conflict, and heightened consciousness; and this abundance he soon discovers cannot be lived out in real life. Consequently the creative personality transforms the chaos of his inner life into forms that convey the inner meanings. What art creates is intensely real not because it is a faithful facsimile of life as it is, but because it *selects* and heightens and shapes truths that are hidden in the clutter of everyday living. Whereupon it follows that those of us who lend ourselves to following the artist's meaning recognize what he is saying and are thereby enriched.

The story opens in the early evening of a hot sultry day on board an English ship anchored in the Gulf of Siam, where the ship waits for a wind to start it on its long homeward journey. On deck with his hand on the rail is the young captain whose name we do not know, who tells the tale in the first person. Utterly alone he feels the immense stillness, the solemnity of perfect solitude, no human habitation visible as far as the eye can reach.

He has been on board only a brief two weeks; it is his first command. He is the stranger; all the others have been on the same ship together as a crew. It is clear at the beginning that he is neither in possession of himself as yet nor in command of his ship—alien, disconnected, isolated. We find him measuring his fitness as he reflects about himself and his ship:

"In this breathless pause at the threshold of a long passage we seemed to be measuring our fitness for a long and arduous enterprise, the appointed task of both our existences to be carried out, far from all human eyes, with only sky and sea for spectators and for judges."

The action begins at midnight when the captain again alone on deck, having himself taken on the night watch in order to give his crew some rest (which in itself was not what a captain should do) hears a slight movement in the otherwise silent water. Peering into the darkness he sees at the bottom of a rope ladder an exhausted swimmer who climbs aboard. We soon learn that the swimmer has escaped from another vessel anchored miles away, where as chief mate he killed a seaman in the height of a raging storm. His name we know: his name is Leggatt.

The dramatic encounter between these two men springs up at once: "A mysterious communication was established already between these two." Stealthily the captain clothes him in a sleeping suit, gray-striped, identical with his own, and at once he senses the identity, the likeness, the double of himself, his "other" self.

For five days, with mounting tension and increasing risk, the captain conceals Leggatt in his cabin. Although there is some indication that the crew suspects, his presence is never actually discovered; but the concealment succeeds only through excruciating attention to every move, in order that the steward may clean the cabin as he always has done. In extraordinary ways the captain and Leggatt sense the intentions of each other, and each moves in such a way that through every perilous moment when discovery seems unavoidable they manage to preserve their secret, but not without mounting suspicion of the captain by his men.

At the end of the story Leggatt leaves the ship as he came, by jumping into the sea at midnight, swimming away to unknown shores. At the moment of departure, despite all the dangers he faces, he is nevertheless "a free man, a proud swimmer, striking out for a new destiny."

At the same time he leaves behind on board a captain who likewise is symbolically "a free man, a proud swimmer" who now is indisputably in command. For the captain, in order to take his ship close enough to land for the escaping seaman, orders it into reckless proximity to these unknown islands, causing his officers and his crew to cry out in fear and protest. But the captain staunchly stays by his command, the crew obeys, and by the miraculous appearance of a white object in the water the captain is enabled to gauge the movement of the wind, the water, and the ship, and thus is able to guide it to safety. The white object is in itself a magical symbol—it is a hat which the captain gave to his second self to protect him from the sun.

Now, upon this bare sketch of the plot, and with the help of Conrad's own words, I should like to construct briefly the psychological movement in this novel as I see it.

Of the two men, it is the captain who experiences the dramatic change. This is after all his story—Leggatt is the secondary character, the double, the other self. What is this change experienced by the Captain, and how did it come about? He tells it in his own words. At the beginning he says:

> "What I felt most was my being a stranger to the ship; and if all the truth must be told, I was somewhat a stranger to myself . . ."
> "I wondered how far I should turn out faithful to that ideal conception of one's own personality every man sets up for himself secretly."

But at the end, these are his triumphant words when the peril was clearly over and the swimmer on his way:

"Already the ship was drawing ahead. And I was alone with her. Nothing! No one in the world should stand now between us, throwing a shadow on the way of silent knowledge and mute affection, the perfect communion of a seaman with his first command."

I have a great reluctance to analyze the meaning, preferring for myself the experience of being moved, of subtle instantaneous recognition and understanding. Once two years ago when Miriam Waddington was on this platform she used the words "shimmering ambiguity" and I have remembered them and treasured them ever since. For it is in a sense the shimmering ambiguity of the whole tale that bewitches us.

Yet I will try, for there is as well great satisfaction in giving form to one's own feeling. It is as if this novel confirms the conceptions in which I believe, whose source is of course in Rank's psychology: concepts (as you will recognize) having to do with likeness and difference, union and separation, and at the apex, the birth of individuality.

One can ask whether this is indeed "real" for life: the time so short, the change so dramatic. Of course it is not real for life, but the dynamics are real, the phases of the experience to my mind authentic.

In this short span of time a powerful relationship is at once present, built upon likeness, identification. "It was in the night," says the captain, "as if I had been faced by my own reflection." All the particulars enhance this impression of a reflection of the self. Yet what I find altogether tantalizing is the prevalence of difference, for on rereading we discover that the captain finds in Leggatt those qualities which he feels to be lacking in himself: Leggatt is calm, resolute, perfectly self-controlled,—most of all "invulnerable," the very opposite of what the captain himself feels. He says it thus: "The self-possession of the man had somehow induced a corresponding state in myself."

They are united not only in this strange identity, but because everything external is against them, or so it feels to the captain:

"The Sunday quietness of the ship was against us; the stillness of air and water around us was against us; the elements, the men were against us—everything was against us in our secret partnership; time itself—for this could not go on forever."

For Leggatt, the precipitant of the change is in his whispered outcry, "You understood thoroughly. Didn't you . . ." and he adds as he is about to leave, "It's very wonderful."

This outcry of a troubled human being "you have understood me" is deeply moving. But there is a danger that we will hear and accept it on too shallow a level, almost superficially, or even worse, sentimentally. If it stays on the level merely of being sided with, being on my side, then it is indeed shallow and on first reading one might gather this from the story. Because what the captain in content *has* understood is that Leggatt although he had indeed killed a man, had killed a brute who threatened the safety of the entire ship; by his act he, Leggatt, did indeed save the ship and substitute for an inept captain.

But it does not satisfy me to leave it on this content level, for the meanings are far more complex; there is a way of "being understood" that sweeps under all content and is to be found in some complex way in recognition, confirmation, assent. But I will leave this here for you to ponder at your leisure if it interests you. It was indeed on this that Leggatt willingly departed, separated, to what future he could not know.

One might ask, what meaning does all this have in a contemporary world, so divided, distracted, and often rent by force? To each of us it will have a different meaning, if any at all. But to me it shapes into words that aspect of living about which I care most, namely the talent and development of the individual self, which, needless to say, demands discipline, aloneness, and pain. That aspect of the Conrad novel which I have not mentioned, and not by oversight, is the mythical belief which Jung fully developed and which is implicit, that every man in order to grow must somehow be tested, must risk his life in order to gain it. Perhaps this is the underlying theme of Conrad's meaning.

REVIEW OF *LOVE AND WILL*

Love and Will, by Rollo May. W. W. Norton & Co., New York, 1969.

I approached the writing of this review of Rollo May's book with pleasurable anticipation. Twice I had been in the audience at meetings of the American Association of Existential Psychology and Psychiatry where I heard Dr. May read papers on subjects that form chapters of his book. Responsive, I listened with mounting interest, with recognition, and the pleasurable experience of a spontaneous "yes" with the gratitude that accompanies it. Later his book appeared. A start on reading and reviewing had to be postponed, and in the meantime I heard Dr. May speak on television presenting some of the same ideas. This only served to increase the positive feeling with which I began to read.

I liked his title, his assertion that "love and will are interdependent and belong together." I liked his Foreword and identified with his early morning reverie:

> During the long summers in New Hampshire when this book was being written I would often get up early in the morning and go out on my patio where the valley, stretching off to the mountain ranges in the north and east, was silver with predawn mist. The birds, eloquent voices in an otherwise silent world, had already begun their hallelujah chorus to welcome in the new day. . . . I feel again the everlasting going and coming, the eternal return, the growing and mating and dying and growing again. And I know that human beings are part of this eternal going and returning, part of its sadness as well as its song. But man, the seeker, is called by his consciousness to transcend the eternal return. . . . My own conviction has always been to seek the inner reality.

In these pages Dr. May does seek the inner reality, in ways that I shall shortly discuss.

But first I must try to disentangle the ambivalent feelings that I have about this book, for the more I read and the further I went the more disappointed I became. Until, in the last few chapters, I felt surfeited and almost overwhelmed by his generalizations. A reaction of this kind on the part of the reader is not altogether trustworthy—perhaps at first not trustworthy at all because the reader may be too tired, or too sharply different in his views from the conclusions being drawn. To reflect on one's reaction is as indispensable as reading the entire book.

In the case of this reviewer the necessity for reflection and reexamination was of double importance because of my absorption in the Rankian theory of the will and my instantaneous reaction that Rank saw this or that point with richer insights, more profound thought, more lucid expression. Also because a book overflowing with allusions to every kind of literature makes almost no mention of Rank's work, and when it does, does so in a way that I find regrettable. There are only two page references to Rank in the index, one of which links Rank and Wilhelm Reich (a false linkage) as two who in the 1920's "Began to point out, there were built-in tendencies in psychoanalysis itself that sapped its vitality. . . ." One moves beyond the superficial protest against omission of acknowledgment to a deeper level of sense of loss, loss of that very communication which Dr. May so fervently extols. Toward the end of his book it is the word "Care" that becomes his shibboleth; in a most genuine way his writing acclaims the fact that he does "care," as indeed do I.

I surmise that what happened between the time when I heard Dr. May read his papers before professional meetings and the publication of his book was a process of preparing it for a wider audience, a reader audience which has certainly proven its existence. For weeks *Love and Will* appeared on the Best Seller list in the *N. Y. Times.* It has received extraordinary attention by reviewers in popular as well as scholarly periodicals. A substantial portion of the book first appeared in the then-new periodical *Psychology Today*. All of this can only be regarded as evidence that some of these penetrating ideas about values in living, values that run counter to the tidal wave of popular ideology, are being recognized, needed, and heard by many.

But what has been a gain for the many in new ways of realizing experience has also been a loss for me in depth, and I think also a loss that results from a shift in position by Dr. May. When I heard him read his papers I thought I heard him take the courageous stand that refused to align himself with those who place the total blame upon society, upon an anonymous "We," and that he rejected the shift of all responsibility upon "the times." As I recall, he went below the instinctive surface reactions to mass destruction and examined what happens to the individual who loses himself in the "daemonic" of a crowd. He was the first person to speak out of his observation that the new sexual "freedom" was no freedom at all but a new kind of "Puritanism" in which the supposedly free individual despaired because he had lost his capacity to feel. All of this of course still runs through *Love and Will* but it is temporized by a repeated sudden taking-off into the clichés of today without the reflection and exploration which Dr. May portrays in other ways.

I hope I can be forgiven not only for having had to work through my negative feelings but also for having had to include them in print as a part of this review. To have omitted them would have cast a false light on everything that follows.

* * *

The organization of this book is in itself worth attention: in three parts, the first deals with "Love," the second with "Will" and the third with the relation of each to the other. The concept of "Intentionality" is central to Dr. May's theme, as is his newly-created meaning given to the simple word "Care," toward which his whole theme is developing and with which the book ends.

I am relieved and gratified that this book, which is about

love, is in itself a gentle, benign, warmly considerate book, an "unwillful" book that does not try to force its point. Thus it is what every work should be, a living experience akin to the topic with which it deals. It speaks to the reader, it points gently to gems of wisdom that may be painful or denied. The allusions are so rich and varied—we range back and forth from the Greeks to the modern drama "Who's Afraid of Virginia Woolf"—the passages from literature always introduced with meaning and pertinence, that the texture of the book is a pattern of complexity. At times this is too much (as in the ending) but usually these passages give interest, breadth, and depth to the reader's responsive thoughts.

Yet this very wide-ranging use of the arts—especially its classic literature timeless in quality, leads me to what I regard as a loss, namely, that May locates this work, this whole theme, in the present, as if the problems with which he deals were a contemporary malady instead of man's humanity. He accepts unquestioningly the contemporary clichés by calling his introduction "Our Schizoid World," in which he repeats many of the diagnostic ailments that supposedly beset us. "The striking thing about love and will in our day is that, whereas in the past they were always held up to us as the *answer* to life's predicaments, they have now themselves become the *problem*." Let me repeat, *now* become the "problem." In sharp contrast, Rank writes universally, timelessly; he writes thus: "Only after a struggle against prejudice of every kind did the acceptance of will as a psychological factor of the first rank seem unavoidable but soon also became a matter of course, so much a matter of course that I had to say to myself that only a tremendous resistance could have hindered the complete recognition and evaluation of will as a great psychic power."

I cannot help but feel, with evidence from the book itself, that Dr. May too intends to write universally, timelessly. The temptation to locate in the ideology of the day must be all but irresistible. But in doing so at least three undesirable tendencies are the result: He contradicts his own deep recognition of the "polarity" of humanity by calling it schizoid; he falls into the trap of excessive blame and condemnation of contemporary culture; and he uses constantly that horrendous word "We" ("we cling to each other and try to persuade ourselves that what we feel is love; we do not will because we are afraid that if we choose one thing or one person we'll lose the other, and we are too insecure to take that chance . . ."). This is a wholly anonymous "We" never including I am certain Dr. May himself—he could not be describing himself, nor will I accept it as a description of myself, the reader. Then who is this "We"—what creature has been constructed onto whom these ideas are projected? Who are the individuals of whom he speaks?

On the contrary when he draws from his therapeutic practice, speaking as a therapist of his patients, observing that the recurrent problem is no longer inhibited sex, but the inability to feel, to experience emotion in the new sexual freedom—this has meaning and a meaning that could have been predicted because it emerges out of a conception of relationship compounded of emotion, development, weathering. An essay review in a current issue of the *Saturday Review* presents a shocking picture of the "search" among some societal groups, for relationship in "swinging," in what the reviewer calls the new "sexistentialism"—the shock is felt not only because of attitudes toward sex (although they too are shocking) but because of the pitifulness of it, the starvation, the artifice, the desperation hidden by glib words.

* * *

I should like now to try to frame my own impression of the answer to the question, what is the major theme of Dr. May's book? What is he most anxious to have us understand and, understanding, live out? How convincing is he? And what does he, in my opinion fail to see?

The quotation from Aeschylus with which Dr. May begins his last chapter conveys in the briefest possible way his aspirations for mankind:

Let them render grace for grace,
Let love be their common will.

He is pleading for "deepened and wider dimensions of consciousness" and this new consciousness would be awareness of and acceptance of the polarity of life, the daemonic, the emotions, the opening of the self to give and to "active receiving" and all of this literally unified, harmonized, by communion, relationship to the other. "For human beings, the more powerful need is not for sex per se but for relationship, intimacy, acceptance, and affirmation."

> We love and will the world, create it by our decision, our fiat, our choice; and we *love* it, give it affect, energy, power to love and change us as we mold and change it. This is what it means to be fully related to one's world.

What is missing in these brief passages, what is missing throughout the book, is the recognition of separation, of individuation. In fact, it is not merely overlooked, but regretted: "Longing, as all individuals do, to overcome the separateness and isolation to which we are all heir because we are individuals" yet "this sadness comes fom the reminder that we have not succeeded absolutely in losing our separateness . . . none of us ever overcomes his loneliness completely."

What matter that one should face the fact of separation squarely? What difference if a human being can read this book and take from the written word some help (which I believe most sincerely can happen) toward loving and being more lovable? Then why push insistently toward a revelation that the principle of separation is as essential a part of humanity as the principle of union? Because to strive toward the one-sidedness of relating, loving, communicating, is to experience defeat, despair, and flaw—to experience what Leslie Farber describes thus: "When man believes in his perfectability, he experiences his own real being almost as a disease, a fatal sickness whose cure—perfection—seems unobtainable."

But in more practical terms, the emotion of love even in its minor forms cannot be sustained unchangingly. It is imperative that it change and everyone knows out of daily relationship how characteristic are the swings from separating to coming together, even in the closest relationships and even on the most trivial of content. For this experience I use the word "weathering."

On yet another level, May uses the word "loneliness" with all the clusterings of meaning that now adhere to it; usually, in common parlance, an accusation against "society" for causing, fostering, making alienation, loneliness, emptiness, apathy,—the worst of ills as indeed they are. But there is another word in the same category namely "Solitude" which when heard thus by every human being must ring with pleasurable tones as well. To repeat what is common knowledge—that in order to create, there must be separation, solitude—may seem banal; to imply that Dr. May does not himself know this (as I am certain he does,) would be to do him a great injustice. He writes one-sidedly as is perhaps unavoidable.

This is what I mean when I say "loss"—loss of the key that unlocks the mind and feeling. I agree with Dr. May that apathy and emptiness are among the most painful states of human existence. But I disagree with his over-emphasis on its source as the "inability to influence others." Indeed, the push is there, *projected*, out of the self on to the other, powerfully, to produce the change in the other or in the environment but not in myself— the last and hardest acknowledgment being that it is myself that must change over the obstacles of fear and guilt.

There are two ways to overcome boredom, emptiness, apathy— one is in relationship, the other is alone. To merge with the crowd is to melt in feeling with the feeling of others, to be lifted by excitement, made whole by the brevity of one single concentrated attention. I can understand wholeheartedly why people go to baseball and football games—I knew it when I was young watching and playing tennis all day long living, talking, watching, playing tennis. It is a wonderfully healing experience.

The other way is harder and it is obviously the way of work; making, creating, searching, first in solitude, with discipline that sets in motion a process, which comes to a satisfying ending of which the feeling of having *used* one's self is a vital part.

Stated in terms of the will, apathy is a powerful negative will expression, not the absence of will. It is "no" to life and even the rebel knows that at some point that no must turn to a yes, if ever so briefly or only occasionally. The "No" is not merely a willful stubborn "I won't"—it starts and has its source in fear—fear in the face of life. And fear in turn produces guilt for the refusal of life. Dr. May recognizes this: "Overwhelming anxiety destroys the capacity to perceive and conceive one's world, to reach out toward it to form and re-form it." He comes out flatly with the statement that the will originates in a "No." Further: "Man can and must . . . choose how he will relate to necessity." He quotes William James:

> 'Will you or won't you have it so?' . . . we are asked it every hour of the day, and about the largest as well as the smallest, the most theoretical as well as the most practical things. We answer by *consents* or *non-consents* and not by words.

Having now opened the subject of "fear" it is time to pursue it further.

When Dr. May was a student some thirty or more years ago, he observed and was impressed by what he chose to call "normal anxiety" in his patients—"not merely as a symptom of repression or pathology, but as a generalized character state." His conviction about this was met by skepticism as late as 1949 when he read a paper on anxiety before the American Psychological Association. But then (he continues with his account), in the 1950's a change was apparent. The concept of "normal" anxiety appeared in the literature, "Everybody, normal as well as neurotic, seemed aware that he was living in the 'age of anxiety.' What had been presented by the artists and had appeared in our patients in the 30's and 40's was now endemic in the land."

Agreeing on the whole as I do with his view of anxiety, I can illustrate by these quotations what I mean by the loss of depth of insight by locating and limiting the human experience in this so-called "age of anxiety" as if it had just happened to man, hence to be overcome, transcended, left behind as an unwanted by-product of the age instead of a part of humanity itself.

It is necessary to digress for a moment in order to return to the subject of "anxiety." The most original, most deeply reflective portions of *Love and Will* are those which deal with Eros and the Daemonic. There are, says Dr. May, four kinds of love: "One is sex . . . lust, libido"; "the second is *eros*, the drive of love to procreate or create—the urge, as the Greeks put it, toward higher forms of being and relationship. A third is *philia* or friendship . . . the fourth is *agape* . . . devoted to the welfare of the other."

Now of Eros—man transcending himself either in relation to others or in new forms of being—and of the Daemonic: every man is possessed of a "Daimon" which "arises from the ground of being" capable of either destruction or construction. Without attempting to draw an exact parallel, Rank's "irrational" is similar enough to May's "Daimon" to regard them as alike. Both plead for the acceptance of this awesome source of life. May quotes an excerpt from a letter of Rilke, written after one session of psychotherapy when he chose not to go on, which makes the point vividly plain:

> If my devils are to leave me, I am afraid my angels will take flight as well.

Both "Eros" and "Daimon" ignite human anxiety which arises from the experience of each, "the anxiety-creating involvements of eros." To me the concepts that he traces are those which I know as the universal experience of "life fear" (and its opposite "death fear"). The source of the fear is obvious in May's shortest definition of the daemonic "any natural function which has the power to take over the whole person." It is the loss of will, the being taken over, that ignites the fear. "The antidaemon is apathy."

Now, one of the most interesting and perceptive observations made by Dr. May is that having to do with "external" and "internal" anxiety. As the "external social anxiety and guilt have lessened" he writes (because of the new freedom) "internal anxiety and guilt have increased." In other words, the primary, genetic source of anxiety and guilt is within the inner self; when the projection on the outside is removed, the experience within the self becomes more intense—as May observes "more morbid, harder to handle, and imposes a heavier burden upon the individual than external anxiety and guilt."

Is it not obvious to everyone that every venture that can be said to be in the most general sense, life-giving, nevertheless inescapably creates some fear? Even the start on a trip long-planned with delight? Even a move into new opportunity? The sources of this fear are complex yet hold the fascination that commands our attention, far too much for this comment on *Love and Will*.

In my opinion, Dr. May explains this too easily. He lays it at the door of influencing others: "The blocking of the ways in which we affect others and are affected by them is the essential disorder of both love and will." Yet at the same time, if I let myself hear the whole of what he is saying I hear too his claim that it is the *self* where one starts, where the feeling of alienation begins, where the emptiness originates. I am certain I heard him say this on the television program to which I referred earlier. One must in a sense accept one's self in order to be able to love others.

* * *

In the ninth chapter of *Love and Will* May takes hold of the concept of "Intentionality" which up to this point he has just mentioned in passing. As he opens the concluding portion of his book, he defines *Intentionality*: "By intentionality, I mean the structure which gives meaning to experience. It is not to be identified with intentions, but is the dimension which underlies them; it is man's capacity to have intentions. . . . Intentionality is the heart of consciousness." And he speaks to the reader thus: "The concept seems to me so important, and has been so neglected in contemporary psychology, that I ask the reader to go with me into an exploration of its meaning."

In the exploration of its meaning, he works with word roots, one of the most interesting aspects of this book. Through the root "tend" he makes the accurate associations with care, with tendency, with "tension." It is clear that he feels at least two levels of experience, that which is clearly conscious in intention—specific, clear-cut, everyday intention—and intentionality which underlies it as the "capacity to intend." To me, this is what I mean by will in its long gradual development; I use the word sub-liminal, not unconscious, because most of the time awareness of its direction lies out of our reach; nonetheless is surely a direction of one's life.

In this recognition of intentionality, Dr. May acclaims without reservation man's volitional responsibility. There is, he says,

> . . . a willing which is not merely against body desires but *with* the body, a willing from within; it is a willing of *participation* rather than *opposition*.

He now introduces the word "care" referring to Heidegger for whom in the German the word is "Sorge." And thus the concept toward which May's theme has been heading, is introduced. Later, of it he writes: "Care is a state in which something does *matter*; care is the opposite of apathy. Care is the necessary source of eros, the source of human tenderness."

He makes two other key points before leaving the subject of intentionality; the first:

> The conflict, which is part and parcel of intentionality, is the beginning of volition, and the beginning of volition is present in the structure of consciousness itself.

And the second:

> By my act I reveal myself, rather than by looking *at* myself. This saves us from the untenable position in therapy of assuming that the patient

develops a sense of identity and *then* acts. On the contrary, he experiences the identity *in* the action or at least in the possibility for it.

Examining the meaning of intentionality is in every sense of the word an exploration.

As I bring my comments to a conclusion, I am left with a question regarding the relation of love and will, and in order to work on this question I reread the chapter "The Relation of Love and Will" and I am left with a nagging puzzlement that is difficult to clarify, let alone to express. At first I know only my dissatisfaction, unfulfilled search for what to me would be reliable meaning.

Let me state it thus: Dr. May leads up to his key point, his intention, his solution: "Man's task is to unite love and will." "I speak of the relating of love and will not as a state given us automatically, but as a task; and to the extent it is gained, it is an achievement. It points toward maturity, integration, wholeness."

Love and will *are* different—very different but constantly dynamically interplaying in human experience. Their union, their wholeness, when it does occur, is brief, temporary, with the downward beat of every true rhythm. The love emotion is a yielding of the will, a giving up of willfulness. Its opposite is will in its creative, shaping, making expression; wishing to mold the object, possess it. In some respects of course the latter describes the love demand, the will demanding the loved object. It wishes to make the loved object like itself, it wishes to find in the loved object the "yes" to what it itself is. But the heights, the depths of the love experience are momentarily tenderness, yielding, melting, loss of self, unwillful, undemanding, existing for the immediate experience, the center and sense of "being." It is the very fact that these descriptions of states of being would have to go on indefinitely, not for the banal reason that they are hard to describe (everyone knows them) but because they are mercurial, in constant movement like psychological atoms. Rank's chapter "Love and Force" illuminates these truths, especially those that reside in the therapeutic encounter, where the love demand is intensified.

I find in May's exposition itself my apology for the preceding paragraph, the release of some daemonic which may or may not convey the meaning it intends. But of one thing I am certain, namely, that I cannot believe that the task of mankind is to unite love and will (which it would do willfully) but to experience their unity in those rare moments when the human being is whole and using himself to the full, either in creation or relationship.

I mean it most sincerely when I state that any book which can keep a reader engaged to read painstakingly, to work in order to understand its meaning, to produce one's own meaning, is a worthy book. I am delighted to find in it the heralding of feeling, of emotion, of the awesome, the "master work" that is man. I am taking the liberty (with permission) to quote two poems by Emily Dickinson, one that equates the will with life, one that gently reveals growth from within.

THE SUMMING UP—WHAT ARE THE
NEW VALUES OF WHICH
RANK SPEAKS?*

When we chose this topic, "Psychology and Social Change" (which as you know is the title of the first chapter of *Beyond Psychology*) and when we framed the question—what are the new values of which Rank speaks—it seemed as if the answers could easily be found. But when I knew I was to shape an ending to this meeting, picking up the threads of recurring ideas, focusing the last part of the discussion and attempting to summarize these new values, it was then I realized the difficulty; difficult for many reasons, principally for the reason so often observed, namely, that words alone tend often to obscure meaning when they exclude the fresh experience which alone can animate a new value. This is uniquely true of the subject of change.

I ran into this problem early when, seeming to be getting nowhere, in some despair I went to Miss Robinson with my complaint, and she said to me, "The trouble with you is, you are stuck in change." Which of course was so exactly true that it produced at once some genuine change in feeling and a fresh start.

I do not want to use our time today retracing the steps by which I became "unstuck"—that happy process which we recognize when talk about change moves to a feeling of change. But there are a few introductory remarks which may perhaps help us avoid dead ends that lead nowhere, and which may at the

*Paper delivered at the meeting of The Otto Rank Association, held on October 23, 1971, in Doylestown, Pa.

same time characterize the underlying assumptions from which we start.

At the beginning I had some notion that it would be an interesting exercise to try to "apply" our psychology to some specific happenings for the purpose of explaining them or fitting them into some rational scheme. I have watched always with interest, at times with excitement, dismay, fear, anger, delight, the whirling evidence around us of the conflict of wills, as if to see there every shading and variation of the will spectrum. But first one sees it one way and then another, and the speed of the experience is so intense, there is no way to convert it to the easily explained, the static or the rational. Then I suddenly remembered (with genuine relief) the theme of the first meeting of this association, held in the spring of 1967, when we took the theme from one of Rank's early Daybooks: "The chief thing is the seeking." This then straightened my direction and mood and I knew that again today the chief thing is the search, the seeking.

The second compelling thought that struck me was that Rank's writing is so rich, so complex, so inexhaustible, so imbued with polarity—the very two-sidedness which was his special interest— that each of us can find in it passages that will substantiate almost any position taken (excepting perhaps only that one which he wholly rejected, namely, that we are victims of our fate.) Any rich and complex writing invites projections of every kind, every individual finds there what has meaning for him. Even so, it is a great temptation to wonder how Rank would have viewed and reacted to contemporary experience; once again it becomes clear that when I speak as I shall of what I think would be a "new" value, I can do so only as the expression of that which I recreate from my own understanding of what he was saying.

Third and last of these introductory remarks: I knew that I must be willing to speak out of my own deepest convictions, otherwise nothing that I say will be in proper perspective. One faces then the deepest conflict and resistance in risking the assertion of what may or may not be difference. Seemingly contrary to most of what I see, hear and read, I do not believe this is a sick society nor a schizoid world nor one that is on the verge of disintegration and collapse—on the contrary I feel we are living in remarkable times, witnessing extraordinary changes that somehow are being weathered and assimilated; that we are witnesses of and participants in a dramatic process unfolding before our eyes. The repetition of perpetually gloomy diagnoses is one of the strange phenomena of this age when judgments voiced in brief phrases seem to be taken up at once and repeated again and again without examination or reflection. The phrase "generation gap" is an illustration of a short-cut to a human experience which can be examined only in the light of "likeness and difference" where the light must first be thrown on one's own youthful experiences until one can truly examine age difference.

When I express my impression that we are living in extraordinary times, I do not mean by this that the end results or the methods used to gain the results are always ones which would win my support or approval. One does not have to like the issues or the arguments used or the goals sought in order to be *for* the fact that conflicts can work themselves out in a process, over which no single individual nor any powerful unit of government can exercise complete and total control—even though the effort to control is ever present. I think that Rank would have been an intense observer of the contemporary scene finding in it all the confirmation he needed of the polarity in society as well as in the individual: the interplay of the rational and the irrational, the evolutionary and the revolutionary, the powerful will expression and the counter will aroused in reaction to it. If to be "involved" is as desirable as it is now said to be, then is it not true today that everyone *is* involved, even though you and I might not be happy regarding the manner of that involvement, nor might we even agree with each other?

How else one might ask, can developments come (world-wide, nation-wide, locality-wide) except through conflict of opposing points of view, conflict out of which development arises often punctuated by extremes that frighten and outrage. But we are, as I have said, witness to and participants in a dramatic process, within a structure of government that, no matter what fault you or I might find with it, gives evidence of capacity both to hold steadfast and to yield to change. The only alternative would seem to be a control at the top so powerful as to keep intact that one single pattern which for the times is judged the best.

Let me take time to develop the detail of one issue, namely the issue of local control of the schools. I choose it first because in my years of administrative experience I was not merely an observer but involved in a similar issue and also because this can be discussed without the explosive distractions that adhere to so many other issues that face us. During the 1930's, in the Roosevelt era, when many of us were involved in the emergency relief program, the issue of local vs. Federal/state control was hotly fought out. The difference between then and now was this: that the liberal-progressive stance in those days was passionately for Federal standards set by government, administered by government from top to bottom. It was Harry Hopkins as head of the Federal Emergency Relief Administration who insisted upon decent standards of relief (by no means always achieved). Opposed were the old-line politicians, the "local" people—let me quickly add that I am speaking of the decent, humane, citizens with integrity who honestly believed that the local people knew best, who wanted to choose their own administrators and set their own standards. In that era the pendulum swung to the extreme. Now, today, anyone can follow this same issue as it is reported almost daily in the press. And the astonishing fact is that now the extreme of the so-called "liberal" point of view (granting how much more complicated it is than this) is fighting for local control. So that we see the irony of opposites pulling for the same goal. This happens to be one issue on which I have no difficulty finding my own place because I have lived through the conflict and know beyond doubt my own belief in the interplay of Federal/state standards worked out through a process of local administration where neither one or the other is controlling. And I feel secure that the extremes will gravitate back to a workable, viable stability of the three level structure even though never without conflict. Many other illustrations could be cited; illustrations of conflict, of opposing points of view, of development arising out of this very set of circumstances and always in motion without allowing total control one way or another.

The problem that I feel today is this: that so many of the values to which we gave our utmost, which seemed so often to be denied in society, are now being heralded and acclaimed, and yet violated in some agonizing way. I am speaking of the acclaim of emotion, the desire for relationship, the honest expression of feeling, the pursuit of identity, the wish to be one's self and "to do one's own thing." I hear Rank's words echoing in my ears: what he needs is to learn to *will*, to affirm his will, to be responsible for it; also the words from "Living and Feeling" that have in a sense become part of each of us: it is the quality of emotion that distinguishes one individual from another and the price we pay for refusal to express negative feeling is the inability to feel at all. Relationship— the experience which we sought to understand through all its rich expressions, now seems to be produced by quick measures and by the erasure of difference.

Everywhere we are witness to behavior, attitudes, acts, events, ideals, goals that seem now at last to confirm our beliefs. But so it seems only at first glance. For at the heart of function is form— that simple, vital component of living that appears in every guise from the most trivial (such as our daily routine) to the majestic as in poetry and music. What often is not only missing but actually intentionally disposed of are structure, limits, boundaries, individual difference. One sees the obliteration of time, as in the marathon, the obliteration of role as of the leader, the giving up of individual difference on behalf of a likeness compelled by the group rules. For those of us for whom form is in every shred of our being, to live in a time when a tidal wave is rushing to its most extreme opposite is to leave us with a heightened sense of difference within a strange sense of likeness. The trend can be followed in almost every content: not just in the sensitivity groups which too will change with time, but, for example, in the theatre where, in an especially interesting pursuit of likeness between audience and actor the intent is to be free of separation, of difference.

At the Pennsylvania School of Social Work as you will remember out of past experience or know from current experience, there was developed as part of the curriculum for training as a social worker, a group experience singularly suited to individual development. (I hope the faculty members present and the students present will forgive me for speaking in the past tense where my own teaching experience lies). In the course variously known as "The Nature of the Self," "Development of the Individual," "Growth and Development," all spoken of as the "personality" class, there was developed what was a unique and wonderfully effective way for individual development to take place as part of a group experience. In that classroom, with, first of all, a known fact that one must be able to understand one's self before trying to understand others, the class worked within unbending limits, with specific assignments, with the structure that would support some limited examination of one's self. A question such as, Can you recover your first memory? becomes a way of shaping one's own sense of one's self. Above all, within those limits which restricted license or if you will restricted freedom, the most exhilerating freedom was in my experience achieved. It seems to me that in the Rankian psychology underlying this training was the priceless insight that freedom is earned out of yielding to some conditions of life and recreating them by one's own will and choice. When I wrote my book on choice I wrote that every individual in order to learn must yield to a strength outside himself, actually seeks it; that he must choose some difference, some piece that is not himself, and assimilate it as part of the growing self. How can one know today when the limit must hold, where it must yield?

Now at last to the subject of values. I am sure that whatever we mean by "new" is also "old"—it is perhaps more accurately the rebirth of old values. Rank's interest was timeless, in that he worked universally and in every age that interested him. But again and again he reminds us that everything to be alive and new must be created and recreated through new experience. And if you hold this belief then you will oppose with all your strength whatever in fixed theory demands that we over-analyze, over-explain, over-control and over-direct.

Now by this route I have come to the point of restating the question, what are the new values of which Rank speaks. These are bound to be values which we wish for ourselves, then for others.

First about change. Our need for change is as compelling as our need for air, water and food. No one can bear the unchanging unmoving fixed situation. Some impulse, if there is any life at all, rises up to make it different. At the same time our need to sustain or protect our resistance is equally powerful. In the normal course of events we choose that change which we are willing to assimilate. But this interplay of the need for change and the resistance to change is fundamental. One of the common fallacies that, in my opinion, really blinds us to true understanding, is the popular condemnation of resistance to change, once sociologically named the "cultural lag" in society. The book in recent times that has attempted to look at this problem is Alvin Toffler's *Future Shock*. What happens to us when change is so swift, so external, so imposed? We have three choices: one to resist willfully; two, to adjust by capitulation without conviction; the third, to know its inevitability and to reshape it by our own sensibilities to something that becomes a livable and interesting movement.

In that first meeting to which I previously referred, we used along with the quotation from Rank's Daybook, a quotation from William James:

> There is an everlasting struggle in every mind between the tendency to keep unchanged, and the tendency to renovate its ideas.

This, I suggest, is a "value" to hold.

Now about the *Will*. No one could ever doubt that the rudiments of the will psychology are being lived out in dramatic ways. Let me remind ourselves as briefly and simply as I can, what some of them are:

First: The experience of willing, the thrust of will, produces a sense of life. It does not matter how destructive the end result may be, while the will is triumphing, the excitement, the freedom (false as it may be) are the exact opposite of boredom and emptiness. The creative will, on the contrary, unlike the sheer thrust of will projected outward, becomes an individual expression, in work, in action, in life experience.

Second: Every growing individual must in some way rebel, that is, declare and live out his difference. Every individual does this in his own way. But differ we must—growth demands it. The will of the growing individual develops and finds new strength by opposing itself to something or someone on the outside which seemingly has a greater strength. When, as sometimes happens, this takes the form of tearing down the structure by which we live, then it takes on frightening proportions.

Third: Any individual upon whom a powerful alien will is projected reacts with a sharpening of his own will to oppose. We see this everywhere around us, again often in frightening and dramatic form, and if you were to ask me what I genuinely fear today it is that the irrational power of the need to say "I will not let this be done to me" (no matter how benign the intent) becomes so great as to move us into a controlled society.

Fourth: The need to be in relationship and the need to be a separate individual are equally powerful needs and sometimes we satisfy one and sometimes we satisfy the other.

This psychology of individuation is the least understood, the least acknowledged in all the new thought whirling around us because its ideas appear to be totally committed to likeness, togetherness, relatedness, all of which, important as they are, are but one side of the picture. In contrast Rank described the fate of the artist: the more creative he becomes the more different he becomes the more separated he becomes the less likely to conform to the prevailing ways of relating. This too is likely to be the direction of any individual who shapes his capacity and his gift, and forges his own insights.

Out of all of these, I believe, old/new values are made. If you take Rank's work as a whole, the conclusion, I think, is inescapable, that he rejoiced in the way man is made. His was no bland "acceptance" nor toleration of what we are unable to change. His words are often alive with hopefulness without any tinge of false optimism. The closing words of *Beyond Psychology* are these:

> Granted an acceptance of the fundamental irrationality of the human being and life in general with allowance for its dynamic functioning in human behaviour, we have the basis for the emergence of everything of which mankind is capable in personal and social capacity for betterment.

PREPARATION FOR THE ANNUAL MEETING

"The Relation of Function to Process"

[Editorial Note: It has been our custom to mail to the O R A membership in advance of the fall meeting, a "Letter" that gave a forecast of the program with selected passages from published material which, read in advance, would provide the reader with background material for the discussion which was to follow.

On the occasion of this annual meeting, October 27, 1974, the theme of the meeting was taken from the title of an article by Dr. Jessie Taft, "The Relation of Function to Process," generally regarded as the first definitive statement of the theory of functional helping. Now, some thirty-five years later, the vitality of this creative and unique process of helping was being affirmed and recognized. At the same time, it became a professional tribute to the 90th birthday of Virginia P. Robinson, as the day has been recalled in the preceding pages of this issue of The Journal.

In this same "Letter" we quoted passages from the writings of Kenneth L. M. Pray, Jessie Taft, and Virginia P. Robinson, arranged within seven headings which venture to state with brevity the underlying conceptions of functional psychology and the practice of functional helping. We are including them in this Journal, in part because they are referred to in the preceding papers, but also in order to reach a wider readership and to preserve them in permanent form for those who are actively engaged in casework, supervision, administration and teaching in this field where the helping process is the center of their practice.

While we did not know in advance that we would be fortunate in having a new paperback edition of Dr. Ruth Smalley's book (Theory for Social Work Practice), *reviewed in the preceding article, by Dr. Saul Hofstein—a book in which principles underlying social work practice are stated—we are pleased to combine these two statements which, with different wording, are at the same time so similar in basic conception.]*

* * *

"The Relation of Function to Process" will be recognized as the title of Dr. Jessie Taft's "Introduction" to the first volume of the *Journal of Social Work Process* published in 1937. In it for the first time she made a definitive statement of the principles of functional helping, introducing nine articles in which:

> One common factor stands clear and that is a degree of accepted understanding and use of "helping" as a technical process basic to the exercise of every social work function. The taking and giving of help are seen as two opposite but complementary currents in a single complex process in which social work must base whatever it hopes to achieve in the way of effective understanding of the client and conscious control over its own procedures.

This article endures as a classic, a starting point for the understanding of functional helping.

Some years earlier, in 1930, Miss Robinson had written in the same vein, looking ahead some fifty years:

> New values [in the case work movement] have developed in the experience and consciousness of case workers as they have come into closer contacts with human problems. These values are psychological in contrast to economic, religious, moral, or sociological values. To articulate these values . . . is a task which social case work might do well to accomplish within another fifty years.

These fifty years are now almost over and the time is auspicious for asking where are we now, do these principles live on in continuity, how might we characterize the climate in which we now live?

To return for just a moment to the 1930's we find both of these authors examining the conflict between outer and inner, economic and psychological, the many and the one. Dr. Taft describes accurately the swings that occur in the sweep of the years:

> There is a universal tendency in all human development to progress by extreme swings from object to subject, from the external, the physical and the social, to the internal, the psychological and the individualistic.

Out of what she called the "quandry which contemplation of the social case work movement in the period between 1928 and 1930 presents," Miss Robinson wrote:

> At the present time it [the social case work movement] is caught between the pressure of its own tremendous absorption in the psychological and the demand from other interests both within as well as outside the field. Endowed as it is with the responsibility of helping to maintain and to improve the social order, it is threatened from without by the change and uncertainty in established institutions, in moral standards and social reforms.

This paragraph might as well be describing contemporary times.

Our point of departure is this same conflict of opposites: we find on the one hand the belief in and conviction about the worth of the one individual and in the value of the person-to-person relationship in the helping process and, on the other, devotion to social reform, to movements involving many in common action, legal reform, institutional reform.

We are looking back over these fifty years, not in order to return to the past, but in order to feel the rich depth of development, the insights that the passage of time may have brought. We speak out of our own experience to find again those "common factors."

First of all, we assume it to be true that now perhaps more than ever, we need to keep alive our conviction regarding growth, lifelong, both for ourselves and others, and our belief in the process within which an individual can seek and use our help.

We believe, despite all of the enormous and powerful external forces, despite all the deficiencies, inadequacies,—even the well-intentioned "new" theories that are the opposite of functional principles—despite all of these we believe in the continuing possibility of setting up a process of functional helping in social agencies, hospitals, psychiatric clinics, public or private services, as well as in the private practice of casework counseling. We must not let ourselves be overwhelmed by what seems to be impossible.

However, we are interested not in a mere restatement of principles (although even this at times can be refreshing) but we are interested in seeing these principles engage with contemporary events and theories, in order to discover whether the principle can survive, whether it is modified, and if so, whether in being modified what occurs is a reluctant compromise, or a new creative way of using the same principle.

Further, we assume it to be true that "function" is a deeply psychological concept, implying an inner sense in the one who helps by which he knows who he is, why he is there, the form within which he works and his separation from the self of the "other." The actual "service" which the agency or institution offers and the conditions that reside in that service are the outer tangible expressions of the helping function which he represents.

Seven principles, with quoted passages, from the writing of Kenneth L. M. Pray, Virginia P. Robinson, and Jessie Taft, follow. * * *

1. "The Source of healing power is in the client himself."

". . . the helping dynamic, the source of healing power, is in the client himself as he reaches out for help. It is not primarily in the worker . . . It is his own will, his own capacity for growth and change, his own selective use of his experience in accord with his own nature and needs, that determine the outcome." K.L.M.P.

"Only the individual himself can reveal the true meaning of his experiences." V.P.R.

"...what each individual wants and needs however slight his capacity, is to possess his own experience and to arrive at his own conclusion, faulty though it be." J.T.

"...No trained caseworker today would deny that the client must not only be free to choose his own goal but should be helped to find it. Just how free this choice is in actual practice depends upon how genuinely the agency and its worker respect the strength and integrity of the weakest applicant, and also upon the worker's capacity to initiate and further a true relationship process in which the inner movement of the client towards a plan, not the decision of the worker, determines the outcome." J.T.

2. *The skill of the caseworker can be taught and learned.*

"Our search for a generic base has led us to define and abstract a process of relationship which we have called 'the helping process'." V.P.R.

"No more difficult skill could be demanded—skill in setting up and controlling a process in which change may take place in a human being.... Certainly no skill could be more desirable; none would be more deeply feared. For man's fear of and resistance to change within is in proportion to his desire to produce it outside himself." V.P.R.

"Three major contributions to social casework stand out as basic to the progress that has been made in child placement in the Philadelphia area during the decade following 1930. The first is a dynamic psychology of the individual which recognizes the creative nature of will and the conditions under which psychological growth takes place. The second is a clear understanding of professional helping as a process in its own right, capable of being understood and controlled in the interest of client and agency, a process that admits the dependence of all such helping on client initiative and client participation. And finally, there is a new conception of the social agency as an organic whole with a clarified function by which the casework process is stabilized and directed towards a goal valid for client, worker, and agency." J.T.

3. *The professional relationship creates a new experience.*

"It is clear that from this point of view, the decisive factor in the helping situation and in the helping process is the offering of a *new* experience for the client, in which and around which old patterns of thought and feeling and behavior—proved inadequate to the existing need—can be broken through sufficiently to afford a new start toward some personal and social reorganization." K.L.M.P.

". . . technique lies in creating a relationship environment in which the individual growth process of the client can be released. This internal process itself then becomes the center, the growing point of change, rather than any external manipulation of the client from point to point." V.P.R.

". . . the dynamics of the immediate relationship is often obscured by the concept of living out, reliving, or solving past relationships on the worker. According to this concept, the worker is being used in the present, but only as a lay figure on which to project experiences and feelings from the client's past. An utter confusion results, a practical denial of the reality of the present which is functioning for the sake of the past. Once more the worker is effectively hidden behind the screen of father, mother, brother, sister, while all the time her value for the client is that she is none of these and he knows it. . . . He may be using patterns developed by him . . . but he is using them now, in immediate reaction to someone who behaves as no one has ever behaved to him before. . . ." J.T.

4. The difference between the one who helps and the one who seeks help must be maintained.

"Certainly no skill in controlling a process of change can develop unless there is a separation between self and object, between the will-to-effect change of the workman and the material with which he works." V.P.R.

"In facing this new experience—in taking in this difference—the client faces the necessity to find a new focus for dealing with his problem; it demands of him some change, at least enough yielding of his individuality to become a part of a larger whole, while it still leaves his own integrity intact. This is a new dynamic, which can reactivate and redirect the potential dynamic in the individual's self, for it introduces that firm barrier to the perfectly free and limitless play of all his conflicting wants and impulses which necessitates deliberation and responsible choice. This is the beginning of his effective use of a helping process." K.L.M.P.

"As I conceive it, the therapeutic function involves the most intense activity, but it is an activity of attention, of identification and understanding, of adaptation to the individual's need and pattern, combined with an unflagging preservation of one's own limitation and difference." J.T.

5. The social agency with its purpose, its conditions, its way of helping provides to the caseworker, the supervisor, the administrator the form and limits vital to the helping process.

"The shift which functional casework has made from client's need to agency service carries with it a new configuration in which the agency itself is the center, a vital organic whole, determining its function and sustaining its service through every worker who is identified with that service and acts as its representative with the client and in the community. This new concept of agency as the supporting matrix and controlling center of operation, working through defined structures but with imagination and flexibility gives to the worker a less powerful but more possible spot in which to exercise whatever of individual skill he possesses." J.T.

"The relationship within which this process results is not simply and strictly a person-to-person relationship, like that which the client has known in all his other experience. A difference has been introduced which carries with it a new dynamic ... that difference is the agency which the worker represents, a fixed and stable structure governing both worker and client in this relationship, presenting limits within which the worker operates and with and against which the client can measure and define his own need, his own will, and his own power." K.L.M.P.

"... the client may if he chooses, in greater or less degree, learn to bear this limited situation which, as he finally comes to realize, is imposed by himself as truly as by me: by his own human nature, no less than mine; or if you like, by the nature of the life process itself." J.T.

6. Only in a process can help be effectively offered and used.

"In every social work process, as in Rankian therapy, there is a common or generic base. In essence, all help, as we mean it, is psychological and depends upon a relationship process, whether it is expressed in the tangible form of relief, of foster home, of hospital service, or is derived from interviews alone. Whether you call the interview form of helping supervision, counseling, casework, or psychotherapy, depends not upon the difference in the nature of the basic helping process as such, but its functional determinants and the way in which they bear upon the helper and the one to be helped." J.T.

"This shift from the tendency to an even deeper and more futile analysis of either side, subject or object, client or worker, to an attempt to grasp the nature of the process itself in all its relativity and immediacy, is as important for the advancement of our understanding of human psychology as it is for social work." J.T.

"...it is not possible now or ever to know a client as he is in himself—or, for that matter, a worker either—except as part of a process in which, with one relatively fixed or known quantity, the other may be defined in terms of what he does..." J.T.

7. *Summation: the belief in growth (not "cure") and in the strength of the will.*

"Under the term 'will' Rank describes the most fundamental reality of psychological experience, the very essence of the self which underlies all expressions of that self, a dynamic concept of energy and motion. Thought of apart from its content, its forms, its objects of projection, it is pure force and movement, too total, too alive, too abstract to become conscious. It can come to consciousness only as it is in operation, positively or negatively, in relation to another will or an object, or as it operates as an organizing or integrating force on parts of the self treated as separate forces. It is impossible to handle as idea or formulate as concept since it is essentially the life principle itself." V.P.R.

"The viewpoint that underlies this advance in practice is not related so much to a particular psychology of behavior as to a new understanding of growth as a living process which can and must be utilized psychologically as well as physiologically in any effort to help human beings, particularly children. This brilliant insight was first realized consciously in therapy with adults by Otto Rank, whose single-minded devotion to the welfare of the patient, regardless of the classical tenets of psychoanalysis, led him not only to a new therapeutic method, but to a new theory of helping, applicable in any field in which the human will is accepted as a potentially creative force capable of overcoming and even of utilizing for growth the external and internal forces with which it must struggle." J.T.

CHANGING VALUES
IN EXPERIENCE TODAY*
The Theme of the Meeting

My task this morning is to shape the beginning—to set in motion the theme which will provide us with some sense of unity for the day—a process in which I shall be stating a question that confronts us not only for this one day, but that may shape our course for some time to come.

The theme of today's meeting "Changing Values in Experience Today" brings together four words suggesting an important relationship: "Changing" which surely is characteristic of the times; "Values" by which we mean both inner and outer values, but especially perhaps inner values; "Experience" which is the daily existence of each of us; and finally "Today" which brings us squarely into the year 1975—where we may or may not want to be! Values, changing so fast we cannot keep up with them; living experiences that are powerful and strange—the question that recurs over and over again, both in the spoken and the written word that comes to the Association is this: Can we find anything, we ask, in this psychology, the sources of which are in Rank's work, that will help us live through these tumultuous times? How can we go about this search, what markings can we find by which to chart our course?

This is, as you know, our tenth anniversary. We received our charter in 1965, our first meeting was held in the fall of 1966 and the first Journal appeared in the fall of 1966. It was a memorable journal, not only because it presented Rank's so-called "Yale paper" which had often been referred to but never published, but also because of Anaïs Nin's portrait of Rank, the experience of her therapy with him, the therapist who saw and recognized the creative woman, not merely the feminine problem. In this journal too is a letter from Henry Miller

* Paper presented at annual meeting of The Otto Rank Association, April 19, 1975.

to Anaïs Nin, describing with excitement his one interview in Paris with Rank.

In that journal, too, wishing to give an account of how the Association came to be formed, I wrote an article entitled "Individuals in Association" and in it I made a point which seems to me all-important to emphasize again today. We are here not primarily to give recognition to Rank, to memorialize his name—in the long run his work will be rediscovered (as is indeed now happening). But we are here to keep alive ideas and experiences that have had deep and profound meaning for ourselves, ideas that convey the highest regard for the individual, for growth and development, in times when mass movements can drown out the one lone voice. I chose the title deliberately and with care intending to imply that individuals who associate can still keep their individuality.

What we have known all along and rediscover anew each day, is that Rank's ideas cannot be "applied"—we have always avoided saying we will "apply" Rank's concepts to contemporary issues. Instead I speak of what I call for lack of better words, the three-step approach: first one takes the idea into the self, there it goes through a process of becoming part of that self which is already there, and finally, is put back out as if it were now one's own—as indeed it is.

Now I want to build a bridge from what I have just said, to the program as shaped for today. In our usual way we select from Rank a passage that illuminates our theme and this time we quote a sentence from the brief preface of *Beyond Psychology,* a sentence which we have used before but whose full meaning we have never explored. He writes: "Then we shall be able to discover new values in place of the old ones which seem to be crumbling before our very eyes—vital human values, not mere psychological interpretations predetermined by our preferred ideologies."

These are bold and ringing words: no hesitation, no doubt—"then we *shall* be able to discover"—words full of hope and promise and almost visionary in their prediction. It characterizes the very positive quality of Rank's thought, so often lost because of his acknowledgment of the darker side of life which is, as we well know, as natural and inevitable as the brighter side. Likewise, in functional helping, our acceptance of limits, of form, of the reality of negative feelings needing expression, of the imperative necessity that to become a helper, change must take place inside the self, often resulted in understatement of the wonderful life-giving possibilities that ensue out of just such acceptance of life the way it is.

What were these values "crumbling" before Rank's eyes, and more important, what were the new values he was so certain we might discover? It must be remembered that he was writing in the decade of the 1930's, forty years ago, a decade through which many of us lived with painful but also exciting experiences. He could have been writing of today when he speaks of "our general bewilderment" "our era of social distress" when in "the torrent of onrushing events. . . . we feel helpless because we cannot even for a moment stop its movement so as to direct it more intelligently."

At the meeting of our board of directors in the fall when program planning begins, this subject of changing values recurred with increasing emphasis, and following the meeting I began to ask myself do I know what a value is? Do I know what values are most important to me? Can I state them? When I think about values do I first think of the outer ones, those that exist in the morals of our society, in the institutions established to sustain them, or do I really hold myself to my own responsibility and ask what to me are the values that I hold most high—do I in fact live them or hold them only as ideals? These are by no means easy questions to answer, but stirring ones, confronting the self with its own deepest convictions.

At this same meeting of the board of directors, we became engaged, truly engaged with the word issues—contemporary issues. And the wish was expressed, in a variety of ways, for bringing together Rankian concepts and contemporary issues. We did not name those issues—there was no need to, conscious as we were of the tide of events and personalities that filled the world in which we live. But again after the meeting I took hold of this word issue, and I lived with it in reflection, realizing how impossible it is to select one issue out of the numberless ones whose impact we felt. But in order to become realistic and specific, I settled down one Sunday with the whole of the New York Times, with the specific focus of identifying and realizing what the issues were, with the result that I was overwhelmed by them,—feeling my own helplessness in the force of their power.

Along about this time a discussion took place between myself and a friend and colleague with whom, at bottom, I feel a likeness that cannot be disturbed on most matters, only to find that on a specific issue of that very day we had arrived at reactions that were widely different and divisive. From this I began to reason that even out of a psychological likeness, it was an impossibility for our attitudes, conclusions, solutions to be the same.

The observation emerging out of this experience is inescapable; it is the impact on the individual by these overwhelming events that can concern us. And we do understand something about the effect on the individual of change imposed by the outside, powerful change for which he is not ready and to which he must nevertheless relate.

To return now, and very briefly, to the question that I posed in my opening remarks—Can we find anything in this psychology, in Rank's work, to help us live through, to find our position, in these tumultuous times? Acknowledging from the outset that values must be our own inner values, developed and integrated into ourselves, what can we find nonetheless in this same brief preface of Rank's that might indicate at least some avenues along which to pursue our goal?

I will give you my version now of what Rank says about the "new values": He offers (and says so) no panacea, no solution: he is "pleading" (and he uses this word) for an acceptance of life the way it is, including and especially the acceptance of the "irrational," saying that we need at the same time and equally, the rational structures that man has built up since time immemorial "in religion and art, in philosophy and psychology" these being "an essential part of human existence." And he suggests that the new values will be old values recreated and relived in new experience in every individual. He urges us toward "an actual living in and with the flow of events, following its changing currents as we swim along fully aware of its dangerous undercurrents." Man lives simultaneously in two worlds, the natural world—a part of nature as are all creatures—and a man-made world and the two are often in conflict within ourselves.

But distinctly the emphasis is on the acceptance of the irrational, and it is extremely important to try to discover what Rank means by that word "irrational." Indeed this is a tantalizing question with which to live, and I can only give you my own version of what I believe he meant. Surely he was not thinking of the episodes that fill our press and screen, of violent acts when the impulse has gone wild with terrible destruction, although I suppose one would need to say they are at the extreme of the spectrum of irrationality.

But these extremes need not, in my opinion, concern us so much as does the "irrational" in our own lives. I think what Rank was speaking of was the realm of the intuitive knowing that lies just below the surface, the emotions, the magic which sometimes occurs in life, the unexplainable, the awesomeness—the opposite of the powerful effort to control or explain or rationalize the essense of the life process.

Of the flood of illustrations that come to my mind, I have selected just one out of my own work and lifelong interest in the process of choice. It still remains a mystery to me how people make the fundamental choices in life, especially let us say the all-important ones, how one chooses a life's work, life-relationships, a career; and I am especially interested in how the woman does that. I listen to parents whose youthful children are trying to decide where to go to college, what to study when they do go, always with the underlying anxiety that this may mean a life-time choice—what, where, and how. And indeed while I readily concede that an enormous amount of reasoning and weighing of pros and cons must go on, I still believe at bottom that when the moment comes to choose, some unexplainable—what I have called the deep stream of life—finally determines the direction.

I am delighted to have come upon a quotation from W. H. Auden which says this in a poet's words:

> When I look back at the three or four choices in my life which have been decisive, I find that, at the time I made them, I had very little sense of the seriousness of what I was doing and only later did I discover what had seemed an unimportant brook was, in fact, a Rubicon.

I know of course that what Rank means by values is to be found only in the whole of his work: in his understanding of the artist, his experience in and understanding of therapy, of what he calls a "philosophy of helping." But one key conclusion I bring today, for whatever value it may have—one that I hold, however, with deep conviction. It is this: that everything we believe and understand about the growth and development of the individual is just as meaningful and true for larger units of experience—the group, the community, the nation, the world. Principles, such as: development ensues from conflict, that process is the all-essential movement in any living organism, that the will is present in every relationship, surrounds us wherever we look, that the assertion of authority and leadership always calls forth the tendency to assert the own will against it, that events are likely to go to an extreme in order to discover where the limit lies, then to move back to seek the balance. Rank makes the point, and I truly believe this, that the individual who rebels against all outer restrictions in order to "do his own thing," will, if he develops at all, seek for and create those limits inside himself because of his deep need for them.

We have shaped the program today in such a way that it does select one contemporary issue to which to turn our attention, namely, the psychology of woman; moves on to consider "Timelessness and Change." This afternoon when Dr. Adamson will chair the meeting, we will consider "Social Work and Social Change" and explore one new method of therapy, namely, Transactional Analysis in the light of Rankian concepts. And at the end we shall try to round out and bring together the threads of the day's deliberations.

PROJECTION—Introducing "CORRESPONDENCE" by Carson McCullers

Years ago when I was teaching at the University of Pennsylvania School of Social Work the course briefly referred to as "personality," described by Miss Robinson in the preceding pages, I was preparing for a class session in which we would explore the meaning of "Projection"—a ubiquitous human characteristic. Commuting as I was then, on a suburban line, I stood on the railroad platform next to a man with two very young children—one boy standing by his father's side, the other being carried. Down the track roared the train. Standing near me, the boy, quivering with excitement and fright, looked frantically down the track at the approaching monster, up at his father, back to the train, then pointing to his baby brother (who was showing little reaction), he shouted to his father above the uproar, "He's AFRAID!" A pure illustration of projection, as is the story "Correspondence" which I am introducing with much pleasure.

If it is of any comfort to teachers, let me say it seemed always to be my experience that if I became absorbed with one subject I began to see abundant illustrations all around me. It was as if they appeared by magic, just when I needed them. But of course it was only because of a heightened awareness with a focus that lasted for a limited time only.

To be discussed in this same class hour years ago were a few brief literary writings, among them "Correspondence." As always, in assigning reading of this kind, we did so with a gentle admonition: do not try to analyze, or explain, or reduce to scientific evidence! Feel your way into the lines as you read, let yourself identify, enjoy the humor, the humanity, and the underlying psychological truths. It is a matter of recognition, of finding one's own likeness and difference.

For myself, in real life, I have always entertained grave doubts about the value of understanding a phenomenon like "projection." Rank, of course, constantly cautions against excessive efforts to "understand" to be overly "conscious," urging instead a living experience. We were always trying to achieve an emotional understanding of an experience without reducing it to a formula. However, for the helping person, an understanding of projection is of great importance, for many reasons, but among them the all-important one that usually the one who comes for therapy, or even to learn, projects on the helper or teacher the responsibility for whatever change is desired. In therapy, the characteristic is likely to be the location of blame on others, or on the outer situation. As we know so well, only when this changes and the will responsibility (along with the power to produce change) moves to the inside of the self, can any development occur. The two-sided relationship that consists of the therapist and the "patient" is not a relationship of likeness, even though the one being helped will find it there, but of difference in role. The concept of projecting upon the other what is in the self is far more meaningful, in our opinion, than the concept of "transference" which is unsuited to Rankian psychology.

"Dear Manoel" begins the "Correspondence" by Henrietta Evans, "going on fourteen" when she chooses a name from a list posted in her high school, ostensibly of South American students interested in starting a correspondence. Apart from the obvious point that the experience is entirely self created—without a reply—there are some touching and deeply human insights.

In her first letter she gives of herself without restraint: what she longs for, what she believes in, even her failures. She is able to tell it to this stranger, whose picture she paints in her mind's eye even to the color of his eyes—inner treasures of her self that she cannot talk about to her schoolmates because "I feel like I am different from them." If we are right in assuming, as I believe we are, that everything Carson McCullers wrote is autobiographical, not necessarily in particulars, in content, but in feeling of experience, then we can indeed assume that she felt her difference intensely. And one of the inexhaustible subjects for our consideration is that of the awareness of difference, which every child in one way or another, to one degree of intensity or another, appears to have experienced in his lifetime.

It is a privilege to have the permission of the New Yorker magazine to publish this story by Carson McCullers. The story can be found, too, in a collection of her writing entitled *The Mortgaged*

Heart, edited by her sister Margarita G. Smith, and published post-humously by Houghton Mifflin Company.

"CHOICE IS THE SOVEREIGN FACULTY OF THE MIND"

The quotation which becomes the title of this article comes from the novel *The Eighth Day* by Thornton Wilder. Seldom does one come upon a work of fiction where the change in a man's inner life and growth is so dramatically depicted. This is a novel of growth and change, of the inner life and the outer impact of fate upon it: of "Fate and Self Determination." That is why it is of such unusual interest to those who reflect upon these matters of life and choice.

Moreover, seldom does one come upon a novelist who prepares the reader so movingly, with such depth of perception, yet so clearly, for the questions on which he, the novelist is at work. People ask over and over again, why does a man or woman write? They seem to ask it repeatedly in literature that concerns itself with creating in the medium of words—yet it seems to me the answer is clear, no matter where one finds it. For in this novel Wilder is creating fictional characters to plumb the depths of his own doubts and conflicts. Is this not always true? The writer, the genius, lives with a rich, complicated, conflicted, widely ranging realm of thought—to it he must give form in order to live. He must shape it into lines, rhythm, development, resolution, and closure. He dispels fragmentation and distraction by creating a whole.

But let us first return to Wilder and ask, what are these questions that he makes and shapes and what does the title of his book mean? They appear first in a Prologue in which the whole story, from beginning to end, is told (excepting for the clue to the mystery that holds the plot together.) Wilder exclaims and asks:

"Life! Why life? What for? To what end?"

Of course he does not answer this question, for indeed as everyone knows, there is no answer. So he divides it into smaller units of questions, but first we need the brief outline of the story we are about to "live our way into."

John Ashley is the principal character whose life is broken in the middle by a stroke of fate. The story opens on a Sunday afternoon in the small Illinois village of Coaltown. Two families, the Ashleys and the Lansings, are doing what they do every Sunday afternoon: whiling away the time on the lawn of the rather elegant home of Breckinridge Lansing, wives and children looking on while the two good friends, John Ashley and Breckenridge Lansing practice rifle shooting. Present are Beata Ashley and her children, Sophie, Roger, Lily and Constance; and Eustacia Lansing with her children: George and Anne. The picture of the town is dull and lifeless: In the center of the town are the two coal mines of which Lansing is the manager and Ashley his subordinate whose job it is to try to invent ways to keep decrepit and worn out mines still operating.

Suddenly on the otherwise quiet afternoon when the only sound is the rhythmic shooting of the guns, one shot rings out and this time Lansing falls to the ground, mortally wounded. John Ashley is tried for murder, convicted within a week in an emotion-laden trial, and sent by train with a heavily armed guard to the state penitentiary where he is to be executed. But in the dead of night a strange and mysterious rescue takes place: a group of men board the train, smash the lights, bind up the guards, take possession of John Ashley, starting him upon an odyssey that is the heart of this book. John Ashley is never found by his pursuers, even though the case becomes a celebrated one and rumors come from everywhere that he has been seen and recognized. Never so; and, to give away the end of the story, five years later new evidence is uncovered that proves his innocence, but all too late because John Ashley is never heard from again when a ship on which he is aboard is lost at sea.

Yet these endings which make the plot are not nearly so important nor so interesting as the inner story of John Ashley's life from the moment of his rescue.

But let me return first to the questions which Wilder poses; then we shall look at the kind of man John Ashley was before that fateful Sunday afternoon.

Nothing is more interesting than the inquiry as to how creativity operates in anyone, in everyone: mind, propelled by passion, imposing itself, building and unbuilding; mind—the latest-appearing manifestation of life—expressing itself in statesman and criminal, in poet and banker, in street cleaner and housewife, in father and mother—establishing order or spreading havoc; mind—condensing its energy in groups and nations, rising to an incandescence and then ebbing away exhausted; mind —enslaving and massacring or diffusing justice and beauty.

Then Wilder asks: "This John Ashley—what was there in *him* (as in some hero in those old plays of the Greeks) that brought down upon him so mixed a portion of fate: unmerited punishment, a 'miraculous' rescue, exile, and an illustrious progeny?"—"Was there a connection between the catastrophe that befell both houses and these later developments? Are humiliation, injustice, suffering, destitution, ostracism—are they blessings?" Simultaneously, he has in mind (as he later describes) the extraordinary success of three of the Ashley children who become world famous—one as a journalist, one as a singer, one as an activist for worthy causes of all kinds.

The title of the book, *The Eighth Day*, has a subtle and illusive meaning: We (man, woman of the twentieth century) are children of the eighth day, the allusion being to the seven days in which the world was created, God resting on the seventh. The words are spoken at a New Years Eve party by a Dr. Gillies, a character both of hope and despair. It is the New Year that welcomes in the new century. He creates hope for those who listen, while his words are actually being spoken, but later one who knows him well, says, "He didn't mean a word of it." So one is never sure, as Wilder could not have been himself—expressing as he was the two sides of his nature. Much later on in the book we find the prophetic words: "There is no creation without faith and hope." "There is no faith and hope that doesn't express itself in creation."

* * *

John Ashley was a man who seemed to make no choices, who went with the stream of events that happened to come his way. One could almost say he was without will of his own—that is to say, without creative will and yet he was, as we shall see later, a creative man. He had been the most brilliant student in engineering in his college in Hoboken, New Jersey. One later section of the book describes his courtship of Beata, his wife.

But here, as I see it, is a classic illustration of what Rank means by "adjustment"—conformity to outer events and decisions, with no precipitant to awaken the promise of creativity which lay in the inner life of John Ashley. Only after the catastrophe, when fate struck an irreversible blow, did the creative elements in John Ashley begin to take over.

But first let us look at what kind of man he was through half of his life. As a young man he went to work as an engineer for a mining company with headquarters in Toledo, Ohio. There he worked puttering on inventions of a minor sort, when suddenly there came a time when he was informed that he was to be transferred to the actual location of two mines, in Coaltown, Illinois. He accepted the decision without protest—whether he knew or not that these were worn-out mines that the company was determined to keep in operation despite the dangers and worn-out equipment.

He arrived in Coaltown and went to work at once—down the shafts, aware of the risks, devising this and that solution. He used whatever he had to do the job he was supposed to—never does any anger, or protest, or discontent show itself. This is one of the subtle and delicate portrayals of character by which Wilder prepares us for what is to follow. Ashley had been "called" to Coaltown as a mere maintenance engineer to mines already in decline—his duty was to repair and shore up delapidated fabric. He used all of his ingenuity,—was delighted with his work. Was delighted with the large house he found for his family (said to be haunted). He accepted without complaint ⅓ of the salary of Breckenridge Lansing who was the top manager, who did nothing of any note—friendly, outgoing, sometimes carousing in the inns along the river. Yet again, John Ashley showed no envy, no resentment. The Lansings and Ashleys were friends; the two men worked together at off hours while John Ashley puttered at new ideas and new inventions, always giving Lansing credit for work he never did—always somehow covering for him and for his faults.

Then Wilder becomes more explicit: John Ashley had no ambition, no dominating will, he was an "invisible" man. He felt no fear, he showed no emotion (not even to his children). He was in every ordinary sense of the word a "happy" man. No doubt he would have been content to go on for the rest of his life without any change, without "growth" as it interests us. A well-adjusted man with whom no one found any fault. He lived in Coaltown in this contentment for seventeen years. He seemed never to have realized that he and Breckenridge Lansing had been sent to Coaltown because they had failed—at least so far as the company was concerned. Indeed, Breckenridge Lansing had failed, and one can conjecture that to send him to Coaltown without Ashley who could actually do the work, was indeed impossible.

This is, to repeat, "adjustment" of the average man to the situation which develops without a choice and without a single sign of rejection of the circumstances imposed upon him. And yet as Wilder (again with brilliant portrayal of the two sides of Ashley's nature) writes: "He rose each day with zest—singing before the shaving mirror," two favorite songs which occur again in his later experiences.

Only a John Ashley could have lent himself for so long to so difficult and even humiliating a role. Devoid of ambition or envy, indifferent to the admiration or contempt of others, completely happy in his family life at 'The Elms' he 'saved' Breckenridge Lansing. He not only did all he was able, to conceal his superior's ineptitude from the company and from the community, he played the older brother to this older man.

*　　*　　*

In the darkness of the night, in that July of 1902, when John Ashley was snatched from his guards and started on his way, he himself did not know and never knew who his rescuers were. They had provided for him a few necessities, very few indeed, but each of crucial importance. A horse, saddled; a suit of denim; a hat, a bag of oats with an apple and potatoes; a compass, a map, and with silent motions pointing westward toward the Mississippi River. It was the horse who took the first step, who began to find her way. This was the beginning of the journey from Illinois to Chile.

Chapter II of the book (from Illinois to Chile) can be read only if one gives one's self over to the wonder, the awe, the mystical which Wilder himself seems to find so satisfying, so true, so poignantly meaningful of what he intends by the man of "The Eighth Day."

His rescuers disappeared, no sound of their departure. "Simple natural, and unearthly." Ashley did the simple immediate things; he changed his clothes, he consulted his compass and map with a lighted match, he opened the bag of apples and oats. And then:

"He was filled with wonder. He laughed softly, 'Gee Whillikers' Gee Whillikers." "Ashley felt younger hourly. He was filled with an indefensible, an impermissible, happiness." . . . "He felt the need to talk. The horse seemed to like being talked to; in the diffused starlight he could see her ears rising and falling." He named her Evangeline "bringer of good tidings" and then prophetically he speaks these words: "You are a sign. We've both been marked for something." "He was overwhelmed with the wonder of it."

The reader could reflect long and deeply in contemplation of this tremendous joyful burst of happiness that followed the separation from all most dear to him, facing all of the unknown ahead. A happiness full of impulse of spirit, different in kind in every way from the early statement that he had lived "happily" in Coaltown.

From here on Ashley uses every shred of intuition, ingenuity, and urge toward life. In most extraordinary ways he does indeed reach Chile.

I think there cannot be any question but that Wilder's interest in "how creativity operates" is given in living experience in Ashley's journey to Chile. This may at first seem strange to the reader, as it was to me. Because the content is in a sense so unimportant, almost trivial one might say. Wilder might have spent more of his reflection on the fact that three of Ashley's children became creators in different mediums: in writing, in music, in activism. Here there was evidence of what the world would call creativity. Yet instead, it is that poignant awesome inner/outer journey of Ashley that engages his deepest thought and attention. At one point Wilder says "Ashley was a genius." But we have already seen how, up to this time, no evidence of the true genius appeared.

The extraordinary fact about this journey—what one can call an Odyssey without exaggeration—is this: that Ashley chooses every step of the way, feels his way along in a process, so that nothing goes amiss. Every piece falls into place. Wilder makes it plain that Ashley is not a man who can plan logically or systematically for his own welfare. He wakens in the morning knowing what he will do and how. The steps come to him intuitively or by talking with his horse Evangeline. All that we read is the opposite of control, of fear, of excessive planning ahead. What he knew was, that he wished to go to Chile. He knew of mines there high in the mountains, and what he knew of them were such disadvantages that he could be certain he would not meet there any of his old associates.

But to me what was miraculous was his urge toward life, to live, to gain his way, to use everything that was in him, past and present, to project just far enough on the future to make his way succeed. Wilder is indeed exclaiming over the urge toward life in every human being—and this in the face of a tragic precipitant.

I have already mentioned the flood of happiness that overcame him when first he discovered he was alone with his horse and on his way. Emotion of this kind was new to him. He felt the need to talk and talk he did to Evangeline—he told her everything that happened. Later when in memory he sees his family in a new light he talks to her of them. Her ears twitch and respond. She protects him; she senses the approach of enemies. She seems to know the way without his direction. Then comes that remark (already referred to); he says to Evangeline,

"You are a sign. We've both been marked for something." This is indeed the recognition of the self—the "being marked for something." It could be, if the reader will not feel it too great a stretch of presumption, what Rank calls in the artist the "Self appointment." It seems to me that every child who suddenly recognizes and feels his own identity is bound to feel in some shape or other, words not unlike this, "I am marked for something" whether he achieves it or not. Remember that Wilder in the early section of the book in no way shows that Ashley feels "marked for something" nor recognizes his own genius. Only later does Wilder describe it.

Ashley travels toward the Mississippi River where he hopes to pick up a barge on its way to New Orleans (as in fact he does). But early in the journey he experiences new strands of himself that were never before expressed. With the sign of a lighted farmhouse at night his thoughts return to his children, feeling and seeing what he had never seen before—with guilt of his omissions. At the smell of bacon in the morning air he "Put his head between his knees. He fell over to one side, then rolled over to the other. He groaned, he lowed, he bayed. The anguish of mind in a mature man is borne in silence and immobility, but John Ashley was not a mature man." Why does Wilder say he was not a mature man? Only, I think, because never before has he known or experienced the emotional depths of his life: now engulfed in loss, in yearning, in love, in protest (later he says at last, why did this have to happen to me?). Guilt, fear, memory, and all now combining to make his way.

The memory of past events plays a strategic role in his choices. As a child he loved more than anyone his grandmother, an "unlicensed veterinary" who had a way with animals that he learned and loved. He knew about horses—"first sniff the oats yourself and taste them before you offer them to the horse." If you have to use the whip, whip your own leg first—never use your foot; do not stroke a horse but slap him gently first slapping yourself. Every shred of knowledge came to his use.

His choice of a barge on the Mississippi River came from a memory of an outing which with his family he had long ago taken to the river's edge, sitting watching the barges make their way down the river. He uses his mathematical skill (that of a genius) to play cards and win at the game, to provide himself with money. Half way along the trip he must sell Evangeline, and this he does to a woman who seems to recognize him and provides the means for his trip across the river to the island where the barges stop.

One could continue to add to the fascinating detail of how he manages and how he moves, always in the direction which he has settled upon in his mind. But the main points are here; and for me there is no question but that Wilder is showing the freeing of creativity by an event of catastrophic tragedy and revealing the self found in the inner life of this his chief character, John Ashley.

*   *   *

Again, it may seem pretentious to call this whole experience a "rebirth" but Wilder himself does so. Several times in Ashley's journey short, touching relationships develop with women who understand him as no one has before. With Maria Izaza: "Their friendship grew in their silences; it was cemented by their destitution. It was nourished by the prevalence of misery in San Gregorio." She lays out cards and tells his fortune. He confirms many of the facts and she says to him, *"That, That*—happiness? No!" Adding, "You are being born."

As indeed he was. He knew his inner life, he felt emotion, he knew what suffering was, his memories (blind to him before) became crystal clear as he saw them in new light. Every move he made, every decision he made, was by his own choice. He was filled with the urge to live, and live he did until the tragic moment again when a man known as a "rat" who hunts escaped men, discovered his identity and he was forced to flee.

But before doing so once more a brief relationship with a woman, Mrs. Wickersham, enriches his life, in such limited sparse ways but always with a depth of understanding seldom found in real life or in literature. She helps him to escape once more and their parting is thus:

> Ashley took her right hand and kissed the back of it slowly. The leave-takings of the children of faith are like first recognitions. Time does not present itself to them as an infinite succession of endings.

The point that I wish again to emphasize is the change that occurs in the memory itself—in the past inner life. Several times I have alluded to the title of the autobiography of Lillian Hellman, *Pentimento* which expresses in a few brief words the movement that occurs in looking back. "Pentimento" is an Italian word used to describe what happens to an ancient painting. The painting on the surface begins to fade and below it begins to appear another painting different in character and form. "It is a way of seeing and then seeing again." The memory that seemed fixed and authentic begins to change: emotions never felt before well up in the consciousness: for John Ashley it was guilt, fear, refusal of the creative elements in the self, omissions in relationships: the failure to climb the hard and perilous road of knowing that one is "marked for something:" the unprotesting conformity to whatever outer circumstances bring. The content of John Ashley's experience in some strange way may not seem to the reader to be worthy of the word "creativity"—yet it can well be that the lack of grandeur in the content makes it all the clearer what Wilder meant when he wrote of his own question "how creativity operates in any one." The will of John Ashley has changed dramatically and taken on a new character.

THE HELPING PROCESS
Where Now?

Part 1

During the time when the committee was at work preparing manuscript for the new edition of Miss Robinson's selected writings, she wrote (and we quoted in the Introduction) "Looking back over these decades, I see that a single focus has dominated my writing, namely, my interest in the development of a professional self." From this the distinctive title of the collected works emerged, "The Development of a Professional Self—Teaching and Learning in Professional Helping Processes." Such a singleness of direction in a lifetime, and the insight that puts it all together thus, in one sentence, at the end of that lifetime is rare indeed.

Why "professional self?" Why not just "The Nature of the Self"—this being the title of the course that she taught year after year to students at the Pennsylvania School? What is this dilemma, this dichotomy, this apparent division between two aspects of the self, personal and professional? And how can we reconcile two seemingly contradictory realities, namely, that in the functional helping process where the professional self is actively engaged there is at the same time the possibility for richness of feeling, heightened relationship, and clarity of insights, often beyond that which prevails in personal relationships?

This article began with my wish to speak in tribute to Miss Robinson, first for myself alone, but with the hope that simultaneously for others it would serve to release and give form to the unique individual memories that belong to each who was a student, or to those who may have known her in other relationships, or who know her only through her writings. As I worked, at first in thought only, then to begin to write, it became increasingly clear to me that the time had come for some new statements regarding the functional helping process—in writing, in discussion and especially in the practice itself. And that this work in continuity would be the most deeply satisfying tribute to the superb human being that she was, always, as she would say, "My best self is my professional self."

Separation is an experience about which we believe we understand something both in theory and in actuality. The ending of therapy, of a deeply meaningful learning experience, was the key to what had gone before and what followed. Every person who has been through the functional process knows this; knows the new sense of life ahead, expanding imagination, energy, and new use of the professional self.

Yet there is an aspect of *this* separation which seems to me to carry a difference that I can scarcely touch and then only with intimations of its meaning. So long as Miss Robinson lived it was as if we could be certain of an unconquerable source, a center, a wholeness, that gave a reassuring certainty that what one cared about most would prevail.

Suddenly she is gone and each is on his own. The source of inner life is a delicate, awesome quality—some have an abundance within themselves; some have it only at times and then perhaps only in relationship; others seem to have it not at all, being always dependent on others to create it. In therapy, it seems to me, the person taking help draws upon the source of life in the other, but in the ending he takes it over into himself.

We know in theory that separation can be followed by an upsurge of inner life in the self. In reality, although this life may appear in sudden impulsive break-throughs, it is nonetheless a slow process that cannot be willed. It takes a kind of yielding to, acceptance of, circumstance that cannot be changed; but also a nurturing of the desire to work again, to live the life of one's own self.

During the time when Miss Robinson was at work on her article "The Influence of Rank in Social Work" her interest in the word "influence" became uppermost in her mind. She was working on the question, "what *is* influence" and it was clear that she could reject without a second thought influence that was imitation. Although it was Rank's influence that was the direction of her train of thought, I am certain that she was thinking as well of herself, (probably of Dr. Taft too) in some wondering thoughts of what would come in generations to follow.

At the same time our attention was drawn to Rank's own clear description of the steps by which "influence" becomes one's own in this professional self of which we are speaking. First there is a new element, non-self, which is encountered, engaged with, taken into the inward experience. There, in a second phase, it undergoes a process of becoming part of the self as it has been and is now changing, and lastly it is put back out in work that is original, different, belonging wholly to one's own self in a fresh creation. This is of course a greatly oversimplified compressing of the many facets of a human process.

*   *   *

When I wrote above that I thought the time had come for some new statements about the functional helping process, I was reacting to what seems to me a widespread and urgent need on the part of those who are reading theory to understand what the process itself is like in experience. With the underlying belief that process is indispensable to growth (and learning in the true sense of the word is growth) and indispensable to therapy, we believed when we were teaching that the process must be experienced in order to be understood. This never failed to bring criticism from the outside, especially when an intellectual concept of knowledge was applied. One might then ask, where now can one experience the process, where does it exist? And the answer is a bold claim that it exists in the hands and experience of those who are helping, their source being in the process which they themselves experienced.

At the same time, I have long harbored the notion, and taught in some seminars some years ago, that process exists in every life, (at least in ordered, aware lives) and that one can find it (particularly in work) recognizing the phases, the movement, which, briefly summarized are: the surface beginning, "cold" and often bungling; the coming up against an obstacle when one either stops or moves to a new level; the movement gradual into more ease and skill; the approach of the ending with conclusion and its resulting reward of a completed experience. I am firmly convinced that every life needs these brief limited experiences of a conclusion even in the trivial affairs of everyday living.

This paper which I am now writing grows out of my urgent wish to begin anew to write about the helping process. But simultaneously and almost with equal urgency, I wanted to count upon the possibility that others will be stimulated to do the same. Also to visualize more and more of the pages of the Journal devoted to this exploration which is implicit in our purpose.

As I began again to write about the helping process, a sudden realization struck me: that in the past I have written from the experience of helping and teaching others (as in my book "The Nature of Choice") not specifically about my experience of being helped even though this lay as the primary source. Now I am re-animating the past, taking back the vivid and alive memories, and I have started in this way in Part 2 which follows, which I have entitled "Portrait of a Professional Self."

I have made some choices in the use of words. At first I thought I must find some wording to substitute for "the helping process" "the one who helps" or "the one who comes for help" because they are cumbersome and not brief enough. I considered using the words "therapy" and "therapist" because they do convey to a reader the depth of experience possible. But I returned again to "the helping process" because it is unique and includes not only teaching, but supervision, casework, and what is now commonly named "counseling" (even though in our true meaning we do not "counsel"). I have also settled upon the use of the word "client" in its literal meaning of one who uses professional services, and student which is clear.

I have also become aware of certain elements of form that have guided me and that feel to be the most rewarding in presenting accounts of what goes on between helper and client or teacher and student. First, I refer to the concentration of attention on what goes on during this session between the one who is helped and the other: especially perhaps what the helping person does and says, what he is in function, how he feels the will, the emotion, and how he responds to the impact of these upon himself. I realized how I felt about an account of biographical data and problem of the client: it tends to divert and erase the immediate, present movement of the relationship and turns attention elsewhere.

Further, an observation of long-time standing has at last appeared to me with more clarity: this is the desirability of living with one small part of Rank's theory, a sentence at a time, even a phrase at a time, in order to bring it to life in experience.

I have (somewhat reluctantly) written about my own way of helping in private practice, not in order to recommend it as the one desirable way, but out of the conviction that a concrete framework is effective, with or against which others can clarify their beliefs.

And lastly, one more expression of conviction: that the Rankian psychology, its outlook on life, its extraordinary value for understanding human experience—even for reading the daily newspaper—is as valuable for the individual in retirement whose professional work may have ended, as for those who are still actively at work.

*　　*　　*

It was as "Miss Robinson" that she was known to successive classes of students. This customary way of addressing her or speaking of her had become over the years a mark of her own unique self (along with her familiar "V.P.R." on memos and notes at the School). In recent years, when the occasion arose, she would say of herself, "I am a teacher, through and through a teacher" whereas (she would add) "Dr. Taft was a therapist." But even as she was thus declaring herself to be a teacher, she would not have differed with one who said she was a therapist. Indeed, she was a superb therapist. But I think she held thus firmly to being a "teacher" because implicit in it was the function of teaching which made possible the therapeutic movement in a genuine learning experience.

If it were not for the formality often associated with the word "professional," I would feel safe in saying that Miss Robinson was her truest professional self in all aspects of living. By this I mean the sense of inner form, of inner discipline, never without some rich awareness of inner pattern. Perhaps this can be expressed in the words of a neighbor, who occasionally dropped in for a visit, "I always felt better when I left."

PORTRAIT OF
A PROFESSIONAL SELF

Part 2

In the early 1940's, in the first semester of my master's degree program at the Pennsylvania School, I had a weekly 4 o'clock appointment for individual conference with Miss Robinson. I was traveling from Baltimore to Philadelphia, and as usual my train schedule brought me to the offices of the School (then located at 311 South Juniper Street) just a few minutes before my conference was to begin. As I entered, one of the secretaries rushed up to me with an urgent message from my office to call "Washington" as soon as I arrived. I was then the Assistant Administrator of the Maryland Public Welfare Department, a high-pressured agency recovering from the depression and launched upon the establishment of a state-wide county unit program. "Washington" was the then Social Security Department, the federal department from which our money, rules, and supervision came.

I stood looking at the slip of paper in my hand; it was 4 o'clock, Miss Robinson was ready for me, and I went into her office intending to excuse myself for a few minutes while I made the telephone call. I sat at the side of her desk explaining the urgency. Miss Robinson made no answer, no comment. She waited. And suddenly a rush of decision clear as a bell, went through me. I said, "I won't return the call now." And I settled down to my conference which (as I shall explain further later) was deeply affected by this incident.

I begin with this autobiographical note for two reasons: the first is the startling realization as I have already mentioned, that as I have, on occasion, written about the helping process I have drawn mainly upon my experiences of helping others, never directly upon the experience of myself being helped. As I reflect on this and call it "startling"—I see at once that in doing so I have been using only one-half of myself, shutting out that deepest level of awareness, a reservoir of memories, rich, elated, painful, sometimes riddled with doubt, sometimes with a clarity of direction that never faltered. In my book, *The Nature of Choice,* I was nevertheless able to write (after regretting the fact that I had not known Rank in person), "Yet I have been advantaged in that I have had simultaneously the unusual experience of being helped in a truly functional process, toward the goal of becoming a teacher, at the same time that I discovered in Rank's writing the exact and precise illumination of the moment in which I lived. To put it in Rank's words, 'for once experience and pure psychological understanding are simultaneous.' " From this (written in 1951-52) I might have reasoned that whenever I wrote I was reaching to the source of my own experience of being helped, at the same time that I was writing of helping (teaching) students. One cannot be one's self without permitting the whole of that self to be in motion in the work.

The second reason for starting with a memory of my own is to highlight a principle of functional helping in the most alive, simple, and clear way available to me; namely, that the helper remains steadfastly identified with the individual's process, standing for it, holding to it, representing it, affirming it, against all interference or interruption, no matter how compelling the reason may seem to be.

In retrospect I see and have known for a long time, that this was that moment of choice that Auden speaks of (and which I have quoted several times before):

> When I look back at the three or four choices in my life which have been decisive, I find that, at the time I made them, I had very little sense of the seriousness of what I was doing and only later did I discover what had seemed an unimportant brook was, in fact, a Rubicon.

What was the choice that I was making? It was first of all, a commitment to myself, to my own process placing it first even ahead of what might have been a crucial point for others. It is that "self-appointment" in a human way that Rank assigns chiefly to the artist but which I believe is true for most of us. For me, it was a far-reaching choice because it was the turning point when the whole direction of my life changed, from outward-directedness, as an administrator responding to and reacting to all the demands from the outside, to inner-directness when the longing to understand the individual (myself and others) took over and shaped the direction for what turned out to have been for the rest of my life.

Before I leave my reflections about this conference on this particular day, I need to add, on behalf of understanding the helping process, that my hour of time with Miss Robinson was affected profoundly by this incident at the beginning. I do not remember the content or the particulars, (they being unimportant anyway) but I do bring to awareness as I write, the emotional aura, of guilt, of fright, the two major emotions that are aroused by a fundamental change. The guilt is the guilt for declaring the interests of the self first, and the fear is the fear of change, of the unknown, of the intuitive sense of growth, of what Rank speaks of as "the conflictual separation of the individual from the mass . . .," the acceptance of one's difference—the guilt for the powerful will expression present in such a choice. One does not understand this at the time—only in retrospect.

Yet another point is illustrated here: that so seemingly minor an incident can become, must become, the dominant factor in what we speak of as "the present experience"—more specifically, for that hour of conference and those following. I must have tried that day to work on the material which I had brought, which I customarily did, but it would have been in a recurring wave of emotion, never with any conscious realization of the long-ranging effects of this day. Miss Robinson had a way of saying, in a time of crisis or even of a mildly troubled day, "We have to make the day," or, more specifically, "Shall we work on the material . . ." whatever the material might be, whether in those days of conference, or later, on articles for the Journal or programs for a meeting.

It accounts in part for my continuous and ever-deepening interest in "work" knowing, first, that if the initial resistance is overcome, work will set a process in motion and being in motion in process will increase energy, interest, wholeness, direction, focus, with, always, an ending in sight which, when once accomplished, creates a change of feeling from fragmentation to unity and wholeness.

As I write about the Helping Process I have already touched upon three points of primary importance: the first is, the identification of the helper with the *function*, with the sustaining of the individual's process without interruption; secondly of the value of process without which no individual can "find himself." I am not generalizing for all of casework practice, or for other helping processes; I am exploring specifically what I understand of the functional Rankian way of helping, rooted in the theory of Rank, expanded into the theory of function.

*　　*　　*

True function is an inner state of being, not an external definition of the service offered. In private practice, it seems to me, the inner reality of function must be even more clearly realized, and the outer aspects of the situation must reflect and be consistent with, the true nature of the help offered. Even in the social agency, where so much support for the student comes from the external structure, the process of gaining more skill is a process of making the function one's own.

I am taking the liberty of using my own private practice (some years ago) to make clear the points that interest me. I shall be adding to this some very recent experience in interviews with "senior citizens" regarding the problems that have entered their aging lives. I hope it will be clear to the reader that I use this content not in order to recommend it as the one way of helping (about much of which I have recurrent questions), but a concrete framework against which and with which thinking and exploration can be stimulated. Even as I write, I know, too, that it is for my own sake, for the on-going clarification of the experience, that I return to it for pursuit of this urgent need to illuminate my own conception of the helping process.

I begin with a general observation: that among the many will expressions of the client, the helping person can know, without fail, that the one who comes for help will try to level the difference between himself and the helper—will attempt to erase the professional paradigm* on behalf of a deeply felt and painful need to make this a "personal" relationship. One can feel this poignant, painful, human desire as a reaction to the vulnerable position of being subject to the other's supposed effort to change him, to fail in responding to his need, to control what happens not only in this hour when he comes but during the days between. To have a "friend," on a person-to-person level of equality, with the supposed "freedom" of

---

*This word is unfamiliar to me, but seems, now that I have encountered it, to present a meaningful way to describe inner pattern with suggestion of movement. I came upon it in use in a book by Robert Jay Lifton, *The Life of the Self,* otherwise, too, a fascinating book.

conversation would, it is supposed, ease the tension considerably. One does not expect this to come out clearly and directly in speech, probably not at all in this recognizable way, but it can be felt in a wide-ranging variety of content, usually, at the same time, with its opposite, the fear that the limits will somehow be removed.

It was for this reason, the support of the outer setting, that my preference in the past was for the clear office arrangement. My interest today is in the possibility of the use of any setting, provided the one who is helping knows and recognizes the possible appearance of this content, and utilizes it as the dynamic that it can be.

My desk was the usual standard office desk—I sat in my place with the client opposite to me. (I ask myself, did I arrange it this way because this was the only setting I knew where I myself was helped?) I worked in a settled time structure: fifteen weeks, with the first three a time of exploring whether to go on. I chose the time structure probably because it was deeply laid down in me as the semester structure, but also with some intuitive sense that it was enough but not too much. The argument is often advanced that the amount of time needed differs for different people, depending on seriousness of the problem and other factors; I did not feel the need to use this variable. The dynamic of the known time precipitates the essentials; the approach of and the actual occurrence of the ending is crucial. I would not have refused a second series of 15 weeks, but only after some living of reality by the individual involved.

It was my custom to take responsibility for the start of each interview. I felt it to be essential to carry the continuity. I found the pieces for continuing by a method that became a habit: rather than writing out a record of the interview, I waited a brief time for the dominant points to linger in my recollections. These I would jot down and pick them up again when the next interview began.

I held firmly to the time of day and day of week, with regularity week after week, and I did so even when there were apparently valid reasons for change. How hard it is to describe the difference between a will struggle because of determination on the part of the helper because this is *his* way, and its opposite, the firm support of the process which suffers from interruption. (Even though the effects of interruption can be handled.)

I remember a vivid illustration. A social worker who had been coming for the usual 15 week period, working on supervisory material, had gone through the weeks only in the most positive manner.

He was learning, modifying his practice, exchanging insights that were exhilerating to both of us. I could find nothing wrong; yet I had an underlying uneasiness. (People will say, we functional helpers will always look for trouble, "must it always be painful?") Unexpectedly, about three weeks before the concluding date, he came in, full of needing to tell me, he could not come on the date set for his last appointment; he had to leave town for some need of a family member (I do not recall what it was). While factually announced to me, the individual knew enough about ending to know this was by no means a casual change of a date. Naturally I do not recall the specifics of the exchange between us (interfering with our efforts to work on material) but from now on this was it. I held to the ending date; I think he was always grateful that I did. The guilt that the helper must feel in standing thus by the process is unavoidable. Miss Robinson deals with it in her second book on supervision.

Lastly (in this illustration of the way in which I worked) I have in mind my avoidance, insofar as possible, of the use of the question. If you pause to think about it, the "question," no matter how gently said, is a request to organize an answer; if there is an answer, it must be assembled. The will of the helper is in the question; the will of the one helped must be aroused. At its worst the question interrupts the train of thought which we desire in order to reach the subliminal memories. The question can be of great use, as for instance in a projection to a class of students, when the intention is to precipitate just this organization of will. And in the one-to-one helping it can serve the same purpose. But for general use in keeping an interview underway, I soon did without it, not by conscious decision but by another way taking its place.

This comment just made about "subliminal" memories leads me again into the subject of the importance of process. By subliminal (rejecting the more complex word "unconscious") I mean, as the literal definition indicates, those recollections that lie below the immediate surface, at the threshold, that can be produced at will or sometimes have to be searched for and waited for. We all have the common experience of forgetting a name, unable to recall it. Even though of little importance, the mind works away at it, until suddenly it is there, out of nowhere. The workings of the human brain are still awesome.

In the process of a known time period the subliminal memories can be gradually recovered from week to week, always then as if clinging to, circling around the present within an intention to understand some aspect of the self. I worked always with a specific focus; when professional helping persons came, it was on their practice (sometimes the will struggle evolved through the effort to abandon that material on practice). Or, if an individual came outside of the profession, I found it always to be true that sooner or later some aspect of a choice to be made began to shape up (like a piece of wood being carved into a meaningful figure) and this specific I always held on to as (to use another metaphor) the blazed mark on trees through the wilderness.

I think this effort to establish in private practice a structure as undeviating as that which I have described, undoubtedly grew out of the undeviating nature of the structure of the School curriculum: where the time structure, the assignments, the essential reading, and especially the literary materials remained the same, class after class and year after year. How could this sameness be fresh? Because, as I have already quoted Miss Robinson as saying, the teacher had to create herself afresh for every class session, and while the basic psychological concepts remained the same, the experience which each unique student brought was always fresh, original, and illuminating.

What does the helping person say? What does he feel? How does he respond? "Silly question!" one should say; how else but by infinite particular illustrations, if one is to value spontaneity and avoidance of clichés. Still, I do believe there are some general observations; I would like to venture to state them.

I have already mentioned above my own preference to avoid the question, unless I intend to call up an effort to assemble an answer to my request. In its place I am likely to use comment: "This is the first time you are here, you may not be altogether clear why you are here and how we go about this." When I said this, recently, to an elderly man he said at once, "I do know—it's because I'm so nervous and I don't know why I'm nervous and that makes me think there is something wrong with me."

I will give another illustration: this time, when I knew at once that I had made a mistake. Another elderly man had come to try to examine the question, whether his wife must be placed in a nursing home. He had described to me her frightening behavior—wandering away from home alone in the early morning. Among the many particulars he recalled was this one: "She doesn't remember where she puts things, one minute something is in her hand, the next minute it is gone." I said something to the effect, (and very mistakenly) how familiar this is, I too could have a paper in my hand and not know soon after, what I had done with it. He reacted at once, defensively. It is clear that I had minimized his account, excused his wife, sided with her, injected myself into the interview. In long after-thought it confirmed my growing conviction that one cannot point out, to the one who is telling, an aspect of the situation that he seems not to see—such as the remark "but don't you think she was upset"— which of course he knows and the remark becomes a separation, resented I am sure even though the resentment may not be shown.

Yet again I must add and quickly, there is no one right way, there is above all the need for the helper to be himself, provided that it is a professional self. And the second point is, that one need never fear "mistakes" if one knows that the main thing is that they be handled—recognized and picked up in some way. I can recall almost word for word a comment Dr. Taft once made to me, "Rank used to say, it doesn't matter what happens so long as you handle it." I think she prefaced this by telling me of a day once when tons of coal were being delivered (in the old days when coal was delivered) in the midst of an interview in therapy with a child.

I have mentioned 1) the avoidance of the question 2) the effect of the injection of one's self into the interview 3) what I speak of as pointing out what the person seems to fail to see and usually with the implication of defense of the person being criticized; 4) I referred above to my practice of carrying the continuity, not hesitating to take the lead in starting a train of thought along a line of content.

And lastly (although there are many more) I want to speak of the healing quality of a shared feeling, even over a trivial matter. One of these same elderly gentlemen whom I have mentioned above is paralyzed on his right side but relatively mobile. At the beginning of the interview he had a lighted cigar which he graciously permitted to go out. As we were finishing he picked up his now half-smoked cigar, looked at me with a kind of questioning look and I said, yes, it is all right for you to smoke your cigar. Whereupon he took from his pocket a book of matches, inserted the whole container into the side of his shoe, leaned down, tore out a match with his left hand, struck it and lighted the cigar. When this feat was completed he again looked squarely at me and we both laughed—he at his ingenuity and I at my admiration of it. The warm feeling remained with me long afterward.

If we accept Rank's premise that the one who comes for help, the client, the patient, is the "chief actor" then we reason from this that he is the one to characterize himself. I have always felt it to be, (as shown in the title of this article) a matter of creating one's own self-portrait. In aging I see this ever more clearly, first for myself, reinforced by observation of others, that the need to look back is not for those denigrating reasons: such as nostalgia, living in the past, diverting one's self from the present. It is instead a powerful urgent will expression, productive, illuminating, to give form and meaning to one's life by retrospect in the light of the present day. One can and probably does examine such questions as, what were the moments of choice? At this point was *I* responsible, did *I* do it, or was it done to me? Especially does it take the past to make lucid the will pattern of the self. In recent times the idea of a "life review" (as advocated by Dr. Robert Butler) has seemed to me not at all like what I have in mind. It is not that one "reviews" one's life, but that one re-forms it, creatively (and I use the word respectfully) in the ending phase of life.

In the ending phase, yes. But also at any time when the person has come to produce some change in himself that will eventuate in an experience of growth: not necessarily more happiness, less pain or fewer problems; only, if anything, the fuller use of the self.

In the early 1940's, at a Summer Session at the Tome School (on the Susquehanna River in Maryland) Miss Robinson taught a course: "The Nature of Service." Early in the sessions, as part of an exploration of the service, she laid down the proposition that helping is a one-way street, not a two-way street—as is often supposed; that it demands an unwavering discipline on the part of the one who is helping. One might ask, what then is the reward for so demanding a role? Recently, I was privileged to have an illuminating illustration. One of the elderly gentlemen already mentioned, had been pouring out the painful realities of his days. I said in response, (a response that was directly to him but also out of the depth of my own feeling) "It isn't easy to grow old." He answered, "It isn't easy to be born, it isn't easy to live, it isn't easy to die." I felt a flood of gratitude as if

I had been given a gift, a sudden discovery, he from his simple human experience, and I for the theory brought to life.

INDEX

Acceptance, of self, 93; of client: aspects and facets of, 99-100; consequences of, 101, 101-105; meaning of, 103; effects of worker's personal characteristics, 103-105; by others, 132; as necessary for love of others, 277; of difference, 324

Activity, as outlet for energy, 146

Adjustment, definition of, 310, 312

Administration, responsibility, authoritativeness, accountability of, 161-167, 195, 197-198, 210; on staff participation, 206-211; as terminal point with coordinating function, 211-213; see Manual

Aeschylus, quoted on love, 272-273

Agape, defined, 276

Aging, meaning of looking back, 330

Agency, The, responsibility to client, 172-173; on clarity of purpose, regulations, 188-191; dependence on worker for representation of, 196; effects of policy modifications, 198-201; discretionary freedom of local offices, 204-205; see Casework

Alienation, feeling of, 277

Antidaemon, defined, 277; see Apathy

Apathy, overcoming of, 274; as negative will expression and source of, 275; as antidaimonic, 277

Application For Service, meaning of, 67; need for several interviews, 67-68, 132, 135; comparison with diagnostic method, 68-69; part of continuing process, 70, 73; on feeling of union, 74; client ambivalence, 85; resulting risks and fears, 171-172

Aristotle, quoted on identity, 231

Assimilation, of policy: two-sided problem involving internal learning process, 198

Auden, W. H., quoted on choice, 303

Beyond Psychology (Rank), quotation from, 239; cited, 300

Buber, Martin C., 243; quoted on will, 250; quoted on difference, 259

Butler, Robert, on reviewing one's life, 330

Buzelle, George B., quoted on poor results of philanthropy and on non-role of client, 24

Care, sense of, 269; as theme, 270; roots and meaning of, 278

Casework, Diagnostic Method, development and underlying principle of, 21-35

Casework, Functional Method, choice as core of process, 15-16; as therapeutic help, 17-19; specific tasks of, 20; origins of underlying concepts, development in three phases: 1. focus on individual and emphasis on external factors, 21-28; *see* Buzelle, Johnson, Richmond, Simkovitch. 2. shift in emphasis to the psychological, three concepts taken from psychoanalysis, causal determinism as underlying principle, 27-35; emergence of differences as to what constitutes the therapeutic factor, divergences in psychological viewpoints, beginnings of differentiation from psychotherapy, 36-45; formulation of functional concepts, 46-55; *see* Rank, Robinson, Taft. 3. development of detail of functional casework process, differentiation from psychotherapy further advanced, casework as a separate entity more clearly established, 59-149; see "A Comparison of Diagnostic and Functional Casework Concepts," Notes, 150

124-125; search for limits, 142; defined, 184; as psychological concept, 293; as state of being, 325; *see* Casework, Functional Method

Generation Gap, on location of problem, 283

Goal, opening to transitory nature of, 232; identification of, 234; kinds of, 235; and ending, 237; experimental nature of, 239

Growth, through reworking of experience, 134; through opposing self with difference, 288

Guilt, on worker's strict adherence to process, 327; *see* Professional Self, The

Happiness, as urge to life, 313
Heidegger, in reference to "care," 278
Hellman, Lillian, *Pentimento,* 316
Hopkins, Harry, on Federal versus local controls, 284

Identification, with client's feeling state, 42; as reflection of self, 265; *see* Double, The

Identity, search, consciousness, affirmation of, and self-appointment, 230-231, 235, 237; discovery of, 323-324; *see* Aristotle, Erickson, Jung, Keats, *Life Magazine, New York Times,* Pindar, Shakespeare

"Individuality in the Work of Charity" (Buzelle), 24

Individuation, confusion regarding togetherness and likeness, 288; essential principles of, 296

Inevitability, discovery of, 142

Influence, three phases of, 318-319

Insight, creation of, 228

Intentionality, as theme and central concept, 270; definition of, 277-278; as voluntary responsibility, 278; further exploration of, 279; *see* Responsibility

Interest, nature of in client's expression, 246; relation to degree of attention, 248; *see* Listening, Search

Interview Situation, ambivalence of client, 84-85; as engagement of the will of the client, 95-96; as designed segment of life, 249; use of setting, 326; *see* Client

Intuition, as responsive understanding, 42

James, William, *The Energies of Men,* quoted on two-sided nature of the self,

248, 256n; quoted on the element of necessity, 275; quoted on changing, 287

Johnson, Alex, quoted on preventive and ameliorative social programs, 25

Journal of Social Work Process, reference to, 291

Journal of the Otto Rank Association, commitment of, 239

Jung, Carl Gustav, on search for identity, 230-231

Keats, John, his self-appointment as poet, 230

Kierkegaard, quoted on choice and isolation, 143

Knowing, distinguished from logical external comprehension, 71-72; contrasted with imagining, 260

Kunstler, Der (Rank, trans. Mrs. Eva Salomon), 223

Lane, Franklin K., quoted on the individual unit, 21

Learning, visual, 187; an internal process, 201-202;'

Life Magazine, quotation on identity, 231

Lifton, Robert Jay, *The Life of the Self,* on the erasure of difference between self and helper, 325

Listening, in context of the helping process, 241; characteristics of, 245-246; *see* Interest, Search

"Living and Feeling" (Taft), 242, 285

Living and Living Systems, organization on many levels, 238; developmental aspects of, 266-267

Loneliness, contrasted with solitude, 274

Love, relation to will, 270, 272-273; unsustainability of, 274; four kinds of, 276; *see* Agape, Eros, Philia, Sex

Manual, The Agency, core of policy structure, beginning point of administration process, 164; changes in and selection of content, 176, 179; on concreteness, mechanization, misrepresentation of policy, 199-200

Marcus, Grace, quoted on new attitude toward behavior, 34

Memory, role in choice, 314-315; after catastrophic experience, 315; change in, 316; similarity to meaning in *Pentimento,* 316; use and recovery of the subliminal, 327-328

Mobility, gaining new freedom of, 76, 84

National Conference of Social Work, papers and authors, 21, 24, 25, 36, 38
New York Times, The, quotation on identity, 231
Nin, Anais, free use of self, 242

Objectivity, absence of, 88; influence of attitudes, 99-100
Other, The, role of, 222
Otto Rank Association (ORA), why and how established, 221-223; purpose of, 225; focus on, 228
Outlines of a Genetic Psychology (Rank, trans. Taft), 222

Partializing, reality problems, 76; *see* Robinson
Past, The, reworking content of, 134-135; crisis point, 136; revealing pattern of union and separation, 247; in what way curative, 247; contrast with the present, 271; erasing the present, 320; revealing the pattern of the will, 330, *see* Goal
Pentimento (Hellman), meaning of, 316
Perfectibility, concept of and comment on, 259-260; unattainability of, 273
Philia, definition of, 276
Pindar, quoted on identity, 231
Polarity, confusion with schizoid, 272
Policy, studied in its movement, 166; represented by, 169; role summarized, 174; forms of resistance to modifications, 175-177, 194-201; essentiality, 177-178, 182; tempo of assimilation, 180-182; validity of and relation to function and practice, 183-186; as definition of Agency function, 184; concreteness, mechanization of, 199-200; introduction of, 203-204; growth through construction of, 206-207; staff participation in formulation of, 209-213
Practice, four points of technique summarized, 328-329; structure in private work, 328
Pray, Kenneth L. M., reference to, 94, 97; his position on some of the seven principles underlying functional casework, 294-298
Present, The, emphasis on, 36
Preventive, programs, 25-26
Principles, five detailed and summarized as basis for psychological explorations, 232-234; in guiding approach to understanding of world situation, 281-289; reexamination of seven underlying

functions of casework, 290-298; movement of in psychological terms, 303
Process, Helping, control of, 52; nature of, 143; significance summarized, 148-149; listening and response in context of, 241; search in, 246-247; rhythm, continuity, development, 247; development through conflict, 283-285; necessity of conflict for growth, 303, 319; as experience, 317; *see* Goal
Productivity, artist's urge toward, 308
Professional Self, The, an ability to hold to process, 22-23; in functional helping: on conceding central position to client, 59; identification with Agency function, 59-60, 137, 319, 325; respect for and quality of listening and responding to client, 69-71; sensitivity to client receptivity, yielding, and assumption of responsibility, 72-73, 86; identification with client's feeling state, 76, 87; on knowing through own experience in taking help, 82, 322-323; worker's containment of own impulses, 84, 88, 326; effects of sympathy, 86-87; objectivity, 88, 99; motivation in assuming helping role, 89-93; aspects of growth in worker training, 93, 95, 98-99, 135, 322-323; phases in growing maturity, 114; on use of content, 125-126; growth, 247-248; on client's own portrait of his two-sided self, 247-248; on his determination of his real wants, 248; pitfalls, 248; on worker's new use of self, 318; three points of conviction in study of the helping process, summarized, 324-325; *see* Process, Helping
Projection, onto worker, 83, 85; defined, 96; danger of, 98; on placing blame externally, 270; ubiquitousness of, 305, 306-307; in therapy: importance of, 306; short story "Correspondence" (McCullers) illustrative of, 306-307
Psychoanalysis, influence of, 27, 28, 29
Psychology, on using Rank's, 282; on the application of, 300; on feeling into truth, 305; on excessive efforts to understand, 306
Psychology Today, mention of, 270
Public Welfare, defined, 173; relation to policy, 174; differentiated from therapy, 174

"Qualifications of the Psychiatric Social Worker" (Taft), 28

negative expression of, 275; union of
love and will, 278-279; relation to
union and separation, 279; difference
on key point between Rollo May and
Rank (see Rank's chapter "Will and
Force" in *Will Therapy*), 279, yielding
of, 279; in producing sense of life and
sharpening of reactions, 288; as present
in all relationships, 303; example of
dramatic change in character of, 316
Will Therapy (Rank, trans. Taft), on

turning reality content into will
content, 131; chapter "Will and Force,"
279
Work, as initiating movement, 20

Yeats, William Butler, quoted on will and
imagination, 255
Yielding, as sign of growth, 73, 132; resulting exhilaration and sense of freedom, 148; defined, 279